SAP PRESS e-books

Print or e-book, Kindle or iPad, workplace or airplane: Choose where and how to read your SAP PRESS books! You can now get all our titles as e-books, too:

▶ By download and online access
▶ For all popular devices
▶ And, of course, DRM-free

Convinced? Then go to **www.sap-press.com** and get your e-book today.

SAP Hybris®

 PRESS

SAP PRESS is a joint initiative of SAP and Rheinwerk Publishing. The know-how offered by SAP specialists combined with the expertise of Rheinwerk Publishing offers the reader expert books in the field. SAP PRESS features first-hand information and expert advice, and provides useful skills for professional decision-making.

SAP PRESS offers a variety of books on technical and business-related topics for the SAP user. For further information, please visit our website: *www.sap-press.com*.

Baumgartl, Chaadaev, Choi, Dudgeon, Lahiri, Meijerink, Worsley-Tonks
SAP S/4HANA: An Introduction
2016, 449 pages hardcover and e-book
www.sap-press.com/4153

Silvia, Frye, Berg
SAP HANA: An Introduction, 4th Edition
2017, 549 pages, hardcover and e-book
www.sap-press.com/4160

Chandrakant Agarwal
SAP CRM: Business Processes and Configuration
2015, 737 pages, hardcover and e-book
www.sap-press.com/3648

Chudy, Castedo, Lopez
Sales and Distribution in SAP ERP—Practical Guide, 2nd Edition
2015, 520 pages, hardcover and e-book
www.*sap-press.com/3672*

Sanjjeev K. Singh, Sven Feurer, Marcus Ruebsam

SAP Hybris®

Commerce, Marketing, Sales, Service, and Revenue with SAP

Rheinwerk
Publishing

Editor Meagan White
Acquisitions Editor Emily Nicholls
Copyeditor Julie McNamee
Cover Design Graham Geary
Photo Credit Icons made by Freepik from www.flaticon.com
Layout Design Vera Brauner
Production Marissa Fritz
Typesetting III-satz, Husby (Germany)
Printed and bound in the United States of America, on paper from sustainable sources

ISBN 978-1-4932-1538-6

© 2017 by Rheinwerk Publishing, Inc., Boston (MA)
1st edition 2017

Library of Congress Cataloging-in-Publication Control Number: 2017011724

Contents at a Glance

Dear Reader,

How do you meaningfully connect with your customers? How do you handle your core CRM processes—sales, service, revenue, marketing, commerce—in the digital economy? Between these pages, you'll see how SAP Hybris can help you answer these questions, with a detailed look at the functionality offered by each of the five solutions.

Before we move on to book itself, I want to take a moment to thank our all-star author team: Sanjjeev Singh, Sven Feurer, and Marcus Ruebsam. It was a sincere pleasure working with you on this book, and I believe your dedication, thoughtful writing, and expertise have allowed us to produce an excellent resource. Thank you!

As always, your comments and suggestions are the most useful tools to help us make our books the best they can be. Let us know what you thought about *SAP Hybris: Commerce, Marketing, Sales, Service, and Revenue with SAP*! Please feel free to contact me and share any praise or criticism you may have.

Thank you for purchasing a book from SAP PRESS!

Meagan White
Editor, SAP PRESS

meaganw@rheinwerk-publishing.com
www.sap-press.com
Rheinwerk Publishing · Boston, MA

Contents

1   SAP Hybris at a Glance   21

2   Sales   37

7

3   Service

4   Commerce

5 Marketing

6   Revenue

7   Microservices and SAP Hybris as a Service

8   First Steps to SAP Hybris

Foreword

Whenever I meet with decision-makers and analysts from around the world, what I often hear is that we're all at an inflection point when it comes to customer experience and how we engage with customers—or, more importantly, how we "produce" engaged customers. There's no question that companies of all sizes are being affected by digital transformation. Yesterday's leading companies can no longer be sure their business models will take them to the next chapters of their business. I truly believe successful companies must accommodate the trends that accompany the new digital economy and find ways to disrupt the market with new solutions and innovative services. Otherwise, they will get disrupted by new competitors in the digital marketplace.

In a company, digital business models are no longer limited to a set of sales and marketing channels. You must have digital engagement in all channels. This has a massive impact on how your organization achieves value and how you think about and design your future products. As matter a of fact, when it comes to products, you should always put digital engagement with your customers at the core of what you're doing. Doing so is not only a matter of product management, communication, and design, but a matter of technology and software—independent of whether you're offering a physical product, digital product, or selling a service.

For example, if you look at Under Armour, one of SAP Hybris's most valued clients, they clearly put the athlete at the center of everything they do. At a very early stage of their company, they set up a customer community where they deliver a professional, special customer experience. For Under Armour, it's all about how to take products, turn them into experiences and services, and weave that together seamlessly into the everyday patterns of an athlete, no matter if it's a professional or casual one. If you look at the ecosystem that surrounds those products, it also becomes very obvious that this ecosystem is driving the distribution and adoption of the products. This is a fundamental shift in the retail and consumer industries, and is happening in other industries as well.

When I look at the numerous conversations I've had with our customers, the questions that are being asked today are vastly different from what people were asking me even a year and a half ago. Several major utilities companies recently came to me asking how the SAP Hybris team can help them translate their power and electricity products into a transportation and mobility model. The next generation is less and less interested in a driver's license; they are interested in a mobility subscription that includes transportation by car sharing, train, plane, etc. Companies have to think about how they participate in these ecosystems of empowered customers.

Almost every product will turn into a service in the future. This transformation can happen at any time, and affects all touchpoints of your company. Consistent, contextual, and relevant engagement with customers around these services, in an almost automated manner, will be a key factor for success for many companies. Technology and software will be at the heart of this change. If companies are open and willing to rethink their business models and provide the necessary technology platform, tools, and conversation, they will succeed with this new type of superior customer experience. Throughout this process, agility is the most important factor to successfully drive this digital transformation at the right speed and deliver positive business outcomes.

At SAP Hybris, we offer flexible solutions that can be implemented on the public or managed cloud, or installed as an on-premise system. Customers can therefore adopt our front office solutions according to their business priorities and their individual pace and customer experience intensity.

Near the end of 2015, we decided to position our customer engagement solutions as being "Beyond CRM". In this context, SAP Hybris is our unique brand which includes a simplified front office covering all functional areas: commerce, marketing, sales, service, and revenue. Undeniably, SAP Hybris offers the most complete solution portfolio in the market when it comes to customer engagement and commerce—and it comes tightly integrated with SAP S/4HANA as the digital core enterprise platform.

As next innovative shift, we're anticipating microservices and the application program interface (API) economy to affect the IT industry. Microservices are the architecture and delivery principle which many will use to develop software in the future. They help you to break applications down to a finer granularity. Microservice-based development teams are able to publish their services faster, anywhere and anytime, and thus speed up adoption of their solutions and services. We're lucky and proud that SAP Hybris has been driving and influencing this development from the beginning. By using SAP Hybris as a Service (or short: YaaS) you can deploy, consume, and commercialize microservices. The business opportunity for companies is almost unlimited. Amazon, for example, delivers millions of software releases per year based on a microservices infrastructure. By nature, SAP Hybris as a Service is infrastructure agnostic, however the preferred deployment is on top of the SAP Cloud Platform (platform-as-a-service).

Finally, we see automation through machine learning and artificial intelligence (AI) as another key theme impacting a company's value chain. With SAP Clea—our machine learning intelligence platform—we apply those innovations in SAP Hybris solutions across commerce, marketing, sales, service, and revenue.

With SAP Hybris you get all ingredients for success: rock-solid, best-in-class cloud solutions equipped with smart, AI-based scenarios and a microservices framework for innovation and extension. At SAP Hybris we're prepared for digital transformation and passionate about leading the digital customer experience market from front office to core enterprise processes together with our customers and partners, while embracing latest technology trends.

Finally, we hope you really enjoy reading through this book and digging into the different aspects of SAP Hybris solutions. So, let's put the customer again into the center of gravity and shape new outcome-based business models together.

Marcus Ruebsam
Senior Vice President
SAP Hybris Solution Management and Strategy

Preface

Welcome to the first book on SAP Hybris. Since SAP's acquisition of hybris in 2013, all customer-facing applications from SAP are branded under the SAP Hybris product portfolio. Due to the popularity of SAP Hybris in the market, SAP customers, partners, and consultants have been demanding more resources to understand fully the depth and breadth of SAP Hybris offerings. In partnership with the SAP Hybris solution management team, we've written this book to provide a complete overview of the SAP Hybris solutions.

In this book, we've provided insights into SAP's strategy for marketing, commerce, sales, service, and revenue and how the SAP Hybris portfolio of products fit into SAP's strategy to go beyond customer relationship management (CRM) and provide integrated front-office and back-office processes using SAP Hybris cloud solutions. This book captures and provides the most comprehensive information on the SAP Hybris offerings for commerce, marketing, revenue, sales, and service, as well as SAP Hybris as a Service on SAP Cloud Platform, and it can serve as your first source of information on the SAP Hybris solutions.

Who This Book Is For

This book is for anyone interested in learning about the SAP Hybris solutions and gaining knowledge about the key components of the SAP Hybris portfolio of products. Customers, partners, consultants, business leaders, and process owners from sales, marketing, commerce, service, and revenue who are planning to evaluate or implement SAP Hybris solutions will find this book a starting point with SAP Hybris. We've kept the book at a high level by focusing on key capabilities of all the SAP Hybris products and their business benefits so that business process owners from sales, service, marketing, commerce, and revenue can use this book as a ready reference guide while implementing SAP Hybris cloud solutions. This book doesn't include details on setup or configuration of SAP Hybris solutions and isn't intended for use as a deep-dive resource for learning SAP Hybris configuration and enhancements. However, this book will help you build a great foundation on which to deep dive in your SAP Hybris learning pursuits.

How This Book Is Organized

We've organized this book around customer-facing business functions and how the SAP Hybris cloud products are aligned with each of these functions. Starting with a glance at SAP Hybris in Chapter 1, we've dedicated one chapter to each business function: sales, service, commerce, marketing, and revenue. We have a chapter dedicated to explaining the importance of SAP Hybris as a Service. Finally, we provide some important first steps to starting a journey with the SAP Hybris solutions.

We recommend reading this book sequentially from Chapter 1 onward; however, if you prefer, you can directly go to any chapter and start reading about that topic. If you're interested in learning about SAP Hybris Commerce Cloud capabilities, you can start reading the chapter on commerce without reading previous chapters. Let's review what is covered in each chapter of this book.

- **Chapter 1**

  This chapter provides an overview of the SAP Hybris solutions, including their deployment options and flexibility for extension using standard and custom development. We provide an overview of how SAP Hybris front-office solutions integrate with each other and with SAP back-office solutions to enable an integrated process across these systems. We also briefly introduce you to SAP Hybris as a Service.

- **Chapter 2**

  This chapter focuses on the sales function and how SAP Hybris Sales Cloud can help businesses go beyond their standard CRM practices and improve their sales productivity. The key capabilities of SAP Hybris Sales Cloud is covered in this chapter along with the mobile sales application, standard reporting, and analytics delivered out of the box with SAP Hybris Cloud for Customer. We also cover how the sales solution integrates with other SAP Hybris front-office solutions and with SAP back-office systems such as SAP S/4HANA, SAP ERP, and SAP CRM.

- **Chapter 3**

  In this chapter, we explain the service processes supported by SAP Hybris Service Cloud such as SAP Hybris Service Engagement Center and SAP Hybris Cloud for Customer (for customer service and field service). Along with explaining the key capabilities of these solutions, we discuss integration of service processes with other SAP Hybris front-office processes and SAP back-office processes. We also review out-of-the-box reporting and analytics capabilities delivered with SAP Hybris Service solutions to measure a service organization's performance and effectiveness.

- **Chapter 4**

  This chapter focuses on SAP Hybris Commerce solutions and their key capabilities with business-to-business (B2B) and business-to-consumer (B2C) activities. In this chapter, we review commerce industry accelerators, customer experience (CX), product content management (PCM), order management, and embedded commerce on SAP Hybris as a Service. We also examine how SAP Hybris Commerce Cloud integrates with other SAP Hybris front-office solutions and SAP back-office solutions such as SAP S/4HANA, SAP ERP, and SAP CRM.

- **Chapter 5**

  In this chapter, we review marketing solutions available from SAP Hybris. The key capabilities of SAP Hybris Marketing Cloud such as consumer and customer profiling, commerce marketing, marketing resource management, marketing lead management, marketing analytics, and loyalty management are explained in detail along with their business benefits. We also explain how SAP Hybris Marketing Cloud integrates with other SAP Hybris front-office solutions such as commerce and sales, and SAP backend systems such as SAP S/4HANA, SAP ERP, and SAP CRM.

- **Chapter 6**

  This chapter introduces the high-volume, subscription, and usage-based billing solution available from SAP Hybris. We cover key capabilities of SAP Hybris Billing such as business model redesign and pricing simulation; subscription order management; usage metering and transaction pricing; billing, receivables, and collections; and partner revenue share. We also introduce SAP Hybris Revenue Cloud, which includes configure, price, and quote (CPQ), order management, and subscription billing. In line with previous chapters, we review how SAP Hybris Billing integrates with other SAP Hybris front-office and SAP back-office solutions.

- **Chapter 7**

  SAP Hybris as a Service is based on microservices architecture, which has emerged as a new trend to build applications in the digital era. In this chapter, we cover the key concepts for this architecture and how SAP is leveraging SAP Hybris as a Service to allow customers and partners to build, deploy, and consume complementary SAP Hybris solutions in the cloud using tools delivered with SAP Hybris as a Service marketplace.

- **Chapter 8**

  In this chapter, we outline some of the first steps you need to take before embarking on your SAP Hybris journey. We discuss some use cases for deploying SAP Hybris solutions and their corresponding target architectures. We also provide an overview of SAP Hybris education and rapid-deployment solutions (RDS) services available from SAP to assist you in successfully implementing SAP Hybris solutions.

Acknowledgments

As mentioned previously, a book such as this one, which covers all different areas and the latest functional and technical innovations of the SAP Hybris solution portfolio, must be a true team effort. First, the book would not exist if Jamie Anderson and Marcus Ruebsam did not believe in the project, provide their enthusiastic support, and make valuable resources on their teams available to us. Several people made especially large contributions to the book, and we would like to offer our sincere appreciation and to thank these leaders and experts: Werner Aigner, Bernard Chung, Chris Dircks, Marco Flores, Ginger Gatling, John Heald, Matthias Heid, Denelle Hicks, Riad Hijal, Volker Hildebrand, Supriya Iyer, Lisa James, Hansen Lieu, Rosa Lu, Sebastien Martin, Nicholas Milani, Shalini Mitha, David Moore, Fergus O'Reilly, Jackie Palmer, Isabelle Roussin, Werner Schmidt, Christian Schönauer, Coraly Signoret, Karan Sood, Andreas Starke, Andrea Stubbe, Tanya van Soest, Vikas Venugopal, Jehan Vichhi, Nora Weber, and Johann Wrede. We would also like to thank Emily Nicholls and Meagan White at Rheinwerk Publishing.

Conclusion

Reading this book will provide you with a comprehensive overview of SAP Hybris solutions and empower you to engage confidently in any SAP Hybris evaluation and implementation conversation. This book will serve as your foundational knowledge source for the SAP Hybris solution portfolio, and you can build on your knowledge with SAP Hybris training and additional resources that are available from SAP and upcoming SAP Hybris books from SAP PRESS. Let's get on board now and proceed to Chapter 1 with a first glance at SAP Hybris.

Chapter 1
SAP Hybris at a Glance

According to Frank Gens (chief analyst at IDC), by 2018, one-third of the top 20 businesses in every industry will be disrupted by digitally transformed competitors. This, then, is the key question: Will you be the disruptor or the disrupted?

In this first chapter, we want to start by looking at mega trends such as digitization and the way it affects how businesses engage with customers and manage customer relationships. We'll also look at modern customers and their expectations in today's marketplace. Finally, we'll see how SAP Hybris solutions help companies of any size transform from traditional customer relationship management (CRM) into a unified and simplified front-office suite designed for end-to-end customer engagement and commerce in the digital economy.

1.1 Digital Transformation and Customer Experiences

Everyone has heard the stories about Amazon disrupting the book business, Uber disrupting the taxi business, and iTunes—and now Spotify—disrupting the music business. The reality is that every industry is experiencing disruption right now. In a few short years, there's a good chance that the industry leaders you know today will have been displaced by digitally transformed competitors.

Figure 1.1 shows how economic transformation in general is driven by interlinked cycles of scarcity and abundance.

To go into a bit more detail on the history shown in Figure 1.1, consider the following:

- **Early 1900s**
  Henry Ford introduces the first assembly line for manufacturing the Model T. Cars had previously been a scarce and expensive product, accessible only to the richest. However, with the lower costs introduced by assembly line manufacturing, the price of a car dropped so that assembly line workers could earn enough to buy one themselves with a few month's wages. It was the beginning of the move toward abundance of manufactured products.

- **1950s**

  The perfection of assembly line manufacturing was driven by World War II, and major industrial nations could mass-produce household goods cheaply. What was now scarce was the desire for those goods. The heads of corporations were no longer product inventors or manufacturing and operations experts, but rather sales and marketing leaders. TV mass media and ad agencies all over the world entered their golden age, and the consumer economy began.

- **2000s**

  People no longer want to be bombarded with an abundance of mass-marketing messages; they refuse to be passive consumers. The consumer economy only lasted two or three generations and is crumbling quickly. Instead, what is now scarce is true engagement in experiences, and, in this digital economy, every act of engagement is now captured to create a data stream that fuels context and drives continuous improvement in the experience.

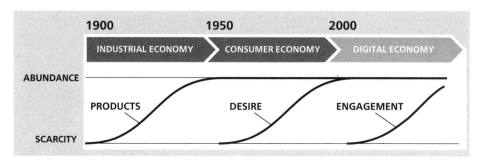

Figure 1.1 Welcome to the Digital Economy

Digital transformation is the new reality, and it's constantly shifting with an unprecedented pace, fueled by innovations across many different technologies. It's changing everything, including how we live, communicate, buy and sell, entertain ourselves, work, collaborate with colleagues, and engage with customers.

The challenge for business and IT leaders isn't just keeping up with this change but seizing the opportunity: How will you reimagine the way you engage with your customers in the near future? Digitally enabled customers will expect you to deliver better, faster, and richer personalized experiences and will unfollow you the moment that you don't meet their expectations and deliver on your promises.

Customers expect you to interact or engage with them in real time, in the moment when it matters to them, with contextual, personalized content that is relevant to them and through their preferred channel, usually via their mobile device. Customer behaviors are changing in how they consume online ads (they are almost completely ignored), perform buying processes (more than half the process is complete before interacting with sales), and abandon a purchase if there's no relevance and personal context.

Clearly, digital customers are changing the rules of engagement, as they are digitally connected, socially networked, and better informed than ever before. They inform themselves and may not even want to talk to a sales rep; they make their own purchases and get assistance when they need it and on their channel of choice. They jump between or simultaneously use web, mobile, chat, Snapchat, text message, Instagram, or the phone (and they expect it to happen seamlessly and instantaneously with each new interaction personalized in the context of the last one). And, if it's not simple and convenient, they expect to have a consistent omnichannel experience, as their tolerance for fragmented experiences, inconveniences, or any delays is lower than ever.

Figure 1.2 shows the new customer journey from awareness to advocacy phases. As each customer journey is individual and snakes and shifts, depending on each customer's needs, businesses have to deliver consistent engagement at each entry point and every phase.

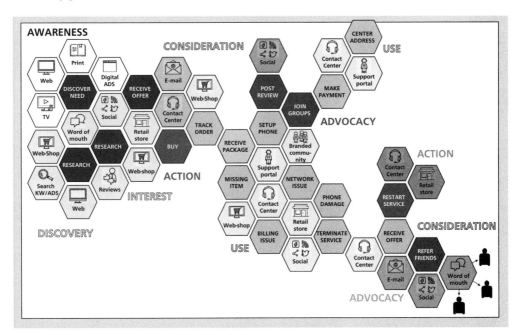

Figure 1.2 Each Customer Wants to Choose His Own Path

Against this backdrop, CRM needs to evolve beyond traditional approaches and technologies. According to recent research commissioned by SAP, two out of three organizations believe that their existing CRM can't support their future vision for customer engagement. So this is the key question: How do you upgrade your existing CRM to face the challenges of digital transformation and get ahead of it?

Traditional CRM technologies are insufficient to bridge the growing gaps among customer awareness, conversion, ongoing engagement, and execution. Previous generations of CRM solutions (no matter whether they are in the cloud or on premise) have become a commodity and primarily address internal operations such as sales processes, call-handling times, and a scattershot approach to marketing engagement. They lack the holistic view of the customer across all touch points and don't include critical business transactions such as e-commerce or billing.

Thinking beyond CRM requires a paradigm shift from managing customer relationships to engaging customers via the following:

- New ways of thinking about your customers and truly putting customer data at the heart of your business
- Blurring the lines among marketing, sales, commerce, and service
- Omnichannel engagement versus supporting multiple channels
- Mobile first versus mobile as an afterthought
- Predicting the future versus reporting on the past
- Blending physical and digital experiences
- Bridging the gap between front office and back office

The foundation to all of this is customer data and customer insight. You need to understand your customers and capture their interactions, contexts, and behaviors to create a continually evolving dynamic profile, surfacing actionable insights for real-time, one-to-one engagements across all touch points. Gaining a complete, single view of your customer has always been the holy grail of CRM.

Recently, big data has captured all the attention. The explosion of data has been at a high volume and is increasing with extreme velocity so that it can be very difficult to filter out the signals in a lot of noise. Even if you're able to capture it all, how do you make sense of all that data?

The real action is in "small data"—the individualization of those large data trends to a single person and the automation of actions at that level. That big data set—store inventory, global shopping trends, the weather, and all the data about the individual (e.g., shopping history, location, service tickets, recent website history, and latest tweets or likes)—is nearly useless without connecting it all.

You need to be able to collect all the information and break it down to the individual level so you can solve the complexity of the modern customer journey and to serve customers contextually and digitally across marketing, commerce, sales, and service interactions. Built on customer intelligence, not just data, you need to gain insight into past behaviors, anticipate each customer's needs, and personalize every interaction in real time by taking advantage of machine learning and artificial intelligence.

All of this presents a huge challenge to every organization. The chief digital officer (CDO) and chief marketing officer (CMO) are emerging roles, along with the chief information officer (CIO), to lead digital transformation. Those roles must serve as change agents not only from a technology perspective but also from a strategic point of view. Breaking down the silos across sales, marketing, service, commerce, and revenue and looking at end-to-end business processes to bridge the gap between front office and back office is critical. In many organizations, the CDO is the only person who can drive this paradigm shift (with support from the CEO).

The trend to shift to more cloud-based solutions has fostered siloed thinking and decision-making when it comes to software solutions. It's time that CDOs, CMOs, and CIOs take the lead and align with the business across departmental boundaries to make the digital transformation happen and to engage with customers like never before.

1.2 SAP Hybris Portfolio and Solutions

Complexity is rampant within enterprises because the strategies, systems, and processes used to engage and transact with customers, and even organizational structures and ecosystems have been built up over time to support the requirements of the consumer economy, not today's digital economy. Historically, the heart of the front office has been the traditional CRM system. This tool was used to enable front-office teams to execute, automating internal processes such as sales forecasting, issue tracking, campaign execution, and so on. To complicate matters, as the customer began to change, and it became evident that these systems were insufficient, companies began to buy point solutions to solve specific engagement challenges, such as managing customer interactions on social media or engaging with customers online. These systems were often implemented as silos, or resources were spent to integrate these systems with the CRM system.

As such, organizations often face the problem of having disparate IT systems and data silos, which makes it impossible to create seamless and exceptional customer experiences across all touch points and leading to high integration efforts and costs.

Key business situations and challenges in front-office areas today are as follows:

- **Sales**
  As modern customers turn to online information, such as business networks, social networks, and communities to inform themselves, salespeople are shut out of more than half of the buyer's journey. To remain relevant, sellers must now deeply understand their customers' businesses and bring them new thinking to earn the right to influence their journey. This requires much more than traditional CRM offers. It requires a new approach to selling and a new set of tools to win the heart and mind of today's empowered customers.

- **Marketing**
  Modern customers have little patience for traditional marketing tactics—turning away from broadcast media and tuning out online advertising. Emails with personalized greetings but irrelevant content are quickly deleted or, worse, unsubscribed. The challenge for marketers has been that the campaign management tools available to them in traditional CRM systems haven't given them the ability to truly personalize content. They haven't been able to turn volumes of customer data into insight that can be leveraged in real time.

- **Customer service**
  Empowered customers have formed higher expectations for effective and seamless customer service. Meeting or missing these expectations has a massive impact on customer loyalty (positive and negative), and the limitations of traditional CRM are causing customer service organizations to struggle with keeping up with changing interaction channels and customer demands as pressure to achieve higher profitability mounts.

- **Commerce**
  Digital transformation has touched every industry, and the pace of change is faster than ever. Today's businesses face tremendous challenges to differentiate, adapt, and meet ever-changing buying behaviors of digitally empowered customers. How customers will engage tomorrow will be radically different from today, which means that commerce teams are asked to go beyond traditional e-commerce to deliver rapid innovation and experimentation in the face of new competitors and new opportunities.

- **Revenue**
  The new data-driven digital value chain has the potential to disrupt the status quo business model in every industry. CEOs are looking to build defensible new revenue models or even to disrupt the entire business model of their industry, such as going from selling products to selling services and outcomes while driving operational excellence and growing rapidly. New models often are characterized by beating the competition with agile subscription- and usage-based pricing, sharing revenues with partners in a new business network, and streamlining high-volume revenue management.

The challenges IT organizations are facing should also be at the forefront of the digital transformation of the entire enterprise. Cloud solutions, however, have empowered businesses to act unilaterally, sometimes complicating the IT transformation strategy. Traditional CRM, long seen as the system of record and the enabling technology for customer-facing teams, is no longer sufficient. Billing systems in place are ill-equipped to cope with business expansion and new revenue models. The challenge facing IT organizations is that more and more often, purchasing decisions are made by the customer lines of business, without input from the CIO. This results in an unnecessarily complex and costly system landscape with multiple integrations and no real consistency. To remain relevant, CIOs need to think beyond CRM and propose innovative engagement solutions to their line-of-business constituents.

SAP Hybris enables businesses to transform how they engage with customers, innovate how they do business, and simplify their IT technology landscape. SAP Hybris does the following:

- **Deliver personalized and relevant experiences**
  SAP Hybris solutions help companies drive relevant, contextual experiences across all customer touch points in real time—from a marketing touch to a commerce interaction, from the contact center to a sales meeting. Leveraging customer context to personalize each touch, and delivering consistently great experiences across channels, creates differentiation, optimizes marketing spend, and capitalizes on the willingness of customers to pay more for a better experience.

- **Simplify the front office**
  With a comprehensive approach to customer engagement and commerce, SAP Hybris solutions unlock opportunities to optimize both the business and customer experience while reducing cost, time, and complexity. Shifting resources

from integration and maintenance to innovation and transformation creates competitive advantage and the ability to compete in the digital economy.

- **Transform and be agile**
  SAP Hybris solutions enable companies to respond to changing market conditions and customer expectations with agility. From adding new channels, to evolving business models, to entering new markets, SAP Hybris solutions help today's businesses experiment and respond quickly to be competitive. Quickly adapting the experience and the business as conditions change empowers companies to become disruptors in their industry rather than being disrupted themselves.

Therefore, SAP Hybris delivers a modular, integrated suite of front-office cloud solutions that is unique in the marketplace. This suite includes the latest technologies— from in-memory computing to predictive analytics—that enable companies across industries to transform how they engage their customers. Using volumes of customer data as the fuel for context, SAP Hybris solutions deliver optimized customer experiences across channels, both digital and physical. The breadth of the suite and the integrated nature of its approach help businesses eliminate the complexity that keeps them from delivering the engaging experiences their customers expect. It also helps businesses regain agility, better monetizing their customer relationships and evolving their business models to stay a step ahead of the marketplace. Figure 1.3 shows the simplified front-office suite with SAP Hybris.

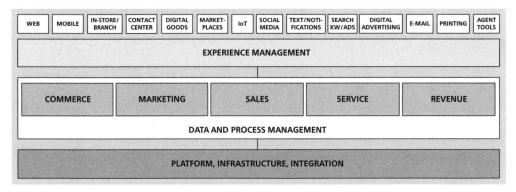

Figure 1.3 Simplified Front Office with SAP Hybris

The essential functionality of each product is as follows:

- **Commerce**
  This solution drives your digital transformation and enables you to become an omnichannel business, delivering contextual customer experiences and unifying

customer processes. It helps integrate all digital and physical customer touch points onto a single, robust platform—including online, mobile, point-of-sale, call center, social media, and print—empowering you to deliver exceptional, seamless customer experiences, in any industry, anywhere in the world. The single-stack architecture ensures a fast time to innovation, drives the best total cost of owner-ship (TCO), and offers you maximum flexibility for extension and customization.

- **Marketing**
  This solution enables marketers to develop a deeper understanding of customers, that is, to know what they have done, what they may do, and, most importantly, what they are doing now. You'll gain real-time insights into the context of each customer in order to leverage these insights to deliver highly individualized cus-tomer experiences across channels.

- **Sales**
  This modern-day cloud sales solution is built for sales professionals on the go. This solution leverages user experience technology that is easily tailored to the way companies want to engage with their customers and run their business. Gone are the days of spending endless hours in the system entering information just for reporting. You can empower salespeople with the agility and power to sell smarter by finding answers easily, engaging in meaningful customer conversations, and delivering the right impact every time to win customers like never before.

- **Service**
  This solution enables the end-to-end service process by supporting seamless tran-sitions between communication channels to resolve customer issues or execute service orders through self-service options, call center agents, or on-site techni-cians. With native mobile access and built-in robust analytical capabilities, SAP Hybris Service Cloud solutions deliver industry-leading support options for every conceivable service issue. You can share timely knowledge with customers, stay on top of their precise needs, schedule the right dispatches or fixes, and collabo-rate with other parts of your operation as needed to accelerate service resolutions.

- **Revenue**
  This solution allows you to launch customer-centric subscription offers rapidly that set you apart from the competition; exploit fast-moving market opportuni-ties by quickly changing customer pricing and partner revenue sharing models; and ramp up efficiency with a billing and revenue management solution that inte-grates the entire order-to-cash process and provides a low TCO.

Organizations of any size and across various industries can become disruptors and power their digital transformation using SAP Hybris solutions.

1.3   Deployment Options

Today, organizations are looking to go to market quickly with a solution that enables them to create highly targeted, relevant, and exciting customer experiences across all touch points. They are looking for fully functional omnichannel marketing, commerce, sales, and service solutions that they can deploy in the cloud to lower costs—without having to set up an extensive IT infrastructure and maintenance or train an operational team to support it—and be able to focus on their core business.

SAP Hybris has developed a next-generation customer engagement and commerce suite that is cloud-ready, high-performance, and adaptable. The solutions deliver the agility that companies need to become leaders in their industries, while its massive scalability enables companies to grow from small trials to enterprise deployments in a simple, reliable way. The underlying platform not only powers the solutions but also is open an evolving ecosystem of partners and customers who use it to develop their own solutions and to expand their business network beyond the walls of their enterprise.

Before we get to the deployment options of SAP Hybris solutions, let's first look at the general characteristics:

- **Public cloud**
  SAP Hybris solutions are fully managed by SAP as cloud service provider with automatic upgrades and support packages pushed on a planned timeline (weekly, quarterly). Customization and configuration depend on the flexibility of individual microservices or key user tools and extension points in the public solution model.

- **Private managed cloud**
  This model (also known as SAP HANA Enterprise Cloud for SAP Business Suite powered by SAP HANA) offers more flexibility for customers in terms of upgrades and administration of their SAP Hybris solutions. Customers can decide with SAP (or other providers) when to upgrade a system and to which level customizations and configurations are allowed.

- **On premise**
  The customer (or outsourcing/hosting provider) installs and runs the software. In this model, SAP Hybris solutions can be customized and configured as needed; however, this affects the TCO because modifications must be tested and adapted each time a software patch or update is applied.

Table 1.1 lists all available deployment options of the SAP Hybris solutions.

	Public Cloud	Managed Cloud	On Premise
Commerce	SAP Hybris Commerce as a Service and further solutions on SAP Hybris as a Service	SAP Hybris Commerce Cloud	SAP Hybris Commerce
Marketing	SAP Hybris Marketing Cloud and further solutions on SAP Hybris as a Service	SAP Hybris Marketing in SAP HANA Enterprise Cloud	SAP Hybris Marketing
Revenue	SAP Hybris Revenue Cloud and further solutions on SAP Hybris as a Service	SAP Hybris Billing in SAP HANA Enterprise Cloud	SAP Hybris Billing
Service	SAP Hybris Service Cloud including. SAP Hybris Service Engagement Center on SAP Hybris as a Service	SAP CRM service functionality in SAP HANA Enterprise Cloud	SAP CRM service functionality
Sales	SAP Hybris Sales Cloud and further solutions on SAP Hybris as a Service	SAP CRM sales functionality in SAP HANA Enterprise Cloud	SAP CRM sales functionality

Table 1.1 Deployment Options of SAP Hybris Solutions

The following provides a bit more detail on each solution's deployment options:

- **Commerce**
  SAP Hybris Commerce provides commerce capabilities for business-to-consumer (B2C) and business-to-business (B2B) corporations worldwide. However, for many small- and medium-sized businesses looking to update their commerce platforms—or break into the digital economy for the first time—SAP Hybris Commerce's enterprise package may simply be too much, providing features that won't be used until the business needs become more sophisticated and complex. SAP Hybris Commerce Cloud is an ideal option for deploying the SAP Hybris Commerce solution without extensive IT involvement.

  SAP takes care of the hardware, software, IT staff, and all operations. SAP will also help you improve operational efficiency and scalability in order to lower costs and maintain high availability and security. You can also start in the SAP Hybris

Commerce Cloud, and then as you grow (or as your requirements change), you can bring your commerce project on premise or remain in the cloud. If you already own a commerce solution, consider SAP Hybris Commerce as a Service based on SAP Hybris as a Service as a possibility to spin-off stores for smaller brands or to enter new markets faster. Powerful integration tools make it easy to connect your enterprise e-commerce solution with SAP Hybris Commerce as a Service.

- **Marketing**
  SAP Hybris Marketing is available as an on-premise deployment, as a managed cloud (SAP HANA Enterprise Cloud) deployment, or as a public cloud deployment (SAP Hybris Marketing Cloud). This is aside from, for example, SAP Hybris Conversion, SAP Hybris Loyalty, SAP Hybris Profile, and SAP Hybris customer journey manager add-on, which are available as separate, pure public cloud solutions with integration to SAP Hybris Marketing.

- **Revenue**
  SAP Hybris Revenue solutions are available on-premise (SAP Hybris Billing) and as managed cloud solutions in SAP HANA Enterprise Cloud. The full scope of the on-premise solution is available in SAP HANA Enterprise Cloud. In addition, SAP Hybris Revenue Cloud combines physical product sales with digital service offerings in a pay-per-use mode. This solution has been developed on top of SAP Hybris as a Service and comprises the functional areas of configure, price, and quote (CPQ) for product/service bundling; commercial order and contract management; retail order orchestration; distribution for physical goods, rating, and billing services; and invoicing for digital business/pay per use.

- **Service**
  SAP Hybris Service Cloud is available as two complementary offerings: SAP Hybris Service Engagement Center and SAP Hybris Cloud for Customer—both available purely as public cloud solutions. In addition, customers can use SAP Customer Relationship Management (SAP CRM) service capabilities either deployed on premise (on any database or SAP HANA) or in the SAP HANA Enterprise Cloud.

- **Sales**
  In the area of sales, SAP Hybris Sales Cloud represents the solution offering in the public cloud. As part of the SAP Hybris Sales Cloud, mobile apps are available out of the box (online/offline), as well as powerful, real-time analytics with hundreds of reports and persona-based dashboards. Alternatively, companies can use the SAP CRM sales functionality either on premise or in the SAP HANA Enterprise Cloud.

Note

In Chapter 8, we'll elaborate further on deployment options and describe how to compare those in terms of data center locations, operational questions, security, and scalability.

1.4   Front Office versus Back Office

SAP Hybris front-office solutions enable businesses to provide customers with a consistent and contextual experience regardless of the channel or device. These solutions offer you unprecedented control over the customer journey and privacy and leverage all available structured and unstructured customer data as fuel to optimize customer interactions in real time. Front-office solutions from SAP Hybris furthermore help you adopt an agile, customer-centric business model with renovated financial processes and bring together marketing, sales, commerce, billing, customer service, and the back office to deliver on your promises to customers.

Figure 1.4 shows how front-office solutions can be integrated with back-office systems from SAP and others.

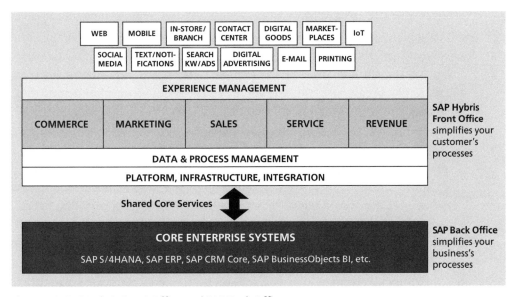

Figure 1.4 SAP Hybris Front Office and SAP Back Office

Following are the key business benefits of SAP Hybris front-office solutions delineated based on organizations and roles within the organizations:

- SAP Hybris Commerce helps organizations specifically to capitalize on the growth of the digital business by engaging and selling to modern customers using any touch points and to deliver contextual customer experiences that attract and retain profitable and loyal customers. Additionally, companies gain agility to meet changing customer needs and expectations as well as the ability to enter new markets and take advantage of emerging opportunities. You'll have the capability to sell directly to consumers (B2C) or to enterprises (B2B) using a single integrated platform. Commerce solutions help to increase conversion by using real-time customer insights and data-driven merchandising technologies and help to simplify customer processes with the prepackaged integration that occurs among SAP Hybris front-office solutions and with SAP back-office systems.

- SAP Hybris helps marketers capture all customer engagement data along each customer's journey to leverage advanced analytics and gain deeper customer insights into behaviors and motivation for accurate targeting and personalization. It enables real-time marketing with increased marketing transparency and internal collaboration, and allows you to play what-if scenarios and use predictive capabilities to optimize offers in the moment. Furthermore, SAP Hybris unifies the customer view and creates a single, always-current source for customer information.

- SAP Hybris solutions help sellers to target customers where they deliver the most value, to discover what they care about most, and to make each interaction relevant, meaningful, and impactful. Sellers can easily advise customers along their buying journey, propose real-time quotes, and go the extra mile for their customers while easing the administrative burden.

- SAP Hybris helps service organizations to meet customers in the channel of their choice and engage in context by knowing who the customers are, the products and services they have purchased, their prior interactions, and their financial history, regardless of the channels and payment modes. Additionally, the solution helps you operate as a single brand across channels, orchestrating customer experiences—both pre- and post-sale—across all touch points. Thus, companies can provide value to customers through very relevant and timely offers, rewards, discounts, and highly personalized treatment.

- SAP Hybris helps revenue managers unleash the creativity of pricing teams to rapidly launch customer-centric subscription offers to meet narrowly targeted customer needs. The solution enables partner alliance teams to exploit fast-moving market opportunities by quickly changing partner revenue-sharing models. In addition, finance teams typically use the solutions to achieve automation of the entire order-to-cash process and accelerate revenue collection.

1.5   Microservices Architecture and SAP Hybris as a Service

Packaged software has been built predominantly for aggregating and optimizing supply and resources in a linear value chain. However, almost all new business models are based on the idea of an open, connected, and nonlinear value chain. The software architecture must reflect such an open, connected, and distributed network to foster growth and capitalize on interactions between participants.

SAP Hybris as a Service was built with this new world in mind and helps you discover and consume software and leverage existing investments by adding new features. SAP Hybris as a Service is SAP's strategic commercial, legal, billing, and development network for microservices based on SAP Cloud Platform. Your developers and product managers can use SAP Hybris as a Service to deliver custom and commercial apps faster and to use leading-edge technology. The key components of SAP Hybris as a Service are as follows:

- **SAP Hybris as a Service Market**
  You can consider SAP Hybris as a Service as a marketplace with secure, trusted, and scalable enterprise-grade apps, application programming interfaces (APIs), and services from SAP Hybris and our partners. You can select the services that really matter to your business, instead of buying one large system that you won't get 100% of the value from. And, you'll be part of an ever-increasing ecosystem of new business functionality.

- **SAP Hybris as a Service Dev Portal**
  This is a centralized information hub and a dynamic community for software developers. The documentation, toolkits, and guidelines contained in the Dev Portal help developers quickly create services and APIs, or even build an entire new solution.

- **SAP Hybris as a Service Builder**
  This is the admin client and its key user interface. With an SAP Hybris as a Service account, you can create a project in the context of your SAP Hybris as a Service organization and manage the projects and resources in which you have membership according to the user roles in the project. Regardless of whether you're a

company (brand) or a developer, the Builder offers a consistent experience for managing your business.

- **SAP Hybris as a Service Community**
  This is the place to stay up to date with SAP Hybris as a Service events, get and share the latest showcases developed on SAP Hybris as a Service, and discuss issues with SAP Hybris as a Service experts in the online forums.

As described earlier, SAP Hybris as a Service is the modular microservices construction system for the SAP Hybris front-office and business process service component of SAP Cloud Platform. It's the foundational target architecture for the future of customer engagement and commerce in the cloud. It also enables customers and partners to extend their existing solutions through services and apps in the cloud. You'll find more information on microservices architecture and SAP Hybris as a Service in Chapter 7.

1.6   Summary

In this first chapter, we've discussed how customers are changing the rules of engagement and how businesses have to react to deliver consistent engagement at each touch point and every phase of an individual customer's journey. We provided an overview of how SAP Hybris solutions for commerce, marketing, sales, service, and revenue are designed to help companies create valuable interactions with customers, in any industry, anywhere in the world. In the next chapter, we'll take a deep dive into SAP Hybris Sales Cloud and learn how sales teams engage better and sell smarter in the digital economy.

Chapter 2
Sales

Traditional selling is obsolete, and the new rules of sales demand new tools. SAP Hybris Sales Cloud helps sales teams sell smarter in this digital economy and accelerate sales productivity through process orchestration and sales enablement.

Sales is one of the critical components of the SAP Hybris portfolio of products. Since the advent of customer relationship management (CRM) solutions in the mid-nineties, the selling process and the need for sales solutions have undergone transformational change. We've seen this change from sales force automation (SFA) to sales enablement. But now, even sales enablement tools don't satisfy the needs of ever-demanding sales organizations. Today, sales reps need the ability to access corporate information from wherever they are and from whatever device they are using, regardless of where information is stored and how information is delivered. Sales managers aren't interested in historical sales and forecast reports. They need predictive capabilities with what-if scenarios to fast-track their sales deals.

With SAP Hybris Sales Cloud, SAP offers the best sales solution for next-generation sales organizations. Built completely in cloud on SAP HANA, SAP Hybris Sales Cloud offers a comprehensive sales solution with an out-of-the-box mobile application, groupware integration, real-time reports, dashboards, and predictive analytics. In addition, SAP Hybris Sales Cloud comes with standard integration with other SAP Hybris front-office solutions, such as SAP Hybris Service Cloud, SAP Hybris Commerce, SAP Hybris Marketing, and SAP Hybris Revenue Cloud, as well as SAP back-office solutions such as SAP S/4HANA's digital core, SAP ERP, and SAP Customer Relationship Management (SAP CRM).

In this chapter, we start with SAP's strategy for sales and how SAP Hybris Sales Cloud aligns with this strategy. We explain all the functional capabilities of SAP Hybris Sales Cloud. We've dedicated a couple of sections to go over the mobility and analytics available in SAP Hybris Sales Cloud and how they can be leveraged by sales teams to drive up productivity. The last three sections in this chapter are devoted to integrating SAP Hybris Sales Cloud with other SAP Hybris front-office processes such as SAP Hybris Service Cloud, SAP Hybris Commerce Cloud, and SAP Hybris Marketing Cloud, as well as SAP back-office processes in SAP CRM, SAP ERP, and SAP S/4HANA.

2.1   Strategy for Sales with SAP Hybris

Before we review SAP's strategy for sales, let's look at the current market trends arising out of the ever-changing buying and selling landscape. These sweeping changes are forcing sales organizations to take a harder look at their traditional selling tools. These trends are as follows:

- **Increasingly knowledgeable customers and buying communities**
  Self-education through online communities and readily available resources have made customers more knowledgeable than ever. They have more information about the products and services before they make first contact with selling organizations. Customers expect sales representatives to be fully informed about their businesses, industry trends, competitive landscape, products, and services to have any engaging conversation.

- **Mandatory social and mobile user experience (UX)**
  Sales representatives are using social media to make new connections and grow intimacy with their contacts. They expect customer information on their mobile devices when they need it regardless of the source and location of the information. Social media and mobility are no longer restricted to our personal lives; they have become mandatory in our professional data consumptions and interactions.

- **Data is king**
  Selling advantages comes from knowing more about customers, markets, competitors, influencers, and so on. Sales representatives need to get critical information from internal and external data sources to draw actionable insights about their customers and sales opportunities. Artificial intelligence, predictive analytics, and big data are disrupting traditional sources of information, and next-generation sales applications must draw on these tools to offer unique selling advantages to sales organizations.

- **Move from SFA to sales orchestration and enablement**
  The traditional sales force applications have been rendered less effective in the digital economy. The trend isn't about automating sales processes to gain effectiveness and efficiency; instead, it's about enabling sales representatives with the tools and

information to be successful in their sales pursuits. It's about orchestrating their activities at various stages of the sales process by using predictive analytics and customer insights to help them move forward toward winning the sales deals.

Figure 2.1 shows SAP Hybris Sales Cloud, the solution designed to go beyond sales enablement and help sales organizations be more effective in their selling pursuits. It's an integral part of the SAP Hybris front-office portfolio.

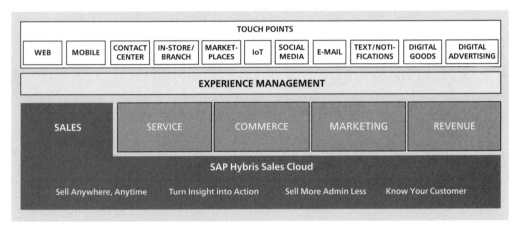

Figure 2.1 SAP Hybris Sales Cloud and Its Key Drivers

The design and SAP's future investments in SAP Hybris Sales Cloud are driven primarily by the following goals:

- **Sell anytime, anywhere**
  Extending their experience from personal life with mobile apps, sales representatives expect instant access to information and tools from the device of their choice irrespective of their location and time. In an SFA implementation, user adoption is key. Sales representatives crave advantage in sales pursuits, and sales tools must help them move forward in their sales cycles. Hence, SAP Hybris Sales Cloud is built to provide full-featured seamless experience across online and mobile devices for sales teams so they can engage with their customers and prospects in real time and manage their activities and track performance even when they are offline. The ability to sell anytime and anywhere is prerequisite for success in the digital economy.

- **Turn insight into action**
  Sales teams need customer insight to plan and execute necessary actions to meet their sales goals. With integrated front-office processes and standard out-of-the-

box analytics, SAP Hybris Sales Cloud empowers sales teams with data and insight in the context of accounts and opportunities to help them engage and connect with their customers in personal and relevant ways. Based on SAP's in-memory database SAP HANA, SAP Hybris Sales Cloud offers a sophisticated analytics infrastructure with standard and customizable reports, dashboards, and key performance indicators (KPIs) in real time. The built-in Deal Finder app helps sales representatives discover new leads and new opportunities on existing accounts. The spiral of influence in opportunity management gives visibility to account relationships and assists sales teams in realigning with customer contacts to maximize the probability of winning sales opportunities.

- **More time selling and less time on administrative tasks**
  In SAP Hybris Sales Cloud, special consideration has been given to requiring the least possible administrative tasks for sales representatives to foster the highest possible user productivity in terms of usability, data entry, and availability of information when needed. Users can personalize their experience to get quick access to the information they need in the least possible number of clicks. Built-in social collaboration and integration with productivity applications, such as Microsoft Outlook, Lotus Notes, and Gmail, offer users the flexibility to keep all customer interactions at one place and avoid redundant data entry in multiple applications.

- **Know your customer**
  Many times sales representatives have to use multiple systems to get information on pricing, inventory, open orders, quotes, service tickets, and so on. The SAP Hybris portfolio simplifies integration between front-office and back-office processes. SAP Hybris Sales Cloud provides real-time access to information from backend systems so that sales representatives don't need to waste time looking for pricing, quotes, and other order-to-cash information from backend systems. Right from the SAP Hybris Sales Cloud screen, they can access backend details from SAP S/4HANA, SAP ERP, and SAP CRM, as needed.

2.2   SAP Hybris Sales Cloud

Built with a mobile-first approach, SAP Hybris Sales Cloud is a mobile cloud solution that empowers sales teams of all sizes to be more effective and more relevant. It provides unified customer views across integrated front-office and back-office processes. The SAP Hybris Sales Cloud user interface (UI) lets users personalize their experiences without any need for programming. Figure 2.2 shows the fully configurable home page in SAP Hybris Sales Cloud.

Figure 2.2 SAP Hybris Sales Cloud Home Page

The modern UI based on the standard SAP Fiori paradigm allows personalization and adaptation based on business roles. It also supports right-to-left (RTL) navigation and layout, as shown in Figure 2.3.

> **Note**
>
> The SAP Hybris Sales Cloud license includes access through mobile applications (for more information, see Section 2.3). Because SAP Hybris Sales Cloud is built on the SAP HANA database, it also comes with standard out-of-the-box reports, analytics, and dashboards (see Section 2.4). Major parts of SAP Hybris Sales Cloud are based on the SAP Hybis Cloud for Customer product line.

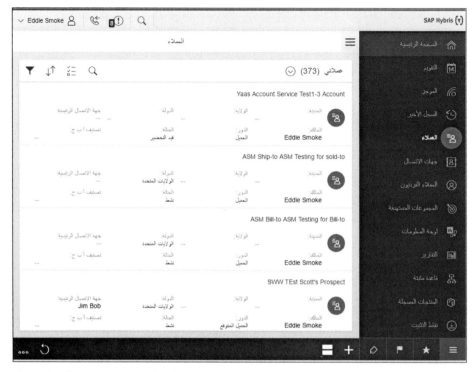

Figure 2.3 Supports RTL Navigation Layout

SAP Hybris Sales Cloud includes comprehensive sales enablement functionalities such as leads, opportunities, activities, visit planning and execution, sales planning, forecasting, and so on. In the following sections, we review all of these key functionalities of SAP Hybris Sales Cloud.

2.2.1 Account and Contact Management

SAP Hybris Sales Cloud offers a comprehensive account and contact management functionality that allows a consistent view of accounts and contacts data across online and mobile devices. Figure 2.4 shows the account screen where account details are presented neatly using tabs, including **OVERVIEW**, **FEED**, **CHARTS**, **ACCOUNT TEAM**, **SALES TERRITORIES**, **RELATIONSHIPS**, and so on.

Integrated account and contact management allows for a complete view of accounts and contacts to keep everyone on the same page with a single source of truth. Sales representatives can capture, monitor, store, and track information about customers, prospects, contacts, and partners. Users can personalize the information to suit their personal experience. The ability to follow, flag, tag, mark as favorite, edit, block, and set as obsolete can be found on the same screen, allowing users to meaningfully work through accounts and contacts as needed. Account and contact management, like the rest of SAP Hybris provides a real-time, consistent view of customers across all channels and devices. Some of the unique features of account and contact management are as follows:

- **Corporate and individual accounts**
  These accounts can be created to represent business and individual customers and support both business-to-business (B2B) and business-to-consumer (B2C) sales processes. The account hierarchy or group of linked accounts can be replicated from the SAP backend (SAP S/4HANA, SAP ERP, or SAP CRM).

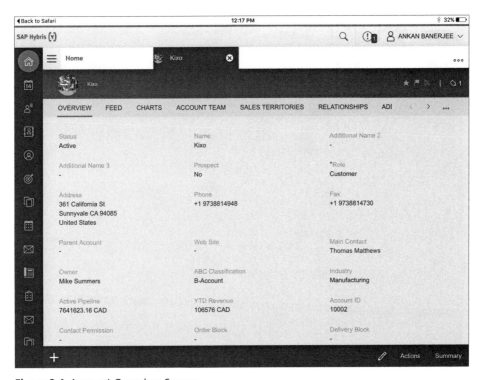

Figure 2.4 Account Overview Screen

- **Account and sales teams**
  The account team or sales team can be maintained for accounts to give visibility to all the team members working on the accounts.

- **Account merging**

  Account merging allows a simple action to merge accounts as needed. Account and contact change history tracks all the updates to accounts and contacts (what changed, who changed it, and when it was changed) and logs details for future reference.

- **Buying Center**

  The Buying Center can map either as a business partner relationship tool or a buying center tool for an account. It can identify the relationship type and attitude of the individual toward products or your organization as well as their strength of influence on colleagues or decision makers. Sales teams can use the Buying Center to build up an accurate picture of customer buying teams and decision making dynamics (see Figure 2.5).

Figure 2.5 Account/Opportunity Buying Center

- **Address maintenance**

  Address maintenance allows you to update account and contact addresses as needed.

- **Account and contact intelligence**

  This can be augmented with additional information from external sources. Using third-party tools integrated with SAP Hybris Sales Cloud (e.g., InsideView), you can get complete information about your accounts and contacts, including company information, news alerts, social profiles, social buzz, connections, financials, and so on. Figure 2.6 shows an example of account information insights.

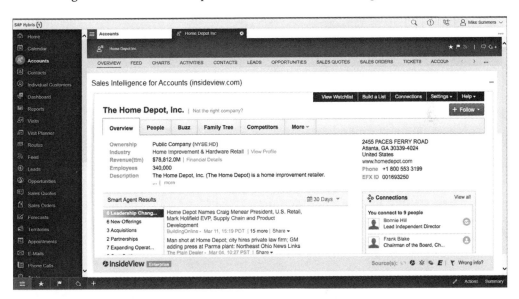

Figure 2.6 Account Insight Information

- **Account 360**

  This view information includes accounts information from SAP ERP and SAP Business Warehouse (SAP BW), as shown in Figure 2.7. Information on sales transactions, order history, and payment history from the SAP backend is displayed for the selected account in SAP Hybris Sales Cloud.

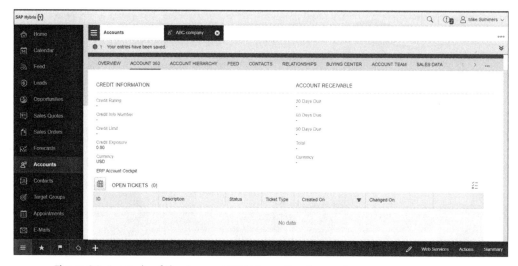

Figure 2.7 Example of the Account 360 View of an Account

- **Account factsheets**

  These factsheets provide snapshots of account details as configured in SAP ERP and SAP CRM, which can be viewed on the **Accounts** screen in SAP Hybris Cloud for Customer. You don't need a virtual private network (VPN) connection to the backend systems to launch and view these factsheets. Figure 2.8 shows an example of how to launch a **CRM Customer Factsheet** in the **Accounts** view in SAP Hybris Sales Cloud.

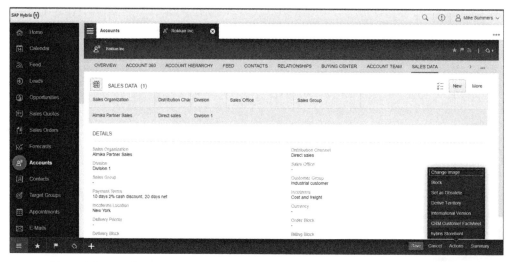

Figure 2.8 Launch CRM Customer Factsheet

- **Account planning**

  Account planning allows your sales team to collaborate and plan sales activities for accounts and prospects.

- **Map view and geo tracking**

  These are available for accounts using third-party mapping services via the GPS functionality of your mobile device. You can display accounts individually on the map or in relation to other accounts, and you can zoom in, zoom out, and pan in any direction as needed.

- **Rule-based employee assignment**

  This feature is allowed for accounts under different roles based on predefined determination rules.

- **Owner realignment**

  This is supported for organizational and territory realignment. The account owners can be reassigned from one account to another based on a relationship timeline.

- **Duplication check**

  The configurable duplication check function enables you to perform duplicate checks based on predefined rules to ensure that the information is unique. If information entered for the account and contact resembles the information of any existing account or contact, the system notifies you about the potential duplicates.

- **Social profile linking**

  Social profiles, for example, for individual customers, can be linked to their records in SAP Hybris Sales Cloud (using third-party integration) to get their social media updates directly in the **Accounts** and **Contacts** view from Twitter, Facebook, LinkedIn, Instagram, and so on.

- **Contact engagement scoring**

  Contact engagement scoring is available through the predictive analytics algorithm in SAP Hybris Sales Cloud to score contact engagement and quality of relationship.

- **Marketing attributes**

  These can be used in fine-tuning target markets for sales and marketing campaigns. You can define and assign various marketing attributes to the profiles of accounts and contacts. You can add **MARKETING ATTRIBUTES** from mobile devices, as shown in Figure 2.9.

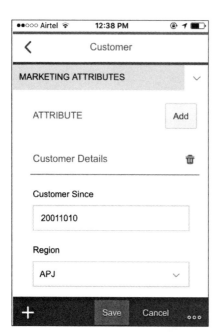

Figure 2.9 Adding Marketing Attributes from the Mobile App

- **Marketing permissions**
  These can be maintained in accounts and contacts to help you avoid contacting customers and prospects who have advised you in the past not to do so.

- **Target groups**
  These groups can be created for accounts and contacts to carry out marketing campaigns.

- **Maintain sales area data**
  Sales area data (**Sales Organization**, **Distribution**, and **Division**) can be maintained on the **Accounts** screen to keep them in sync with their sales area data in backend SAP systems.

- **Customer-specific price lists**
  A customer-specific price list can be maintained in SAP Hybris Sales Cloud, similar to how it's done in the SAP backend (whether SAP ERP or SAP S/4HANA).

- **Contextual reports**
  Contextual reporting helps you get real-time customer information and insight.

- **Read access logging (Eurozone compliance)**
  This empowers you to track users who viewed sensitive information about

customers and contacts such as personal information, bank details, pricing details, and so on.

- **Contacts and relationship management**
  This functionality can be used to manage time-bound relationships between accounts and contacts using configurable relationship management.

- **Groupware integration**
  Via syncing and the side pane, standard out-of-the-box integration is possible with groupware applications such as Microsoft Outlook, Lotus Notes, and Gmail. Accounts and contacts can be synced using drag and drop with SAP Hybris Sales Cloud for the side pane in groupware. Figure 2.10 shows an example of Microsoft Outlook integrated with SAP Hybris Sales Cloud as visible in the right side pane. In addition to the client-side integration, SAP Hybris Sales Cloud offers server-side integration with additional offerings like the MS exchange server.

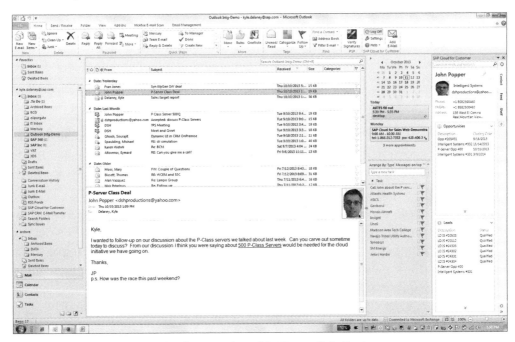

Figure 2.10 SAP Hybris Sales Cloud Integration with Microsoft Outlook

- **Business card scanner**
  The business card scanner using the ABBYY third-party application can scan business cards to create leads in SAP Hybris Sales Cloud.

- **Influencer map**
  Predicting top influencers is possible using the influencer map. You can easily identify the top influencer for a given contact and employee using embedded predictive analytics, which helps build successful sales teams and creates sales opportunities.

- **International address support**
  International addresses are supported for both accounts and contacts in SAP Hybris Sales Cloud. You can enter addresses in different country formats as needed.

- **Territory management and alignment**
  These are available for customers and prospects depending on the territory rules, such as postal codes, regions, area codes, product categories, and so on. Accounts can be aligned with active territory rules automatically.

- **Communication preferences**
  Setting communication preferences for each contact, such as whether the contact prefers phone calls, emails, text messages, and so on, helps you effectively communicate with contacts.

2.2.2   Sales Marketing

SAP Hybris Sales Cloud includes some marketing functionalities, including the ability to plan, create, and execute campaigns. For a comprehensive look at SAP Hybris Marketing Cloud, see Chapter 5.

Within SAP Hybris Sales Cloud, you can either create a campaign in the system itself or create a file export that can be used by an external agency to carry out a campaign. Campaigns can be executed to send emails or create a lead or activity. You can also create multistep campaigns with triggers and responses to automate campaign outcomes. The campaign responses can also be used to create target groups for subsequent campaigns. SAP Hybris Sales Cloud lets you leverage customer insights to create target groups and design campaigns to trigger creation of leads and follow-up opportunities.

Some of the key marketing functionalities for SAP Hybris Sales Cloud include one-click creation, the ability to update target groups from account and contact data sets, and integration with SAP Hybris Marketing Cloud. Figure 2.11 shows an example of an email campaign from SAP Hybris Sales Cloud.

Figure 2.11 Example of Email Campaign

The key features of the marketing functionality available in SAP Hybris Sales Cloud are as follows:

- **Target groups**
  These can be leveraged to identify target markets. Using required attributes to carry out specific campaigns, you can filter customers and prospects per specific marketing attributes and create target groups.

- **Measure campaign performance**
  Marketing campaign performance can be measured using standard delivered analytics and reports.

- **Multistage sales campaigns**
  These can be orchestrated based on various criteria for customer action and responses.

- **Campaign responses**
  These responses can be captured individually as shown in Figure 2.12.

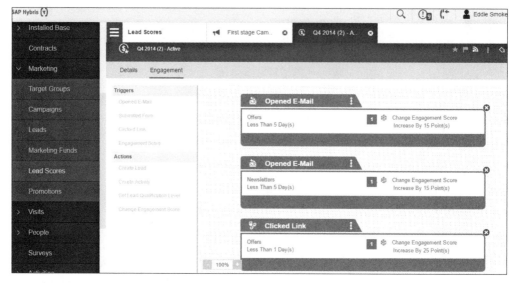

Figure 2.12 Email Campaign and Responses

- **Specific marketing promotions**
  Promotions can be used for specific marketing initiatives.

- **Mass text campaigns**
  Mass text messages (SMS) can be sent to contacts through a campaign.

- **Tasks and activities from campaigns**
  Tasks and activities from campaigns can be created in SAP Hybris Sales Cloud.

- **Target groups based on responses**
  Target groups can be created based on campaign responses to carry subsequent campaigns for the respondents.

- **Maintain and update target groups**
  Target groups can be maintained and updated per changes in marketing attributes, accounts, and contacts.

- **Graphical view of promotions calendar**
  A graphical view of the promotions calendar can be used to keep track of all current and future marketing campaigns.

- **Email blasts**
  Marketing automation email blast campaigns can be used to send mass emails to contacts in a target group.

- **Managing leads**
  Marketing campaigns can be used to create, manage, and update leads in SAP Hybris Sales Cloud.

- **Tracking sales campaign funds and spends**
  Marketing funds and spendscan be tracked for all marketing plans.

- **Marketing response analytics**
  These analytics include standard reports and analytics to provide real-time insights into all the campaigns and target groups, as shown in Figure 2.13.

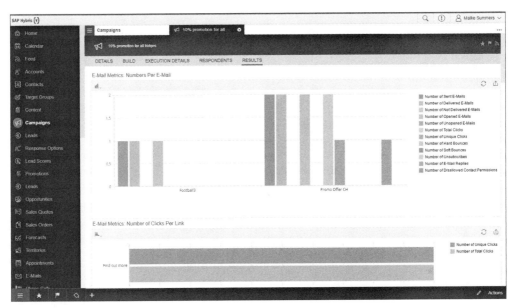

Figure 2.13 Email Campaign and Results

- **Integration**
  Integration to SAP ERP, SAP CRM, SAP Hybris Marketing Cloud, and SAP Jam allows completely integrated and simplified front-office and back-office processes.

2.2.3   Lead and Opportunity Management

Lead and opportunity management are at the core of sales. Leads are fuel for sales; more importantly, the quality of leads define sales performance and lead conversion to tangible business opportunities. Lead and opportunity management are integral parts of SAP Hybris Sales Cloud, and they enable the lead-to-cash process with integrated

SAP S/4HANA and SAP ERP. Figure 2.14 shows the lead and opportunity process flow in SAP Hybris Sales Cloud integrated with an SAP backend.

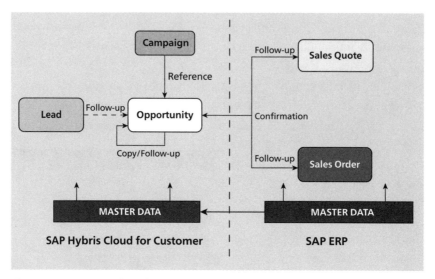

Figure 2.14 Integrated Lead-to-Cash Process

After leads are qualified, they can be converted into accounts and contacts or into opportunities. Using the opportunity functionality in SAP Hybris Sales Cloud, you can create sales quotes or sales orders in SAP S/4HANA or SAP ERP. In the following sections, we'll review the lead and opportunity management functionality in SAP Hybris Sales Cloud.

Lead Management

SAP Hybris Sales Cloud helps you manage business opportunities with automated tools to create, qualify, score, route, and nurture leads to orchestrate their conversion to sales. Using standard workflows and notifications, the system can automatically notify sales representatives and sales managers when leads aren't processed or qualified in time. With integrated lead processing and predictive analytics, you can score existing leads and suggest potential new leads to sales team. Figure 2.15 shows an example of the **Leads OVERVIEW** screen with all the details laid out in facets such as **FEED, PRODUCTS, ACTIVITIES, CONTACTS, SALES & MARKETING TEAM**, and so on. These areas can be personalized.

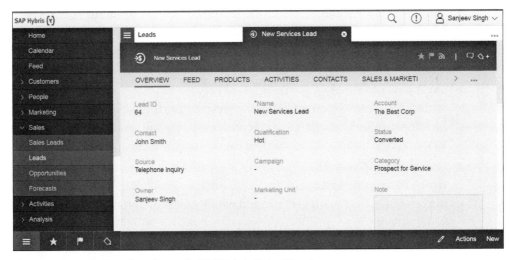

Figure 2.15 Leads Overview Screen in SAP Hybris Sales Cloud

The unique capabilities of lead management in SAP Hybris Sales Cloud are as follows:

- **Lead routing**
  Lead routing can be leveraged to route leads to sales representatives or lead qualifiers who can either accept or reject leads as appropriate.

- **Lead scoring**
  Lead scoring using a predictive engine based on predefined algorithms in SAP HANA predictive analytics helps improve the lead conversion ratio.

- **Lead acceptance/rejection**
  Lead acceptance/rejection is managed through lead status. When leads are assigned to sales representatives, they can either accept or reject them.

- **Lead nurturing**
  Lead nurturing can be done to qualify the leads further with additional information until the point that you either convert the lead to an opportunity or an account and contact.

- **Lead surveys**
  Lead surveys can be assigned to leads with a predefined questionnaire to allow structured information gathering and lead qualification processes.

- **Integration with lead-generation systems**
  Standard integration with lead-generation systems is available to import leads from third-party systems.

- **Various roles for teams**

  Sales and marketing teams can have various roles regarding leads. You can automate the determination of sales and marketing team members in leads from the sales team maintained on the accounts.

- **Lead conversion analytics**

  Standard lead conversion analytics help you measure the quality of leads and their conversion ratio. SAP Hybris Sales Cloud delivers standard lead conversion analytics that can be updated with additional reporting parameters as needed.

- **Lead notifications**

  Workflow and rule-based notifications are delivered out of the box for leads. You can configure these to trigger tasks and notifications to appropriate parties in lead management.

- **Lead-to-opportunity workflow and conversion**

  The lead-to-opportunity workflow and conversion allows one-click action to convert a lead to an opportunity and update the document flow for both the lead and opportunity.

- **Mobile lead management**

  Leads can be managed on mobile devices just as they are on the browser version. Standard SAP Hybris Cloud for Customer mobile apps can be used to process leads.

- **Deal Finder app**

  The Deal Finder helps you to identify opportunities from potential leads and gain insights into customer transactional and external activities. The Deal Finder applies a lead score to highlight high probability wins.

- **Lead engagement**

  Lead engagement scores are based on the marketing interactions between companies and their customers. You can configure engagement scores for leads to represent customer behavior patterns. For example, if lead engagement scores exceed 50%, then the lead qualification level can be marked as **Hot**.

- **Integration with SAP Hybris Marketing Cloud**

  Integration with SAP Hybris Marketing Cloud allows the creation of leads and activities out of campaigns. You can replicate contacts, accounts, leads, and activities from SAP Hybris Marketing Cloud to SAP Hybris Sales Cloud and measure the success of campaigns based on related leads, opportunities, and activities.

- **Partner channel support**

  Support for partner channel-based lead management is provided. With partner channel management, you can leverage the lead management functionality to drive partner engagement and partner channel revenue streams.

Opportunity Management

Opportunity management in SAP Hybris Sales Cloud delivers improved sales effectiveness and pipeline visibility. You can create, edit, view, and delete sales opportunities, as well as maintain accounts, contacts, products, sales and marketing teams, involved parties, appointments, activities, tasks, statuses, sales stages, and so on for opportunities in easy-to-navigate facets and work centers. It helps you leverage best practices to orchestrate effective and consistent sales processes. Figure 2.16 shows the **Opportunities Overview** screen.

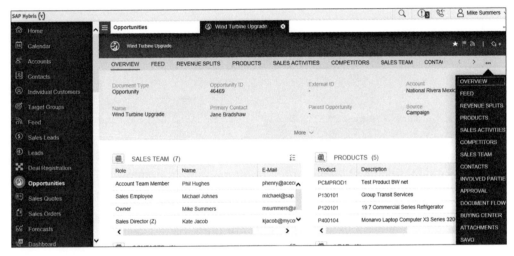

Figure 2.16 Opportunities Overview Screen

The most compelling features of opportunity management in SAP Hybris Sales Cloud are as follows:

- **Opportunity characterization and tracking**
  Opportunity characterization and tracking with required details are used to accurately reflect the sales opportunities and gain visibility into the sales pipeline.

- **Activity Advisor**
  Flexible sales methodology can be implemented in opportunities by modeling the recommended activities and tasks through **Activity Advisor**. You can model sales

methodology such as Miller Heiman or target account selling (TAS) to enable guided selling. For each sales stage, you can configure a set of mandatory or optional activities and tasks through **Activity Advisor** (see Figure 2.17). Sales representatives are provided with recommended activities and tasks at each stage in the sales process to achieve consistent and predictable sales outcomes.

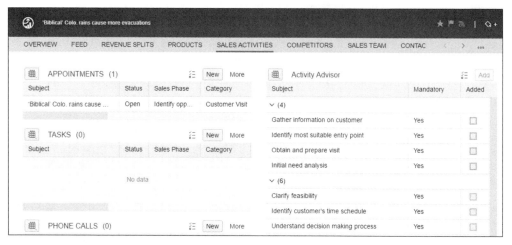

Figure 2.17 Activity Advisor for Opportunities

- **Lead management integration**
  Lead management integration with opportunities allows you to create opportunities as follow-up transactions from leads. In this process, the data are copied over from the source lead to the target opportunity.

- **Rule-based or manual opportunity distribution**
  Rule-based or manual opportunity distribution can be used for opportunities to be either manually assigned to the responsible sales representatives or auto assigned based on the account owner or responsible organization or territory structure.

- **Organizational and partner data determination**
  Organizational and partner data determination, such as responsible **Sales Organization** and **Involved Parties** (e.g., **Employee Responsible**, **Contact Person**, **Opportunity Approver**, **Sales Managers**, etc.) are supported through configuration.

- **Consolidation view**
  A consolidated view is provided of related activities, tasks, and transactions. Information in the **Opportunities** view is presented in intuitive facets and work centers.

All the preceding documents, as well as follow-up transactions, such as leads, activities, tasks, and appointments, are displayed in **Opportunities** to provide a complete document flow. Figure 2.18 shows the complete **Document Flow** view of an opportunity.

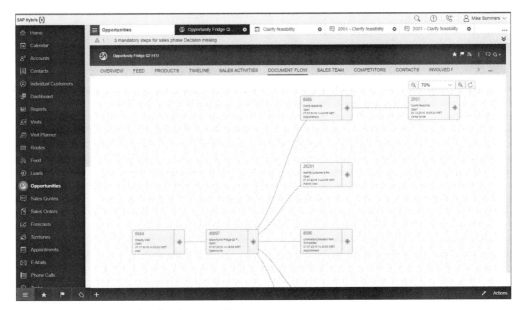

Figure 2.18 Document Flow for Opportunity

- **Attachments**
  Attachments and attachment distribution allow you to attach documents, images, and web links to opportunities from a local machine or from the library and ensure information visibility across the entire team working on the opportunity.

- **Opportunity hierarchies**
  Opportunity hierarchies on the header and item levels enable opportunities to be linked at both levels.

- **Opportunity relationships**
  Opportunity relationships allow opportunities to be linked together if needed.

- **Simple creation of follow-up documents**
  Simplified creation of follow-on documents is supported directly from the oppor-

tunity so you can create follow-up documents such as another quote, sales order, or opportunity.

- **SAP CRM/SAP ERP sales quote follow-ups**
  An SAP CRM or SAP ERP sales quote can be used as a follow-up. With the integrated SAP backend, you can create a follow-up sales quote and sales order in SAP CRM, SAP ERP, and SAP S/4HANA.

- **Spiral of influence**
  The spiral of influence capability can be used for stakeholder analysis. The influencer map on the **Top Influencers** opportunity allows you to visualize contacts and employees associated with opportunities. The spiral of influence shows which employees are closer to the decision makers, and it helps in planning activities to move employees closer to the decision maker to improve the chances of winning the deals. Figure 2.19 shows the spiral of influence for a particular opportunity.

Figure 2.19 Spiral of Influence for an Opportunity

- **Sales team assignment to opportunities**
  Sales team members working on opportunities can be assigned to the **SALES TEAM** category in the opportunity as shown in Figure 2.20.

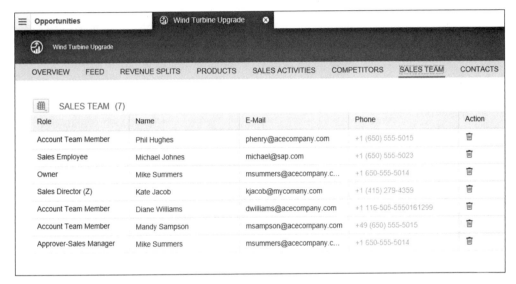

Figure 2.20 Sales Team Assigned to an Opportunity

- **Live updates on opportunities**
  Native social collaboration with feed updates in opportunities helps all the involved parties keep up with opportunity updates. If the opportunity owner added a note or moved the opportunity to the next sales phase, then everyone working on the opportunity can get live updates about these changes.

- **SAP Jam collaboration**
  Enhanced collaboration enables teams to collaborate on opportunities by creating groups in SAP Jam. These groups can be used to collaborate on team meetings, sales proposals, price negotiations, customer discussions, and so on.

- **Credit checks**
  Credit checks (through integration) on customers can be performed from the **Opportunities** view through integration with credit sources.

- **Survey assessments**
  Opportunities can be assessed through surveys attached to opportunities. Answers to survey questions can be leveraged to assess and qualify the opportunities.

- **Opportunity notes**

  Opportunity notes are free texts you can maintain on opportunities, and they are logged with user ID and time stamp for future reference.

- **Timeline**

  The opportunity **Timeline** and activity view provide a snapshot of scheduled activities within an opportunity either manually or through **Activity Advisor**. Figure 2.21 shows all the activities on an adjustable date horizon planned for an opportunity.

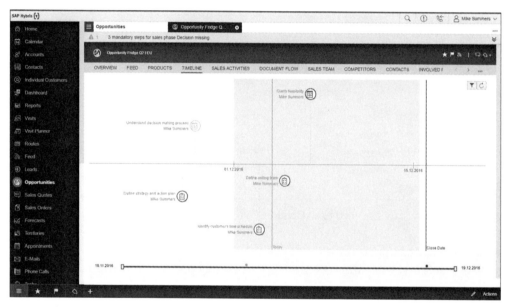

Figure 2.21 Activity Timeline for an Opportunity

- **Pricing flexibility**

  Pricing (in SAP Hybris Sales Cloud or optional pricing from SAP ERP) flexibility allows you to maintain and price opportunities natively in SAP Hybris Sales Cloud or from backend SAP ERP pricing.

- **Approval and notifications for opportunities**

  Workflow rule-based approvals and notifications (tasks and emails) can be used for opportunities to create tasks for team members or to send notifications for approval.

- **Email approval**
  An email-based approval process can be configured so that the approver gets a link in an email to approve the opportunity.

- **Revenue scheduling**
  Revenue scheduling can be used for all the opportunity items to show revenue forecasting. The revenue can be forecasted monthly for each product in the opportunity.

- **Pipeline performance management**
  Pipeline performance management is available. Depending on the sales stages and their corresponding chances of success, sales managers can prepare their pipeline reports in SAP Hybris Sales Cloud.

- **Defining competitors and products**
  Competitors and competitor products can be freely defined and then assigned to opportunities to better track the competitive landscape.

- **Configurable products**
  Configurable products can be used in opportunities through backend integration.

- **Analytical content**
  Comprehensive analytical content is delivered with a comprehensive list of reports, predictive analytics, and dashboards for opportunities.

- **Extensibility**
  Extensibility in SAP Hybris Sales Cloud allows customers and partners to build and deploy additional sales functionality in SAP Cloud Platform and extend opportunity functionality to realize unique sales processes.

- **Mobility**
  Mobility in opportunities is enabled through standard mobile apps available for iPhone, iPad, Android, and Windows.

- **Revenue planning and split allocation**
  Revenue planning and split allocation are supported to split sales revenue from an opportunity among all sales team members. The revenue splits can be performed for each opportunity item. Figure 2.22 shows an example of the **REVENUE SPLITS** view of an opportunity.

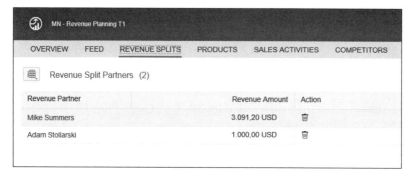

Figure 2.22 Opportunity Revenue Split among a Sales Team

- **Relationship mapping**
  Relationship mapping (graphical mapping) in the opportunity buying center graphically maps account relationships through relationship attributes. Standard out-of-the-box relationship attributes delivered with SAP Hybris Sales Cloud include **Attitude**, **Level of Influence**, **Description**, **Strength of Influence**, and **Interaction Frequency**. Figure 2.23 shows an example of the **BUYING CENTER** view of an opportunity.

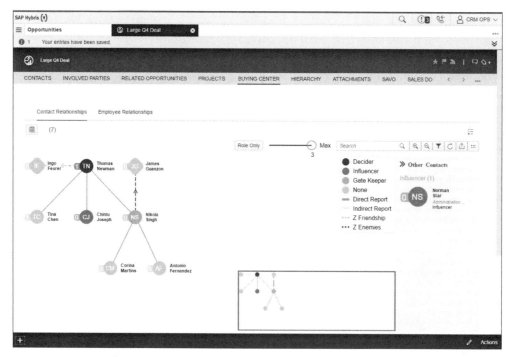

Figure 2.23 Buying Center View of an Opportunity

2.2.4   Sales Planning and Forecasting

Integrated sale planning and forecasting in SAP Hybris Sales Cloud lets you plan, define, create, and edit forecasts based on multiple dimensions such as accounts, products, product categories, sales organizations, territories, and sales teams. Sales planning enables you to define and monitor sales targets while providing seamless monitoring of sales targets, forecasts, and revenues. Out-of-the-box integration with Microsoft Excel enables you to work on your sales planning and forecasting in that familiar format.

You can also run what-if analyses based on real-time data and standard analytics delivered with SAP Hybris Sales Cloud. The key features of sales planning and forecasting are as follows:

- **Multidimensional sales planning by revenue and quantity**
  This provides the ability to sales plan for various dimensions such as **Products, Product Categories, Sales Organizations, Territories, Accounts**, and so on.

- **Target attainment analytics**
  These are available with sales planning and forecasting to help you track plan verses actual forecasts against monthly, quarterly, and annual targets.

- **Real-time Excel-based planning**
  This is available with standard out-of-the-box integration with Excel. By installing the Excel Add-In for SAP Hybris Sales Cloud, you can perform real-time calculation for sales planning and forecasting in Excel.

- **Opportunity revenue forecasting**
  Opportunity revenue forecasting by categories such as **Best Case Scenario Forecasts** or **Committed Forecasts** can be used to prepare different revenue forecasts for your opportunities.

- **Multidimensional forecasts**
  Multidimensional forecast override allows manual updates across all the dimensions of sales planning and forecasting.

- **Mobile forecasting**
  This is available on mobile devices just as in web browsers.

- **Variance analysis reports**
  These reports are available to track deviations in plan and actual forecasts.

- **Multiversion forecasting and submission workflows**
  Multiversion forecasting and submission workflows (e.g., multiple versions of sales plans and forecasts) can be prepared in the system. For example, you can create an optimistic version and a pessimistic version and submit both for approval before they become active. Only one version of a forecast can be active at a time.

- **Special feed integration with forecasting**
  This enables interested parties to receive updates on forecasts if there are any changes.

- **Forecast data sources and analysis reports**
  These are delivered to report on sales planning and forecasting. Some of the data sources are sales forecast planning, sales forecast, forecast and opportunity header, opportunity forecast and sales planning, and so on.

2.2.5 Activity Management

The activity management functionality in SAP Hybris Sales Cloud allows simplified planning, creation, viewing, and editing of all types of customer interactions during the customer relationship lifecycle across all devices. You can create multiple activities at once and manage calendars across multiple channels and teams. From activities, you can create follow-up documents such as leads, opportunities, or other activities as needed. Activities integrated with opportunities can be used to deliver recommended activities and content to sales representatives for each sales stage. The four types of activities available in SAP Hybris Sales Cloud are **Appointments**, **Phone Calls**, **Tasks**, and **Emails**. You can view, create, and update appointment and phone call activities by dragging and dropping them on your calendar. Figure 2.24 shows **Appointments** and **Phone Calls** activities on SAP Hybris Sales Cloud **Calendar**.

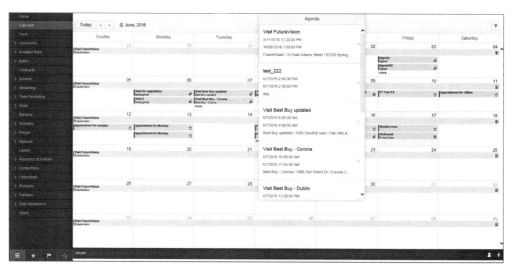

Figure 2.24 Appointment and Activities in Calendar View

You can view, create, and edit all four activity types from the **Activities** work center. The key activity management features in SAP Hybris Sales Cloud are as follows:

- **Categorization of activities**

  Activities are categorized to differentiate between the various types, such as **Customer Meeting**, **Product Presentation**, **Annual Visit**, **Courtesy Phone Call**, and so on. Categories can be defined through configuration per your business requirements.

- **Activity Advisor**

  This functionality works in conjunction with opportunities. You can include recommended mandatory or optional activities and tasks for each sales stage under **Activity Advisor** in **Sales Assistant**. While processing opportunities, you can add the recommended activities and tasks through **Activity Advisor**.

- **Activity Planner**

  This work center is used to plan activities for accounts based on recommended visit frequency and visit history.

- **Rule-based activity plans and routine rules**

  These can be used to determine recommended tasks in visit planning.

- **Grouping activities of certain types**

  Using **Activity List**, you can select multiple items and add accounts and contacts to create activities automatically. You can also assign and unassign owners to all the activities in the list.

- **Integration with Microsoft Outlook, Lotus Notes, and Gmail**

  As explained in the previous section, activities are integrated with groupware applications to allow you to drag and drop activities and tasks between SAP Hybris Sales Cloud and these groupware applications.

- **Activity Factsheet**

  This provides a snapshot of the activity, which can be shared with the activity partners.

- **Color-coded integrated calendaring.**

  This allows appointment and phone call activities to be displayed on the SAP Hybris Sales Cloud native **Calendar** view, and they are color coded to distinguish between the various activity types.

- **View and plan account-specific activities**

  You can view all the activities either planned or completed and if needed create new activities in the **Accounts** view.

- **Follow-up documents**
  Tasks, appointments, phone calls, leads, opportunities, and sales documents can be created as follow-up documents.

- **Visits as follow-up items**
  Visits can be created as follow-up items in the **Activity** view for a customer.

- **Holistic views of meetings**
  A holistic view of the meeting is available by providing information on appointments, such as attachments, involved parties, categories, related items, attendees, document flow, and so on, to provide complete details to all attendees.

- **Turn on/off summaries to external parties**
  Fine-tuning can be used to turn on/off sending summaries to external parties. For customer appointments, you have the option of checking in and checking out from a meeting and sending meeting summaries to all the attendees. Through configuration, you can turn off sending meeting summaries to the external parties.

- **Viewing sales as a timeline**
  Sales activities can be viewed as a timeline. You can view all the planned and completed activities in a calendar horizon.

- **View/edit consolidated activities and visits in a timeline**
  Consolidated activities and visits can be viewed and edited in a timeline in the **Opportunities** view. The **Activities Timeline** in **Opportunities** provides a snapshot of all the planned activities and tasks for that particular opportunity.

- **Assign campaigns and responses to tasks**
  Campaigns and responses can be assigned to a task. You can create tasks as a response to the campaign. For example, you can send an email campaign with a web link for the recipients to click. If a recipient clicks on the link, in response, you can create a task in SAP Hybris Sales Cloud to contact that recipient.

2.2.6   Visit Planning and Execution

Visit planning and execution enables field sales personnel to effectively plan their customer visits and record those visits and activities while on-site with customers. Using mobile devices to plan visits can be optimized to enable more customer visits in fewer miles. With visit planning and execution, you can configure and personalize sales route planning, surveys, and audits to meet the needs of any field sales organization. Figure 2.25 shows an example of a visit plan.

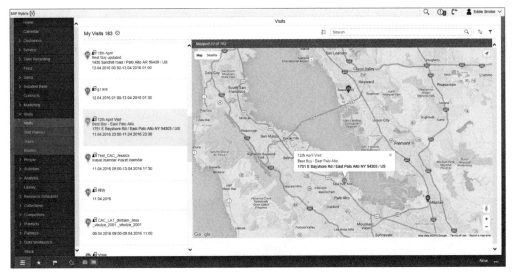

Figure 2.25 Example of a Visit Plan in SAP Hybris Sales Cloud

The key features of the visit planning and execution functionality in SAP Hybris Sales Cloud are as follows:

- **Create, view, edit, and delete customer visits**
  Visit planning and execution enables field sales personnel to plan, create, display, edit, and delete customer visits.

- **Add and create visit routes to maximize customer visits**
  Routes act as the single point of entry for visit planning. Sales personnel can create custom route plans by using templates and onscreen map to regenerate route plans for frequently-used scenarios. Routes can then be used to generate mass visits for the specified sales representative.

- **Inclusion of routes with other visits/appointments**
  In **Calendar** view, routes can be included with already planned visits and appointments to optimize the route.

- **Map integration and display using GPS coordinates**
  The visit planning and execution functionality in SAP Hybris Sales Cloud is integrated with GPS and provides coordinates of accounts on the route.

- **Route planning**

  Route planning can be based on the recommended frequency of customer visits, days since last visit, visits on basis of proximity, and so on. Driving directions are included in the route map, so by using the integrated route map, sales personnel can get driving directions for their customer visits.

- **Rule-based assignment of tasks and surveys**

  Recommended tasks and surveys are assigned to visits via activity routing rules. Figure 2.26 shows a visit with preassigned tasks.

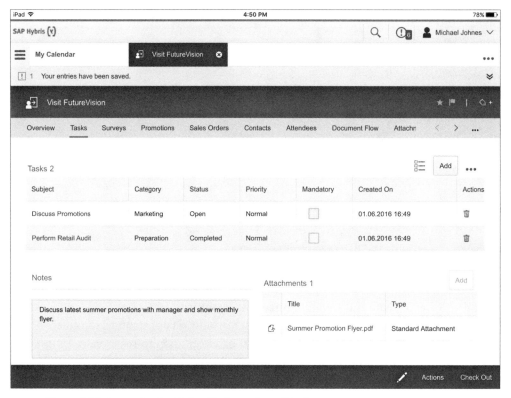

Figure 2.26 Example of a Visit with Preassigned Tasks

- **Capture check-in and check-out information, including GPS coordinates**

  For customer visits, sales personnel can capture check-in and check-out for the start and end of a visit, including start and end times and GPS coordinates.

- **Check ongoing and upcoming campaigns**
  For the accounts to be visited, sales personnel can check current and upcoming marketing campaigns.

- **Offline execution of visits from mobile devices**
  Visit execution is supported in offline mode from mobile devices. Sales personnel can still update their visits in the SAP Hybris Sales Cloud mobile application without any connectivity to the network.

- **Add pictures or other attachments to the visits or survey responses**
  Like any other activities and tasks, sale representatives can add pictures and attachments to the visits as well as responses to the attached surveys. Figure 2.27 shows a **Product Audit** survey and how you can attach photos from the local library or by taking and attaching a picture right away.

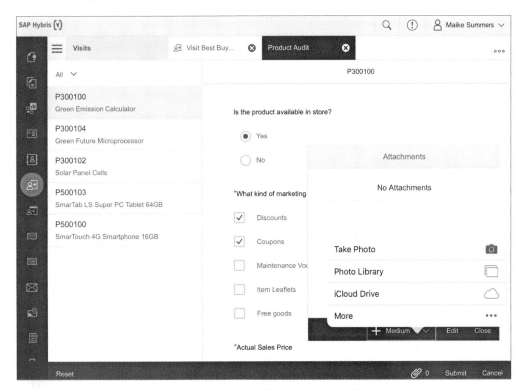

Figure 2.27 Example of a Product Audit Survey with Access to Attachments or Camera

- **Create follow-up items**
  A follow-up visit, activity, task, or any other sales document can be created as a follow-up documents from a visit.

- **Immediate assignment of tasks and surveys on visit refresh**
  Whenever a visit is refreshed, the system updates all planned visits, tasks, and surveys per determination rules.

- **Value helps for target groups and account hierarchy in routing rules**
  The routing rules for visit plans can be created for accounts in a target group or accounts hierarchy. The target group and accounts hierarchy are available as value help for selection while creating routing rules.

- **Manage follow-up actions**
  Follow-up actions can be managed, including opportunity, sales quotes, sales orders, service tickets, appointments, and phone calls.

- **Visit summaries**
  Visit summaries are available from previous visits for use in preparing for the next visit.

- **Notes on visits**
  As for all other activities, the **Notes** field for sales representatives to create visit notes as free text.

- **Involved parties**
  On visits, like appointment, the involved parties can be maintained per determination rules configured for all the parties involved in the visit or appointment.

- **View last visit's date/time and last visit's notes**
  View these details to refresh your memory before commencing with the next visit.

2.2.7   Quotation and Order Management

The quotation and order management functionality lets SAP Hybris Sales Cloud users create sales quotes and sales orders directly in SAP S/4HANA, SAP ERP, and SAP CRM. Quotes or orders can be created as a follow-up document from an opportunity in SAP Hybris Sales Cloud so that data are copied from the source opportunity to the target quote or sales order. Figure 2.28 shows an example of a quote in SAP Hybris Sales Cloud.

Figure 2.28 Sales Quote in SAP Hybris Sales Cloud

The key features of the quotation and order management functionality in SAP Hybris Sales Cloud are as follows:

- **Quotation and order capabilities**
  These capabilities, such as create, view, edit, and delete, can be accessed from an intuitive and modern UI in browsers as well as mobile devices. Integration with opportunity management allows you to create follow-up quotations or orders from an opportunity. Seamless integration between SAP Hybris Sales Cloud and SAP backend SAP S/4HANA, SAP CRM, and SAP ERP allows you to create a quotation and sales order as a follow-up transaction from an opportunity, and the data from that opportunity are copied to the quotation and order, hence reducing the risk of data entry error.

- **Pricing and price check**
  Pricing and price check capabilities are used with native SAP Hybris Sales Cloud so that quotes and orders are priced using native pricing. Basic pricing includes list

prices, discounts, and surcharges (fixed and percentage based). External pricing is integrated with SAP S/4HANA, SAP ERP, and SAP CRM (live call by order simulation) to get pricing data in quotes and orders in SAP Hybris Sales Cloud from the SAP backend system. Customer-specific product lists can be created so that quotes and orders include product descriptions as understood by customers.

- **Support for configurable products (through SAP ERP integration)**
  Support is available for configurable products (through SAP ERP integration) with a bill of material (BOM), provided configurable products are set up in the backend SAP ERP system.

- **Involved party determination**
  Involved parties are configured and determined for various party roles involved in quotes and orders (e.g., sold-to, ship-to, bill-to, payer, forwarding agent, etc.) based on preconfigured determination rules.

- **Notes and attachments**
  These can be added to quotes and orders as needed. They are logged with time stamp and user details for future reference.

- **Cross-selling, up-selling, and down-selling recommendations for various products**
  While creating quotes and orders, these recommendations are proposed to you to offer customers additional products and increase the sales value.

- **Product substitution for discontinued products in quotes and sales orders with new products**
  Adding products from past orders or quotations is allowed to reduce the order entry time.

- **Available-to-promise (ATP) checking from SAP S/4HANA and SAP ERP**
  The availability of products can be checked in appropriate plants and storage locations using ATP rules defined in SAP ERP while creating quotes and sales orders in SAP Hybris Sales Cloud.

- **Fast product entry option for both quotes and orders**
  This option requires limited data entry. Figure 2.29 shows how you can create sales orders based on a fast product search, direct access to past orders, predefined product lists, product promotions, or scanning a product barcode using the device camera.

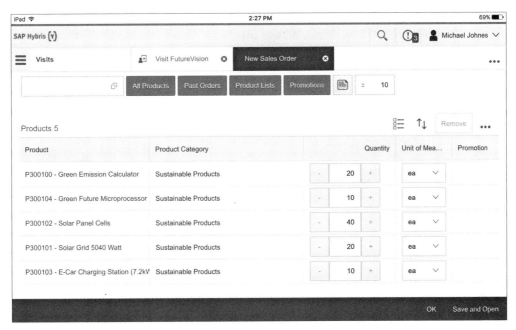

Figure 2.29 Fast Sales Order Entry in SAP Hybris Sales Cloud

- **Rule-based multistep approval workflow for both quotations and orders.**
  For example, if quotes may need approvals from management depending on the quote values, you can enable the approval process in SAP Hybris Sales Cloud depending on those rules.

- **Flexible notifications (internal and external) from quotes and orders**
  These notifications can be sent to both internal and external parties as needed per the predefined triggers.

- **Output management, format templates, and language selection**
  Using these capabilities, outputs can be created in various formats and languages from both quotes and orders, similar to the outputs of SAP ERP.

- **Mobile device support**
  This support includes digital signature capture in Sap Hybris Sales Cloud mobile applications. The mobile applications also allow capturing signatures in quotes and orders as needed.

- **Follow-up documents such as quotes, orders, and activities**
  These follow-up transactions are updated in the document flow for both quotes and orders.

- **Document flow**

  The document flow shows all the preceding as well as follow-up transactions linked to the referenced quote or order. For example, if a quote is created from an opportunity as a follow-up transaction, then the opportunity will appear under the document flow for the quote, and the quote will appear under the document flow for the opportunity. Figure 2.30 shows the **DOCUMENT FLOW** of a sales quote with direct access to SAP backend documents such as sales order confirmation, outbound delivery, and customer invoice.

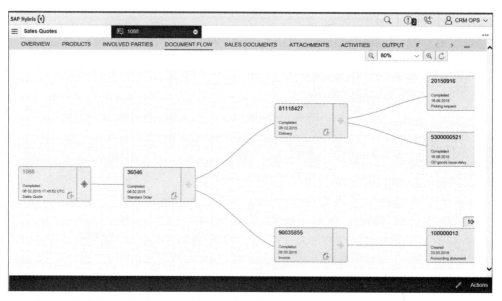

Figure 2.30 Example Document Flow of a Sales Quote

- **SAP Jam integration**

  This integration allows sales team to collaborate on quotes and orders by creating groups in SAP Jam, and information can be exchanged between quotes or orders and the SAP Jam group as needed.

- **Change history for quotes and sales orders**

  Change history provides details about what was changed, when it was changed, and, most importantly, who changed it. Having complete audit of change logs ensures accountability and transparency among the team members.

- **Application programming interface (API) support**

  This provides support for importing quotes and orders from external sources such as the Electronic Data Interchange (EDI) or other systems.

- **Standard analytical content delivered with SAP Hybris Sales Cloud for quotations and sales orders**
  These reports can be updated with additional reporting parameters as required.

- **Quote assessment**
  Quote assessments are made by assigned survey with predefined questionnaires and answers.

- **Credit limit and credit exposure**
  These can be set on accounts so that when quotations and sales orders are created for those accounts, they go through a mandatory credit approval process.

- **Replication of quotes and orders to SAP Hybris Sales Cloud from SAP ERP, SAP S/4HANA, or SAP CRM**
  To give visibility to quotes and orders created in the backend of SAP ERP, SAP S/4HANA, and SAP CRM in SAP Hybris Sales Cloud, you can replicate those transactions from the backend SAP system to SAP Hybris Sales Cloud. Standard out-of-the-box integration between SAP Hybris Sales Cloud and the backend SAP system supports this transaction replication.

- **Item types not relevant for pricing**
  Similar to nonprice-relevant items in SAP ERP, this can be configured in SAP Hybris Sales Cloud.

- **Offline sales quotes**
  These can be created in the SAP Hybris Sales Cloud mobile application.

- **Barcode scanning**
  Barcode scanning enables streamlined product entry for quotes and orders.

- **Incoterms, payment terms, order status management, and multiple schedule lines**
  These are all similar to standard SAP S/4HANA or SAP ERP quotes and sales orders. Multiple schedule lines in orders are supported to enable multiple delivery dates for an item.

- **Order transfer statuses**
  Statuses such as **Not Started**, **In-Process**, **Finished**, **Interrupted**, and **Not Relevant** help you identify objects sync information between SAP Hybris Sales Cloud and SAP S/4HANA or SAP ERP.

- **Pricing date and requested delivery date**
  These dates are set on quotes and sales orders.

2.2.8   Partner Channel Management

Businesses can extend SAP Hybris Sales Cloud to their partners to effectively collaborate with them and drive up the sales revenue and market coverage. Partner channel management offers an intuitive and personalized user experience for partner users, streamlined partner program management, lead routing, and opportunity management. The key features of partner channel management delivered standard out of the box with SAP Hybris Sales Cloud are as follows:

- **Partner program management functionality**
  Available in SAP Hybris Sales Cloud, partner program management can be used to automate the complete process, including partner application, partner application review and approval, partner registration, partner collaboration on leads, opportunities, and so on. Partner Portal lets partners review partner programs, company information, marketing, sales and activities information.

- **Partner channel manager page**
  This page allows you to review information about partners, as shown in Figure 2.31.

Figure 2.31 Partner Channel Management

- **Partner account and contact management**
  These functionalities let partners create, view, and edit accounts and contacts information. These accounts and contacts are specific to partners, and their information isn't shared with other partners.

- **Lead management functionality**
  Lead management lets partners create, view, and display leads from their **Partners** portal.

- **Opportunity management functionality**
  Opportunity management enables partners and partner managers to collaborate on opportunities and create, view, display, and share opportunities as needed.

- **Deal registration**
  Deal registration allows companies to formalize the deal registration process with partners to avoid channel conflicts and foster better cooperation on joint sales pursuits.

2.3   Mobile Sales Scenarios

The SAP Hybris Sales Cloud license includes access through mobile applications. Standard mobile applications are available for iPhones, Android phones, Windows 10 phones, iPads, and Android and Windows tablets (Windows 8.1 or higher). These apps can be downloaded from their respective app stores, and their UIs are consistent with the browser versions. Additionally, most of the functionalities from the browser versions are supported. Figure 2.32 shows an example of the mobile applications for SAP Hybris Sales Cloud (SAP Hybris Cloud for Customer).

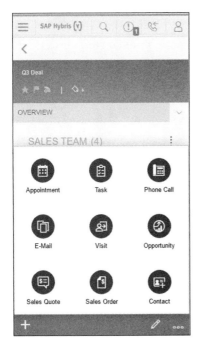

Figure 2.32 SAP Hybris Sales Cloud Mobile Apps

The key features of the SAP Hybris Sales Cloud mobile applications are as follows:

- **Tablet access**

  Access is provided for iPad, Android, and Windows tablets with similar user experiences.

- **Smartphone access**

  Access is provided for apps from iPhone, Android, and Windows devices.

- **Offline view**

  Transactions from SAP Hybris Sales Cloud mobile applications can be created and updated when offline through this view. Advanced offline capabilities such as high-volume scenarios and data distribution rules are available can be used with apps without any network connectivity.

- **Mobile customization and administration**

  Customization and administration allow enhancements to applications for specific business requirements.

- **Mobile dashboards and KPI monitoring capabilities**

  The mobile application allows dashboards and KPI monitoring capabilities to track various sales performance metrics.

- **Advanced analytics**

  Analytics with multilevel drilldown capabilities are supported on mobile devices.

- **Metadata-driven mobile extensibility**

  This enables custom extensions to the cloud for SAP Hybris Sales Cloud mobile applications.

- **Store check-in for retail with GPS capture**

  In the Retail Execution mobile app, users can check in for the retail visit and capture the GPS location for the store, as well as view the **Planogram**, as shown in Figure 2.33.

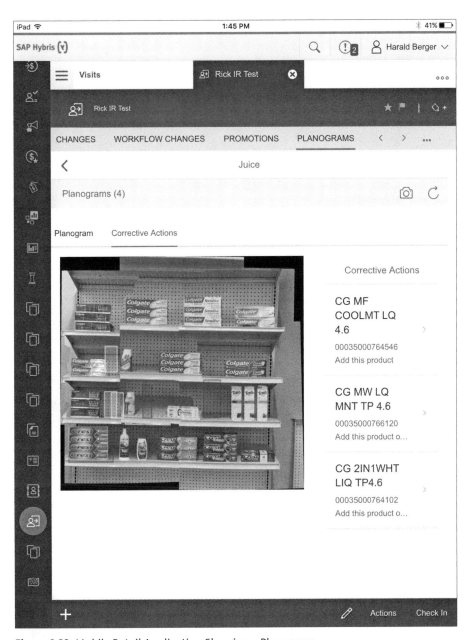

Figure 2.33 Mobile Retail Application Showing a Planogram

- **HTML mashup support**
  Similar to the browser application, this enables the display of data from multiple sources in an HTML mashup.

- **Barcode scanning**
  Barcode scanning of scan products in quotes and sales orders avoids errors in data entry.

- **Multiple tab support**
  Support is provided for multiple tabs to display information about master and transaction data so that you can easily navigate from one tab to another to find the required information.

- **Smartphone layout optimization**
  This enables the applications to sense the target device and adjust the display layout to suit the device.

- **Business card scanner**
  Contacts in mobile application can be created by scanning business cards.

- **Lost connectivity detection**
  When the connection is lost, you'll get a prompt notifying you, and offline operation is enabled until the connection is established.

- **Enterprise device management**
  Single Sign-On (SSO), upgrades, and the ability to enable consistent security policies and application management across all the mobile devices are all available.

2.4   Reporting and Analytics

Standard reporting and analytics delivered out of the box with SAP Hybris Sales Cloud (SAP Hybris Cloud for Customer) offers real-time insights for sales teams. You'll find embedded reports with real-time analysis and reporting on internal and external data sources, along with easy-to-use tools so you can create custom reports by line of business to deliver information when and where it's needed. Interactive dashboards and KPI tiles to view and carry drilldown analysis deliver intelligence to improve business decisions and maximize revenue and customer satisfaction. Figure 2.34 shows an example of some of the reports and dashboards available in SAP Hybris Sales Cloud.

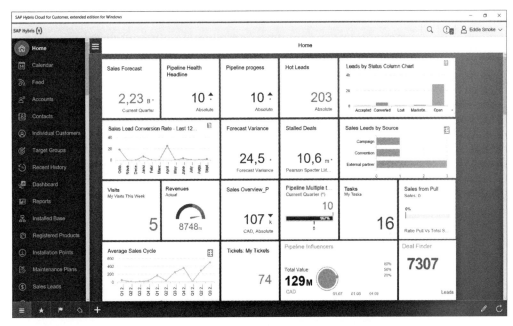

Figure 2.34 Standard Analytics and Dashboard for SAP Hybris Sales Cloud

Following are some of the key features of sales analytics and predictive applications delivered with SAP Hybris Sales Cloud:

- **Standard and custom reports**
  These reports are available for all the key functionalities within SAP Hybris Sales Cloud such as leads, opportunities, activities, forecasts, visits, and so on.

- **Join and combine data sources**
  Data sources can be joined to create reports per your requirements.

- **Data source/content documentation**
  Data source and content documentation are available, which allows you to review and select appropriate data sources for your reports.

- **Monitor KPI reports**
  KPI reports feature traffic light thresholds and contextual reports so you can easily identify the actionable indicators.

- **Schedule broadcasts for reports and dashboards**
  Broadcasts can be scheduled for recurring reports and dashboards to individuals and team members, as needed.

- **Interactive dashboards**
  These dashboards let you drill down on reports, as shown in Figure 2.35.

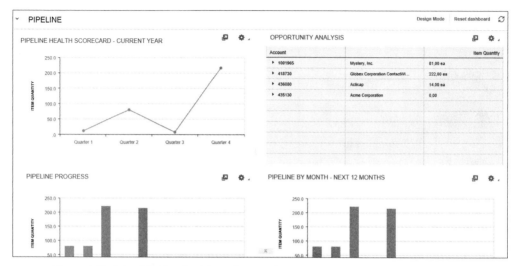

Figure 2.35 Sales Pipeline Dashboard Example

- **Online analytical processing (OLAP) analytics**
  In Sap Hybris Sales Cloud, these analytics allow advanced reporting and KPI text headline analysis.

- **Advanced real-time analysis**
  This analysis is possible in Excel using the add-in available in SAP Hybris Sales Cloud.

- **Collaboration**
  Team members can collaborate around reports, KPIs, and insights because they are all working on the same source of data.

- **Integration**
  SAP Hybris Sales Cloud can be integrated with SAP BW to either expose data sources to SAP BW or embed SAP BW web reports for additional insights.

- **Embedded reporting**
  Focused reports can be embedded in sales object facets.

- **Work center and role-based assignments for report security**
  This ensures that reports can only be used by authorized individuals.

- **Report object administration**
  Administration can be performed on local and global report objects.

- **Export to Excel**
  Report object work lists can be exported to Excel, as shown in Figure 2.36.

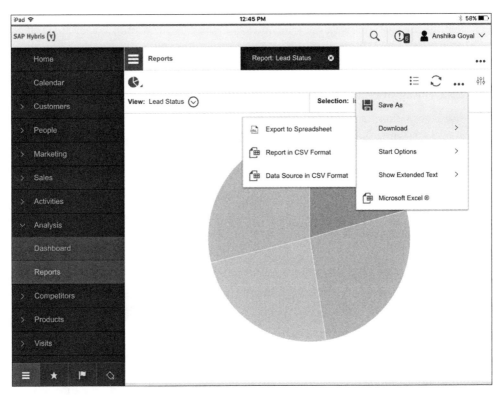

Figure 2.36 Report Export to Excel or CSV Format

- **Report migration**
  Report objects can be migrated between tenants (test and production).

2.5   Integrating with Other SAP Hybris Front-Office Solutions

SAP Hybris Sales Cloud includes prepackaged integration with other SAP Hybris front-office components such as SAP Hybris Service Cloud, SAP Hybris Commerce Cloud, and SAP Hybris Marketing Cloud. In the following sections, we'll review the front-office integration options for these solutions.

2.5.1   Integration with SAP Hybris Service Cloud

SAP Hybris Sales Cloud and SAP Hybris Service Cloud share the same data model. Sales transactions in SAP Hybris Sales Cloud and service transactions in SAP Hybris Service Cloud also share a common customer database. For any account, you can see a list of all the sales and service transactions from one view. No extra effort is needed to integrate SAP Hybris Sales Cloud and SAP Hybris Service Cloud, as they are built on same system and the same database (SAP Hybris Cloud for Customer).

2.5.2   Integration with SAP Hybris Commerce Cloud

SAP Hybris Commerce Cloud offers a ready-to-use integration framework to integrate SAP Hybris Sales Cloud with SAP Hybris Commerce Cloud. Integration between the two is orchestrated either through SAP Hybris Commerce Cloud's data hub or directly through synchronous HTTP access via URL with SSO. Some of the compelling advantages of this integration are as follows:

- Synchronizing customer and contact data between these two systems is easier due to the consistent view of customer information across sales and commerce channels.

- Sales representatives in SAP Hybris Sales Cloud can access product catalogues and the storefront in SAP Hybris Commerce to offer interactive selling to customers.

- With integrated SAP Hybris Commerce Cloud's Assisted Service Module (ASM), sales employees can offer real-time sales support to customers when they are stuck during their online buying process, using the same website storefront across the omnichannel framework both in store and virtually online.

- SSO can be enabled across SAP Hybris Sales Cloud and SAP Hybris Commerce Cloud to improve user experience and efficiency in the sales process.

2.5.3   Integration with SAP Hybris Marketing Cloud

SAP offers standard integration between SAP Hybris Sales Cloud and SAP Hybris Marketing Cloud. Some of the advantages of integrated front-office processes across the two are as follows:

- Closed-loop marketing campaign planning is enabled in SAP Hybris Marketing and campaign execution is enabled in SAP Hybris Sales Cloud. You can plan campaigns and sales initiatives in SAP Hybris Marketing Cloud and then execute them as leads in SAP Hybris Sales Cloud.

- By using target groups based on customer segmentation algorithms in SAP Hybris Marketing Cloud, you can create prequalified leads for sales representatives to develop further sales opportunities in SAP Hybris Sales Cloud.

- Changes in leads and opportunities in SAP Hybris Sales Cloud are synchronized back to SAP Hybris Marketing Cloud and stored as interactions, hence providing real-time full transparency to marketers on their marketing campaigns and execution.

2.6   Integrating with SAP S/4HANA and SAP ERP

SAP Hybris Sales Cloud offers prepackaged integration using SAP Cloud Platform Integration to enable end-to-end business process integration with SAP S/4HANA and SAP ERP. These prepackaged integration contents are delivered in the form of iFlows, which are user-defined functions required for standard integration. iFlows contain predefined mappings with many standard fields and user-defined functions and routing rules. Each iFlow contains logical and technical settings. iFlows run on SAP Cloud Platform Integration as well as SAP Process Integration (SAP PI). Customers already running SAP PI can extend it to integrate SAP Hybris Sales Cloud; otherwise, they can leverage SAP Cloud Platform Integration to integrate SAP Hybris Sales Cloud with SAP S/4HANA and SAP ERP.

In addition to prepackaged integration contents (iFlows), SAP offers APIs to integrate SAP Hybris Sales Cloud with any third-party applications in cloud or on premise. These APIs are sets of public Simple Object Access Protocol (SOAP) web services and OData/RESTful APIs. These APIs can be used by customers and partners to build integration on SAP Cloud Platform Integration or any standard third-party integration platform. You can choose whether to deploy these integrations in the cloud or on premise. Prepackaged integration between SAP Hybris Sales Cloud and the SAP back-end system allows you to integrate front-office with back-office processes as follows:

- **Master data synchronization**
  Integration between SAP Hybris Sales Cloud and the SAP S/4HANA or SAP ERP allows unidirectional replication from SAP ERP to SAP Hybris Sales Cloud for account hierarchies, products, pricing, sales organizations, currency conversion rates, employees, and system configuration. In addition, it allows bidirectional synchronization of accounts and contacts between these two systems as shown in Figure 2.37.

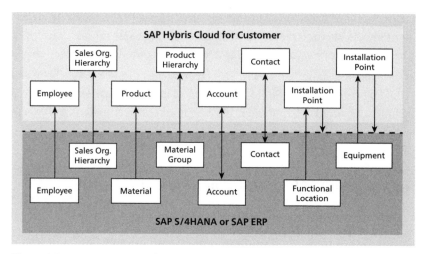

Figure 2.37 Master Data Replication between SAP Hybris Sales Cloud and SAP S/4HANA or SAP ERP

- **Opportunity to order integration**
  The integration provides sales professionals with real-time access to pricing checks in the backend system from opportunities in SAP Hybris Sales Cloud, quote and sales order processing in real time, ATP, and other sales process details from SAP S/4HANA as shown in Figure 2.38.

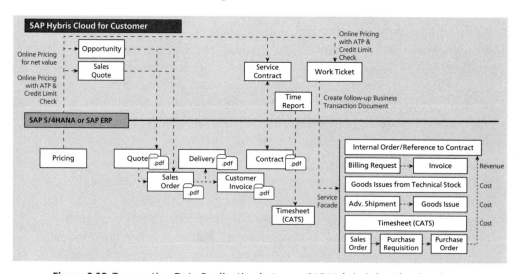

Figure 2.38 Transaction Data Replication between SAP Hybris Sales Cloud and SAP S/4HANA or SAP ERP

2

- **Processes orchestration across SAP Hybris Sales Cloud and SAP S/4HANA**
  The integration provides real-time full accessibility to order fulfillment and document flow information in SAP Hybris Sales Cloud. To enable the **Account 360** view in SAP Hybris Sales Cloud, recent sales orders can be replicated from the SAP backend (SAP S/4HANA or SAP ERP) to SAP Hybris Sales Cloud.

- **Launch customer cockpit from SAP ERP to get a comprehensive view of accounts and prospects in SAP Hybris Sales Cloud**
  Using the **Customer Cockpit**, you can quickly edit SAP S/4HANA and SAP ERP documents as if they were in SAP Hybris Sales Cloud. It also allows drilldowns into backend documents. Figure 2.39 shows the **Customer Cockpit** screen from SAP ERP in SAP Hybris Sales Cloud. In contrast to the customer factsheet integration described earlier, you need a virtual private network (VPN) connection to your backend system to lauch the **Customer Cockpit** user interface.

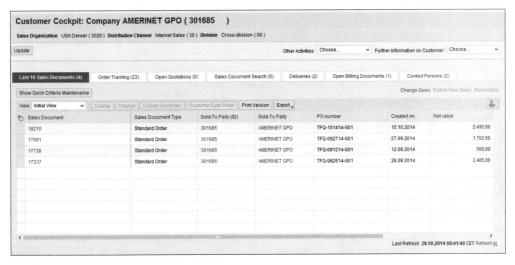

Figure 2.39 Customer Cockpit

2.7   Integrating with SAP Customer Relationship Management

To help customers protect and leverage investments already made in SAP CRM and at the same time take advantage of innovations constantly delivered with SAP Hybris Sales Cloud, SAP delivers standard integration between SAP Hybris Sales Cloud and

SAP CRM. Similar to the previous section, you can integrate SAP Hybris Sales Cloud with the SAP CRM system using prepackaged integration contents delivered in the form of iFlows. These iFlows can be implemented using SAP Cloud Platform Integration or through SAP PI.

Integration between SAP Hybris Sales Cloud and SAP CRM helps you mesh the front-office processes as follows:

- SAP Hybris Sales Cloud can be implemented as a layer on top of SAP CRM to offer a modern and intuitive UI to users across browsers and mobile devices. Hence, for users of both SAP CRM and SAP Hybris Sales Cloud, it appears as one system.

- Real-time master data synchronization between SAP Hybris Sales Cloud and SAP CRM allows one-direction data replication from SAP CRM to SAP Hybris Sales Cloud for business configuration, account hierarchy, products, pricing, sales organizations, marketing attribute definitions, employees, and territory assignments. In addition, it allows bidirectional data replication for accounts and contacts between SAP CRM and SAP Hybris Sales Cloud, as shown in Figure 2.40.

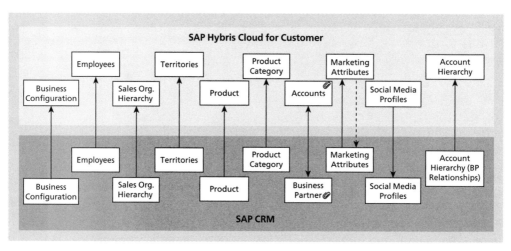

Figure 2.40 Master Data Replication between SAP Hybris Sales Cloud and SAP CRM

- Real-time transaction synchronization occurs between SAP CRM and SAP Hybris Sales Cloud for opportunities with attachments, campaign headers, leads, activities, quotes, and sales orders, as shown in Figure 2.41.

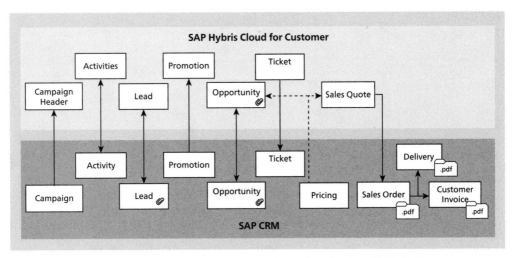

Figure 2.41 Transaction Replication between SAP Hybris Sales Cloud and SAP CRM

2.8   Summary

In this chapter, you've learned how SAP Hybris Sales Cloud can help organizations sell smarter, act faster, and be more relevant anytime, anywhere. SAP Hybris Sales Cloud offers in-depth sales functionality; standard out-of-the-box integration with SAP Hybris front-office processes and SAP back-office processes; standard mobile apps on iOS, Android, and Windows; and, finally, SAP HANA predictive analytics and dashboards. In the next chapter, you'll learn how SAP is redefining the customer service application landscape with SAP Hybris Service Cloud offerings.

Chapter 3
Service

Technology has changed the service landscape. Customers pick the time, place, channel, and touch points to communicate with businesses. The SAP Hybris Service Cloud portfolio delivers end-to-end service excellence across channels and devices.

Customer service is no longer considered a post-sales activity. In this social media era, in which everyone is always connected, brand reputation and customer loyalty are more fragile than ever. Customers are using social media as a tool to look for information and engage with online communities to provide feedback about their customer experiences. Businesses take years to gain customers' trust and build brand reputation by consistently delivering quality products and services to the marketplace. However, one negative social media post from a dissatisfied customer can cause a severe dent in a company's financials and market share. Social media amplifies customer feedback and experiences, and it's critical for businesses to provide seamless customer services experience across all channels and customer touch points.

Traditional approaches to serving customers are unsustainable in the digital economy. Customer service expectations have grown exponentially. Customers want to communicate with companies through new channels and touch points. It's not enough to provide multichannel services; customers today demand omnichannel service experiences. SAP Hybris Service Cloud is the answer to enabling the next generation of service engagements. It allows you to intelligently integrate and simplify service processes across the spectrum from self-service to customer contact center to field service.

In this chapter, you'll learn about SAP's approach to enabling end-to-end service engagement through SAP Hybris Service Cloud. The need for service processes varies widely from company to company and from industry to industry. At the lowest end of spectrum, SAP offers online self-help to customers, and, on the other end, SAP provides fully equipped mobile field personnel to provide on-site service to customers.

SAP Hybris Service Cloud covers the entire spectrum of service processes with SAP Hybris Service Engagement Center and SAP Hybris Cloud for Customer. Later in this chapter, we'll review their key components, unique capabilities and business benefits, deployment options, and, most importantly, out-of-the-box analytics. We'll also cover integration capabilities for SAP Hybris Service Cloud with other SAP Hybris front-office solutions and with back-office SAP S/4HANA, SAP ERP, and SAP Customer Relationship Management (SAP CRM).

3.1   Strategy for Service with SAP Hybris

SAP's strategy for service is primarily driven by the sweeping changes in customers' expectations resulting from the digital transformation. They expect customer service personnel to be more knowledgeable and be ready to engage with them in the channel of their choice. Customers feel entitled to more options to resolve their issues, and customer service agents need contextual real-time customer insight throughout the entire customer journey. To complete field service repairs on the first visit, field service technicians need scheduling, parts management, and collaboration with experts on the job as needed. Service management teams need operation insight and the ability to work anywhere and anytime to run a profitable service operation business.

With SAP Hybris Service Cloud, the strategies behind these solutions are as follows:

- **Omni channel service**
  Service solutions must allow customer service agents to serve customers in the communication channel of their choice. Each customer chooses his own methods of interacting, and businesses must provide a seamless service experience across all communication channels. Whether it's online community, phone call, chat, email, self-service, or social media, you need to meet customers in the environment they prefer to interact and answer their inquiries seamlessly across all channels.

- **Provide insight when needed**
  Customer service agents must be empowered with the right information to help them successfully complete customer interactions on first contact. Real-time visibility into the availability of field service technicians is required to schedule appropriate resources to open service demands and maximize their utilization. Service agents need collaboration tools and instant access to the knowledge base to successfully solve customer issues. Having access to the right insight at the right time is crucial for providing an engaging service experience to customers.

- **Personalized interactions**
  Customers shouldn't be expected to give their information every time they contact a different service agent in your organization. The interactions with customers must be personalized every time they make contact, regardless of which channel they are using to interact with your company. Service solutions must offer service agents instant access to customer profiles, order history, service history, feedback, and preferences at the point of interaction to demonstrate care and commitment to customers.

- **Be mobile**
  Field service without mobile applications is considered primitive and outdated. Field service technicians must be equipped with service applications and tools on their mobile devices to quickly and efficiently address customer issues. They should be able to look up spare parts inventory, products, and technical specifications right from their smart devices while they are at the customer site. Their productivity to resolve service calls can be greatly enhanced with field mobile applications. It's critical that field service mobile applications support offline capabilities because online connectivity isn't always be guaranteed or even allowed at service locations.

- **Integrated with enterprise**
  Service touches both front-office processes, such as sales, commerce, and marketing, and back-office processes, such as order management, logistics, finance and controlling, inventory management, human resources, procurement, and so on. Service processes tightly integrate with logistics for warranties, parts availability, parts shipments, parts consumption, and so on, and they integrate with finance for cost collection, profitability analysis, calculating cost of goods sold, and so on. Integration with Human Resources (HR) allows you to capture service technician's time activities such as travel time, work time, idle time, and vacation time. Service teams must be integrated with the entire organization to operate as a single brand across channels and touch points.

End-to-end customer service engagement has three parts: self-service, customer contact center/call center, and field service. Depending on the industry, companies may implement service processes partly or fully across this spectrum. For example, a company selling online may only need to implement self-service and customer contact center processes. However, a company selling home appliances may need to implement all three.

SAP Hybris Service Cloud covers the entire spectrum of service processes. Figure 3.1 shows the complete portfolio of SAP Hybris Service Cloud. On one end of the spectrum is self-service and SAP Jam Communities to enable low-touch, high-volume service engagements. On the other end, is the high-touch, low-volume field service management. All the components of the SAP Hybris Service Cloud portfolio are integrated with each other to help implement the omnichannel service engagement model across all channels and customer touch points.

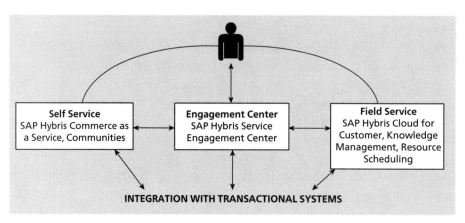

Figure 3.1 SAP Hybris Service Cloud Portfolio

SAP Hybris Service Cloud is available as two complementary offerings: SAP Hybris Service Engagement Center and SAP Hybris Cloud for Customer. SAP Hybris Service Engagement Center can be used for customer service and self-service in conjunction with SAP Jam Communities and agent desktops. SAP Hybris Cloud for Customer can be used for customer service and field service. Using SAP Hybris Service Engagement Center and SAP Hybris Cloud for Customer, you can deliver service excellence across the entire spectrum of service processes from self-service to engagement center to field service.

Figure 3.2 shows the building blocks of SAP Hybris Service Cloud. Built from as a cloud solution, both customer service and field service solutions are integrated with other SAP Hybris functionalities such as self-service, knowledge management, and collaboration. It enables service engagements with customers through web storefronts, mobile devices, social media, email, text-messages (SMS), chat, and customer contact center. Most importantly, however, it helps you develop a holistic customer view for complete contextual interaction. With closed-loop enterprise processes across both the front-office and back-office solutions, SAP Hybris Service

Cloud enables end-to-end integrated process automation to reduce the cost of service operations and improve customer satisfaction.

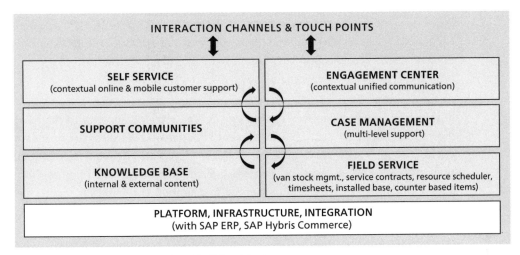

Figure 3.2 SAP Hybris Service Cloud Building Blocks

Some of the benefits of SAP Hybris Service Cloud are as follows:

- **Customers can resolve service requests on their own**
  Equip your customers with the tools they need to search and find answers with ease. Create a self-service experience that improves customer satisfaction and reduces support costs through microservices offered via SAP Hybris as a Service. Allow customers to search communities, view recent purchases, register products, create incidents or engage with a service agent in the channels of their choice to resolve their inquiries at their convenience.

- **Support communities**
  Build an interactive community with SAP Jam Communities to foster collaborative service issue resolution. Through Q&A forums and discussions, your community members can get the answers they need. Integrated into both the SAP Hybris Service Engagement Center and SAP Hybris Commerce products, online communities offer insights into customers' needs and interests and offer relevant content designed to influence and accelerate purchase decisions and seamlessly go from a service inquiry to a storefront. Increase customer engagement and satisfaction and lower the total cost of customer support by inspiring low touch service engagements through communities.

- **Knowledge pool**
  With embedded solution finder functionality through SAP Jam Collaboration, service agents and customers can search for relevant articles in a knowledge base based on subject, categorization, or text analysis derived from keywords and sentiment indicators. You'll be able to quickly deliver product information to customers and agents across multiple channels using content ranking technology, and powerful analytics.

- **Agent desktop**
  With the SAP Hybris Service Engagement Center, enable your service teams to deliver consistent, contextual, and relevant experiences regardless of channel or device throughout the customer journey. Serve customers on their terms through their preferred communication channels and simplify the customer journey with expert guidance. Provide customer service and support through chat, video chat, social channels, SMS, and traditional phone conversations. Allow your agents to retain the customers' context from channel to channel, including integration to the SAP Hybris Commerce storefront, to engage with customers more effectively and to come to issue resolution at the first point of contact.

- **Omnichannel customer support for case and ticket management**
  With SAP Hybris Cloud for Customer, incidents can be created manually or triggered by inbound e-mail messages, chat, SMS, and social media messages, including Twitter, Facebook, and YouTube. All channels can identify customers based on data available from social media profiles, e-mail addresses, or phone numbers. Create new tickets and update existing ones automatically. With native integration to SAP Jam Collaboration, search and share content from within agent workspaces and stay up-to-date on the latest service requests, comments, discussions, and decisions online. SAP Hybris Cloud for Customer automatically assigns tasks to a ticket based on relevant attributes to help guide agents through complex processes and create workflow rules with ease that can generate notifications, update fields, and trigger requests for multilevel approvals based on context and time.

- **Provide the right resources**
  With SAP Hybris Cloud for Customer, manage comprehensive field service engagements from work orders and service level agreements (SLAs) to contracts, warranties, and service parts, as well as telephony integration and universal routing. Enable real-time communication among field engineers and the back office, quick access to relevant information, and automatic tracking of time and resources for accurate, timely billing. Optimize scheduling of work orders to meet SLAs and increase first-time fix rates while minimizing costs. Provide a single,

comprehensive source of customer-related data, including contacts, sales orders and opportunities, service contracts, installed base and equipment, past work orders, and insights gathered from previous interactions. With mobile applications, gather, store, track, and deliver knowledge that field engineers and back-office reps can use to solve problems quickly, anywhere, anytime.

- **Simplify the customer journey**
  With the embedding widgets of SAP Contact Center Cloud you can bring communication channels (phone, email, chat, IVR) and omnichannel contact routing as an integral part of your business applications, improving the customer experience and customer service performance. SAP Contact Center Cloud capabilities are inbuilt to SAP Hybris Service Engagement Center and embedded with SAP Hybris Cloud for Customer to increase first contact resolution and customer satisfaction throughout the customer journey.

The key advantage of SAP Hybris Service Cloud comes from the fact that it's a cloud-based flexible deployment option. Using the SAP Hybris as a Service on SAP Cloud Platform marketplace, you can pick and consume complementary applications from SAP Hybris as a Service and integrate them with SAP Hybris Cloud Service to implement any new service process that fits your unique business requirements and service operation.

3.2   SAP Hybris Service Engagement Center

SAP Hybris Service Engagement Center enables service teams to deliver continuous service support to customers throughout their journey. With integrated assisted and unassisted service, it supports high-volume customer interactions across the channels and touch points.

The SAP Hybris Service Engagement Center solution is offered through SAP Hybris as a Service, and it allows you to implement a low-touch, high-volume service scenario through self-service solutions; to create online communities to enable collaboration across your enterprise, partners, and customers with SAP Jam communities; and to provide omnichannel support with the service agent desktop. In the following sections, you'll learn about the unique capabilities of these three scenarios, which are available through SAP Hybris Service Engagement Center.

Figure 3.3 shows a ticket creation example in the SAP Hybris Service Engagement Center.

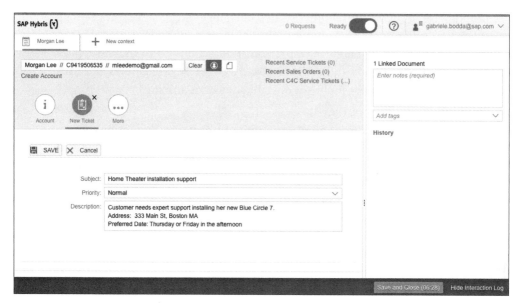

Figure 3.3 Ticket Creation in SAP Hybris Service Engagement Center

3.2.1   Self-Service Scenarios

The self-service portal available through SAP Hybris as a Service is a cloud-based solution for businesses to offer online self-service capabilities to their customers. High-volume and low-touch self-service offers greater flexibility to customers to create service requests, register products, see the status of their service tickets, and search for products details and product manuals themselves without contacting customer service agents.

Self-service empowers customers to download instruction manuals and how-to guides, and request service at a convenient time. The SAP Hybris self-service portal provides a convenient and cost effective method for business-to-customer (B2C) customers to quickly and easily perform tasks related to customer service through an asynchronous low-touch channel. Unique features of the SAP Hybris self-service portal are as follows:

- **Service ticket creation and deflection**
  Customers can register and create service requests or service tickets from the SAP Hybris self-service portal. Instead of contacting customer service agents, customers can check the status of their service requests through the self-service portal. With SAP Jam integration, service tickets can be easily deflected to SAP Jam

communities for potential solutions. Community posts can be monitored and routed to a service agent as well, so customers are getting expert guidance in the channel of their choice.

- **SAP Jam communities integration**
  SAP Hybris self-service integration with SAP Jam communities augments the service experience for customers. Customers can view all crowdsourced content in communities for selected products in self-service. They can also view crowdsourced content in communities for registered products in self-service. Before creating service requests for their issues, customers can search for potential resolutions in SAP Jam communities. They can even post their queries to community members for suggestions. Users can also be prompted with possible issue resolutions in communities for a selected product based on any keyword in the issue description, resulting in ticket deflection. SAP Jam communities complements the self-service portal in providing engaging service experiences to customers.

- **Product registration**
  Though product registration is key for manufacturers to activate service entitlements, it's the most overlooked post-purchase activity for customers. Offering product registration capability through the self-service portal allows customers to register products at their convenience. They can register products through the self-service portal by providing their personal and product details to activate warranty and service entitlements. Products can also be directly registered from details in the sales order. With integration between the self-service portal and SAP Hybris Service Engagement Center, service agents can also view and edit product registration details previously created by customers from the self-service portal. If needed, service agents can also register products on behalf of customers. Product registration information allows customers to easily initiate service requests their entitled to without any hassle.

- **Shopping cart refresh**
  About 50% of customers drop from storefronts due to inconvenient catalog navigation when adding products to shopping carts. Integration with storefront shopping carts enables service agents to hold the hands of customers in their buying journey. A customer's shopping cart in self-service can be updated by service agents if needed based on their interaction in the SAP Hybris Service Engagement Center.

- **Parameterization of product details**
  To allow products to be registered through a QR code scan in self-service, products can be parameterized with the required details. Customers can avoid entering all

the details required for product registration by merely scanning the QR code for the products to register.

- **Flexibility to integrate**
  The SAP Hybris self-service solution can be integrated on a company's web page without the need to build a separate self-service solution to enable seamless service experiences for customers.

3.2.2 SAP Jam Solutions

Crowdsourcing is becoming more popular and extremely powerful. Customers prefer to look for information online to solve their problems and issues before contacting manufacturers and suppliers. Online communities create more market awareness and brand loyalty than all the marketing media put together. Not listening to and collaborating with online communities could be suicidal for businesses and their brands.

SAP Jam is a leading cloud-based content and collaboration tool to connect customers, partners, and suppliers. It can be used across the enterprise to streamline processes by bringing all the involved parties—external or internal—together to collaborate, contribute, and share to solve problems and drive business results. SAP Jam can be used to enhance service line of business processes to improve collaboration between customers and partners by creating SAP Jam communities and knowledge bases. The SAP Jam out-of-the-box integration with SAP Hybris front-office solutions allows you to collaborate with customers throughout their engagement journey. SAP Jam can be licensed with other solution offerings from the SAP Hybris Services portfolio to enable engaging and satisfying service experiences for customers. The key advantages and capabilities of SAP Jam are as follows:

- **SAP Jam Communities**
  SAP Jam Communities build foundation for companies and their customers to collaborate and resolve issues in a whole new and interactive way. Through question-and-answer forums and discussions, community members can get what they need to resolve their issues without contacting customer service agents. Figure 3.4 shows an example of an SAP Jam online community for service. Customers can search for potential solutions to their issues, answer queries from other members, and post new queries if they can't find a solution in the knowledge database.

  Companies can keep the communities active by ensuring customer questions are answered promptly. Integration between SAP Jam Communities and SAP Hybris Service Engagement Center allows questions that haven't been answered in a timely manner to be routed to service agents to build credibility and ensure members are actively engaged with the community. Online communities provide insight into customer needs and interests and help businesses offer relevant content and offerings to steer them to the storefront and accelerate buying decisions. SAP Jam Communities enable stronger customer engagement, lower cost of support, and improve customer satisfaction through low-touch, community-based support. You learned in the previous section that integration between SAP Jam Communities and the self-service portal further expands community and helps customers resolve their issues themselves without needing to contact customer service agents.

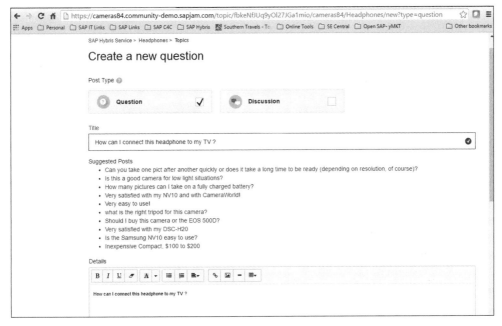

Figure 3.4 SAP Jam Community

- **Knowledge base**
  Knowledge base with SAP Jam Collaboration allows customers and service agents to search and find solutions to their issues. Companies can publish all the work instructions, user manuals, and how-to documents to SAP Jam Communities to create the most up-to-date knowledge base. With natural language search and processing tools, customers, partners, and service agents can search for relevant articles in the knowledge base via keywords, subjects, and categories through the

solution finder functionality. Embedded content-ranking technology and powerful analytics help community members find information when and where they need it. The power of the knowledge base can be leveraged across channels by customer service agents and field service technicians. Service agents in SAP Hybris Service Engagement Center, field technicians, and self-service and storefront customers can tap into the knowledge base to get answers to their queries. The knowledge base attracts new members and keeps current members active and engaged to constantly grow and build a powerful online community.

3.2.3   Agent Desktop

SAP Hybris Service Engagement Center provides a next-generation agent desktop available as software-as-a-service (SaaS). It helps provide services to customers continuously as they move from one channel to another. It allows agents to retain a customer's interactions and contexts from channel to channel, including the storefront, and to resolve their issues more effectively on their first point of contact.

The SAP Hybris Service Engagement Center agent desktop allows service agents to view comprehensive customer profiles, order services, and interaction histories with a modern navigation UI. It lets service agents create, view, and edit service tickets, service orders, complaints, and requests; intelligently route tickets to the appropriate team; and respond to community posts though SAP Jam. In line with customer expectations, agents can engage with customers in the channel of their choice, including chat, video, social media, email, and phone. The key capabilities of the SAP Hybris Service Engagement Center agent desktop are as follows:

- **Communication as a service**
  Agent desktop helps you establish software-based and sophisticated front-office communication processes without requiring an expensive telephony system. These communication services are available in the cloud as services.

- **Embedded communication**
  Agent desktop comes with a prebuilt, embedded communications UI. A customer chat and video UI can be embedded into SAPUI5 applications.

- **Omnichannel routing**
  This is one of the key capabilities of SAP Hybris Service Engagement Center agent desktops. Customer requests are routed intelligently in real time based on service qualifications, skills requirements, and available service queues. You can set priorities for customers and channels so that customer requests are routed to agents per predefined priorities. If you want certain types of customers to be handled by

only specific types of agents, then you can use contextual customer insights to intelligently route calls to the appropriate agents.

- **Customer insight**
  This is key for service agents to satisfactorily resolve customer issues on first contact. SAP Hybris Service Engagement Center agent desktop provides customer profiles, service requests, service and sales orders, interaction history information, complaints, and returns history information for agents to interact intelligently, and predefined interaction transcripts help agents guide service calls effectively with customers. Access to product registration and warranty information enables agents to verify customer entitlements before creating service requests or complaints.

- **Modern UI**
  Based on the SAP Fiori UI, the agent desktop improves agent productivity and average customer handling time.

- **Mobile**
  Mobile support for enterprise applications is one of the key requirements to keeping employees engaged. Based on SAPUI5 technology, agent desktop is supported by iOS, Android, and Windows mobile devices. It gives agents the flexibility to work from anywhere and from any device.

- **Native social media**
  The native social media capabilities in agent desk help service agents seamlessly transition from social channels to traditional channels to keep constantly engaged with customers.

- **Workflow and notification**
  Workflow rules can be created to generate notifications, update fields, and trigger requests for multilevel approval based on context and time as needed.

- **Real-time analytics**
  Delivered out of the box with SAP Hybris Service Engagement Center, real-time analytics lets you monitor SAP Hybris Service Engagement Center performance in real time. Readily available standard dashboards and reports help you provide unified reporting across the channels.

Some of the key benefits of using agent desktop are as follows:

- **Optimize agent productivity**
  Communication channels are integrated with productivity tools to enable easy access to contextual customer information when needed by agents during interaction with customers. Agents can quickly access service tickets and sales

information with simple analytics to effectively help customers resolve their issues. Because agents are supporting customers in multiple channels through agent desktop, all communications are intelligently routed with screen popups, which optimize agent productivity.

- **Comprehensive and contextual interaction handling**
  Through automatic identification of customers and the ability to handle multiple interactions simultaneously, service engagement agents can improve customer satisfaction through consistent and repeatable service experiences. Right from their application, agents can quickly capture interaction notes and reasons, view all past interactions, and easily access any linked business documents (orders, tickets, posts, etc.). Agents interact with customers through service tickets, service orders, sales orders, complaints and returns, social media response/posts, and community posts. Figure 3.5 shows a customer's previous interactions with additional details for the service agent to intelligently address the customer's concerns.

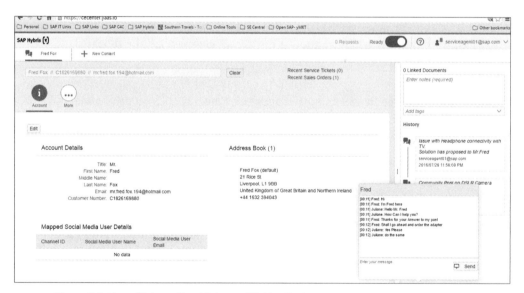

Figure 3.5 Use of Interaction History with the Customer

- **Enable contextual interactions**
  First contact resolution rates can be increased by effectively supporting customers in the channel of their choice. Agent desktops have embedded text chat, video chat, phone, and social media communication capabilities. Agents can visually see

the number and type of interactions in the queue, and they can easily control a phone call within the customer's context. For known customers, automatic customer identification screen popups enable agents to delight customers and improve customer satisfaction. Most importantly, it eliminates the need for expensive computer telephony integration (CTI).

- **Improve performance with multichat conversations**
  Customer service agents can engage in multichat interactions simultaneously and view chat interactions histories for a holistic view of customer conversations, all within the context of each customer. You can also embed the chat widget on your website to allow customers to get help from service agents in real time.

- **Engage with real-time video chat**
  Customer satisfaction can be greatly improved by engaging with customers through live video chat. Live video chat conversations with customers can assist with quickly resolving support issues or sharing product information. Figure 3.6 shows an example of a service agent video chatting with a customer. Agents can also track the video chat interaction log to carry forward meaningful conversation with customers. The video chat widget can also be embedded on websites to allow customers to request video chat for any help with service requests or product information.

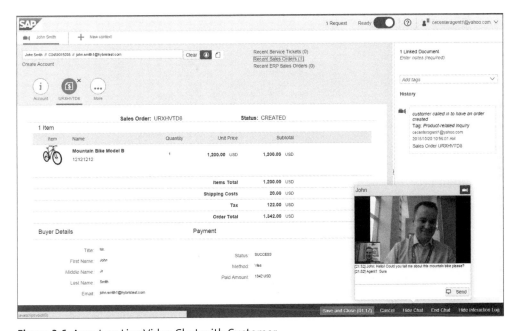

Figure 3.6 Agent on Live Video Chat with Customer

- **Support self-service**
  Customer service agents can support self-service customers by helping resolve and route service tickets submitted through the self-service portal. Agents can see customers' service requests from any channel. Self-service capabilities can be augmented by agents through agent desktops. For example, if a ticket is created by a customer on the self-service portal, agents can contact customers if needed to resolve the tickets through SAP Hybris Service Engagement Center. Agents can also collaborate using SAP Jam communities to augment the self-service capabilities and knowledge base.

- **Service ticket management**
  Service agents can quickly create and track service tickets with follow ups and service notes history. Agent desktop also provides quick access to a customer's service tickets directly from the interaction log. With seamless integration with SAP Hybris Cloud for Customer, agents can simultaneously handle multiple service tickets from SAP Hybris Cloud for Customer, as shown in Figure 3.7.

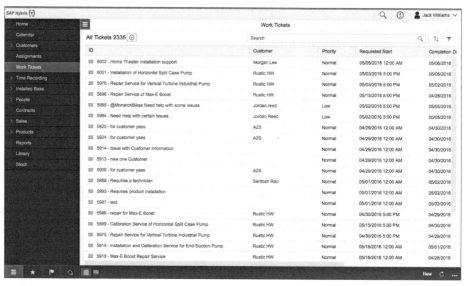

Figure 3.7 Service Tickets from SAP Hybris Cloud for Customer

- **Storefront orders support**
  Integration with SAP Hybris Commerce Cloud allows service agents to create sales orders from agent desktops. It provides direct access to a customer's sales order directly from the interaction log, as well as the ability to track customer sales

orders and email customer order notifications, as shown in Figure 3.8. Embedded order entry allows agents to handle multiple orders simultaneously.

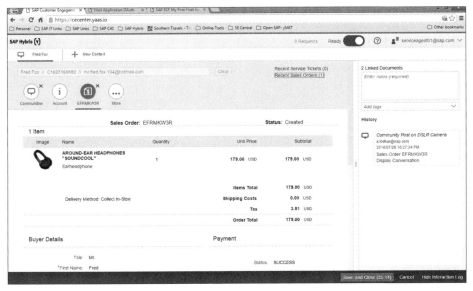

Figure 3.8 Example of an Agent Entering a Sales Order in SAP Hybris Service Engagement Center

- **Real-time insight**

  SAP Hybris Service Engagement Center delivers standard analytics to measure key performance indicators (KPIs) for agents. Managers can view daily interactions handled by agents, volume of interactions in each queue, average interaction handle time for each agent, and so on. They can get real-time insight into their team's customer service performance with standard analytics and dashboards. It also allows them to measure and track response times, handle times, priorities, and escalation trends using prebuilt reports and dashboards. Agents can also see the availability of their colleagues.

3.3   SAP Hybris Cloud for Customer

In this section, we'll discuss the key service capabilities of SAP Hybris Cloud for Customer. It offers guided configuration with a business adaptation catalog to implement contact center and field service solutions. It's built for the cloud on SAP HANA to enable ultrafast real-time processing and analytics. SAP Hybris Cloud for Customer offers a modern and responsive UI, out-of-the-box mobile access, and comprehensive service capabilities integrated with SAP Hybris front-office and SAP ERP back-office solutions. Figure 3.9 shows the SAP Hybris Cloud for Customer home page for a user.

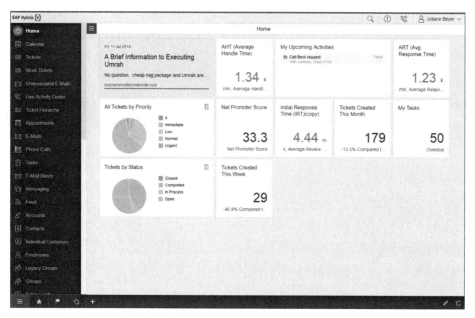

Figure 3.9 SAP Hybris Cloud for Customer Home Page

In the next two sections, we'll review the unique capabilities of customer service and field service scenarios available in SAP Hybris Service Cloud.

3.3.1 Customer Service

Figure 3.10 shows the functional capabilities of customer service scenarios for SAP Hybris Cloud for Customer. Customers can contact service agents through any channel (phone, chat, email, SMS, social media, and self-service), and service tickets are created in SAP Hybris Cloud for Customer and then routed to service agents. Productivity tools such as mobile access, social collaboration, workflows, notifications, routing, and escalations enable service agents to promptly resolve customer issues.

Standard delivered analytics based on SAP HANA database and out-of-the-box integration with SAP Hybris front-office and SAP back-office solutions help customer service agents find answers to customer questions from the SAP Hybris Cloud for

Customer screen. In the following sections, we'll discuss the capabilities and benefits of using the customer service process in SAP Hybris Cloud for Customer.

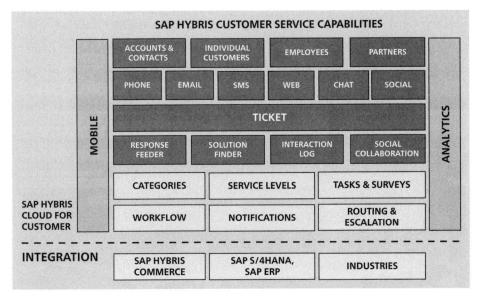

Figure 3.10 Customer Service Capabilities in SAP Hybris Cloud for Customer

Omnichannel

Using SAP Hybris Cloud for Customer, you can deliver omnichannel customer service capabilities so that customer service agents can engage with customers across all channels, including email, phone, social media, self-service portal, chat, and SMS. You can set up different email addresses in SAP Hybris Cloud for Customer so that customer emails can be forwarded to those addresses. For each email address, you can configure different routing rules and default customer and branding templates. For business-to-business (B2B) emails, you can choose between routing unknown email addresses to a common inbox (unassociated) or to a default account. For known customers, you can create routing rules to send tickets to a specific team or team members. For B2C emails, you can either automatically create a new customer in the system or use a default customer to create tickets. Default customers can be different for each incoming email address. For emails to customers from a specific email addresses in SAP Hybris Cloud for Customer, such as ticket acknowledgment or service confirmation, you can use predefined branding templates to ensure consistency.

You can leverage HTML to include brand-specific colors and themes in emails. All the brand templates can be managed centrally using the template data sets. The branding templates can be defined separately for each email address. SAP Hybris Cloud for Customer doesn't depend on your mail server to send outbound emails to customers. Emails are directly sent from the SAP's mail server with the "from" address picked from the channels settings in SAP Hybris Cloud for Customer.

SAP Hybris Cloud for Customer can be integrated with SAP Contact Center (cloud or on-premise) or third-party providers to enable CTI. The CTI Client Adapter and **Live Activity Center** pane are delivered with SAP Hybris Cloud for Customer. The CTI desktop client can be either the SAP Contact Center solution or any third-party CTI vendor such as Avaya, Cisco, Genesis, and so on. It provides phone-related controls such as accept, reject, and transfer calls. The CTI client receives or sends phone events and attached data between SAP Hybris Cloud for Customer **Live Activity Center** pane and CTI Client Adapter. To help customers and partners customize CTI Adapter behavior during implementations, SAP provides a copy of the source code for the SAP Hybris Cloud for Customer CTI Client Adapter. By modifying the source code for this CTI Client Adapter, you can implement your unique CTI requirements.

Service Ticketing

SAP Hybris Cloud for Customer offers powerful service ticket management functionality with ticket document types, ticket lifecycle management through ticket status, ticket partner determination, ticket routing, and escalation. Using various customer touch points, service tickets in SAP Hybris Cloud for Customer can be created through email integration (Microsoft Outlook, Lotus Notes, or Gmail), CTI, Facebook, Twitter, or a combination of web services. Easy navigation in a responsive UI lets users easily find and promptly work on the service tickets from the queue. Figure 3.11 shows the list of service tickets in an agent's inbox for the past seven days.

SAP Hybris Cloud for Customer offers many filters to display service tickets from the queue, for example, **My Tickets**, **My Team's Tickets**, **Open Tickets**, **High Priority Tickets**, and so on. You can also display the service tickets on the map to see the geographical distribution of tickets, as shown in Figure 3.12.

The system allows flexibility in creating and managing service tickets per your requirements. The service tickets can be managed contextually and created from customers' comments on social media channels such as Facebook and Twitter. For example, if there is a negative comment posted by someone about your product or services on social media, you can create a service ticket in SAP Hybris Cloud for Customer and contact that customer to promptly resolve the issue. Using sentiment analysis, tickets can be prioritized so that service agents can address tickets requiring urgent attention. The customer service functionality in SAP Hybris Cloud for Customer enables seamless ticket and case management.

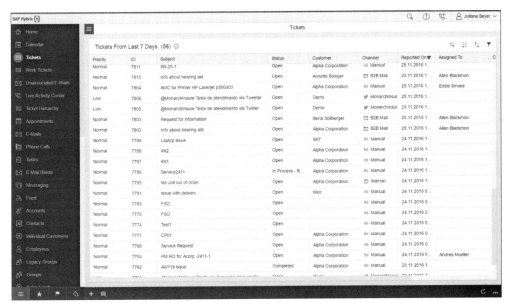

Figure 3.11 Example of Service Tickets in the Queue

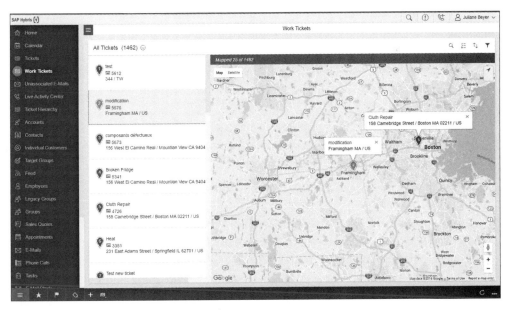

Figure 3.12 Displaying Service Tickets on the Map

The information maintained on service tickets provides complete details about the issues reported and actions taken by service agents toward timely resolution. The service tickets can be used to capture customer details, activities planned or completed, attachments, notes, service entitlement details, various dates, knowledge articles shared with customers, and so on. In one service ticket, you can also maintain multiple ticket items to include different types of service requests such as standard maintenance or repair. Figure 3.13 shows an example of a service ticket with two service items.

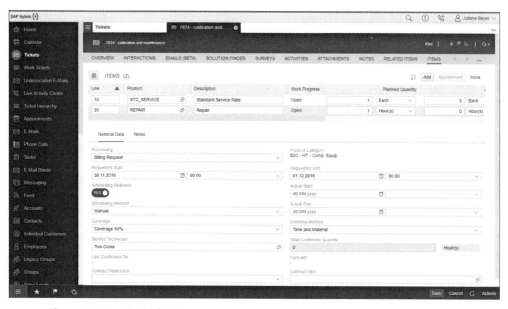

Figure 3.13 Service Ticket Items

SAP Hybris Cloud for Customer ticket management lets service managers efficiently monitor, control, and manage contact center operations in real time. Service tickets can be filtered on various criteria to keep track of types and volume of tickets in various queues. Figure 3.14 shows an example of a list of service tickets displayed in a queue.

As explained earlier, SAP Hybris Cloud for Customer enables integration with CTI through CTI Client Adapters. The **Live Activity Center** pane in SAP Hybris Cloud for Customer displays the live status of various interactions with customers, as shown in Figure 3.15. SAP Hybris Cloud for Customer helps you integrate communications with business processes.

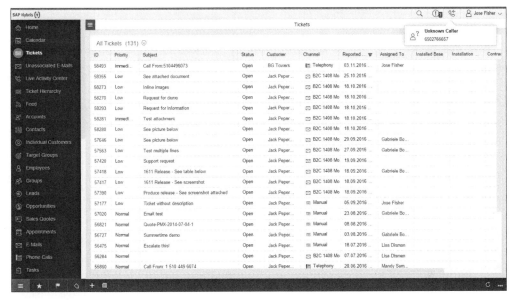

Figure 3.14 List of Service Tickets in the Queue

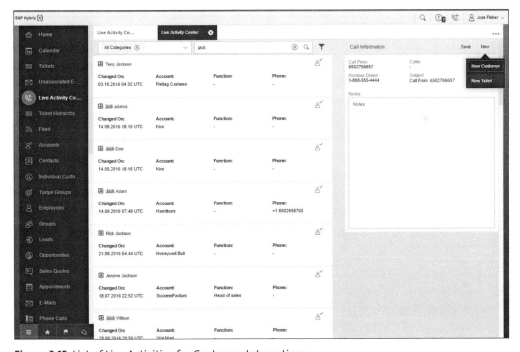

Figure 3.15 List of Live Activities for Customer Interactions

Service Level Agreements

Service Level Agreements (SLAs) can be defined with a set of rules for initial response and completion of service tickets. The ability to define and track SLAs is crucial to the successful operation of a customer service business. SAP Hybris Cloud for Customer lets you define and configure SLAs and determination rules for service tickets based on **Account, Country, ABC Classification, Ticket Status, Priority, Service Team, Product, Product Category, Service Category, Incident Category**, and so on. The initial ticket response and ticket resolution due date can be calculated based on the reaction time and the customer's operating hours as defined in the SLAs. The system allows you to define due dates for initial response and completion of tickets for each ticket priority level.

Service categories can be configured to facilitate a process to align service resources based on service categories for faster resolution of service tickets. The distribution of service tickets to agents and their escalation rules can be defined based on **Service Organization, Territory**, or **Employees**. Routing the tickets to the right team is critical for timely resolution of a customer's issues and to achieve the highest possible customer satisfaction. SAP Hybris Cloud for Customer lets you define routing rules for tickets based on **Customer Category** or **Classification, Specific Customer, Customer Country, Service Category, Priority, Escalation Status, Channel**, and so on.

Knowledge Management

SAP Hybris Cloud for Customer offers the knowledge base as a centralized repository of information to house details about customers' known problems and resolutions. The knowledge base is shared across SAP Hybris Service Engagement Center (as covered earlier in this chapter) and SAP Hybris Cloud for Customer.

SAP Jam integration with SAP Hybris Cloud for Customer delivers a knowledge platform to enable contextual access to most relevant support information needed by service agents to solve customers' issues. The knowledge base content is ranked based on user feedback, so agents can easily identify the most relevant content for specific customer problems. Agents can also track and analyze customer needs and behavior through knowledge management.

The SAP Hybris Cloud for Customer solution extension SAP Hybris Knowledge Central by MindTouch, allows you to configure the OpenSearch standard as mashups with Service Agent Assistant to help service agents handle service tickets promptly and efficiently. The knowledge articles can be set up to include incident-specific documents, enriched content with embedded images, and rating features to provide feedback on the quality of the knowledge articles.

Knowledge articles can be set up to go through a multistep review and approval process before they are published in the knowledge base. Only published knowledge articles will be available for viewing by agents. You can extend existing SAP Jam integration for feeds and groups to the knowledge base in SAP Hybris Cloud for Customer so that service agents can search and attach knowledge articles to tickets or emails as needed.

Full-Feature Mobile Experience with Off-Line Support

Access to mobile applications is included in the SAP Hybris Service Cloud license giving users flexibility to use and access applications from any device they want. Service agents can manage service tickets on any iPhone, iPad, Android, or Windows tablet anytime and from anywhere. Mobility helps agents improve productivity through access to real-time information while resolving customer issues and collaborating with service and nonservice teams on important issues. The service managers can monitor and track the performance of service operations through real-time analytics on their mobile devices.

Employee Service Capabilities

Employee service capabilities are supported through employee ticket creation by agents in SAP Hybris Cloud for Customer and through SAP SuccessFactors Employee Central integration. Employees can create tickets via SAP Cloud Platform Portal, which is integrated with SAP SuccessFactors Employee Center. Service center tickets are created, tracked, and updated by employees in Employee Central, and those tickets are processed by HR agents in SAP Hybris Cloud for Customer.

You can also embed portal widgets in Employee Central, created by SAP Hybris Cloud for Customer on SAP Cloud Platform Portal for Employee Self-Service (ESS). As shown in Figure 3.16, employee records are replicated from the HR system to SAP Hybris Cloud for Customer. Employees can create help requests in SAP SuccessFactors Employee Central, which creates help desk tickets in SAP Hybris Cloud for Customer. The service center agents are able to see the HR tickets, can look at additional employee information if needed, and then provide a response through ticket updates. The employee will see the updated tickets with the response from service agents. Service agents will finally resolve the tickets, and ticket resolution can trigger a satisfaction email survey to the employee in Employee Central.

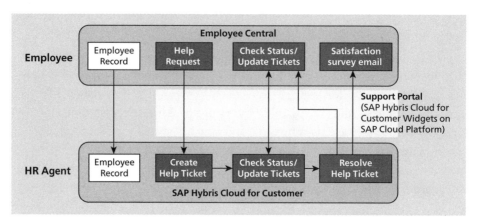

Figure 3.16 Employee Central Integration with SAP Hybris Cloud for Customer

3.3.2   Field Service

You can use the field service capability in SAP Hybris Cloud for Customer to manage service work orders across multiple channels, run rich service analytics, and manage contracts, warranties, and SLAs with customers. It comes with standard integration to front-office SAP Hybris solutions and SAP S/4HANA, SAP ERP, and SAP CRM. Figure 3.17 shows the building blocks of the field service capability in SAP Hybris Cloud for Customer.

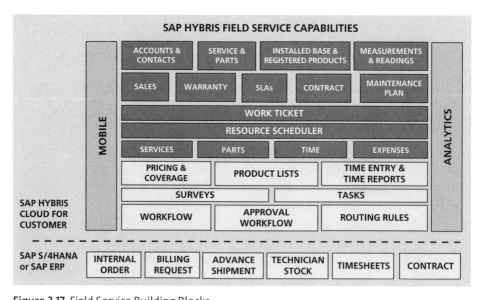

Figure 3.17 Field Service Building Blocks

The installed base, registered products, warranties, SLAs, contracts, maintenance plans, resource scheduler, pricing, workflow, and routing rules are some of the key components of the field service capability available in SAP Hybris Cloud for Customer. Integration with backend SAP allows you to use internal orders as cost collectors for service items, replicate contracts to SAP ERP, create advance shipments for parts, maintain technician stocks, collect time sheets, and create billing requests in SAP ERP.

Figure 3.18 shows how SAP Hybris Cloud for Customer enables end-to-end field service management to manage service orders and SLAs more effectively and increase service performance efficiency. Integration with SAP Multiresource Scheduling (SAP MRS) allows field service managers to find suitable resources for work orders and assign those resources to service demands as needed. With advanced predictive analytics based on the SAP HANA database and mobile access, service organizations can anticipate and meet service demands, as well as collaborate anywhere, anytime.

QUOTE & SERVICE CONTRACT	OMNI-CHANNEL CUSTOMER SERVICE	TECHNICAL & REMOTE SUPPORT	PLANNING & RESOURCE SCHEDULING	FIELD SERVICE EXECUTION & CONFIRMATION	FINANCE, LOGISTICS & ANALYTICS
Manage customer installations	Omni channel support	Routing, queuing and escalation	Planned labor and parts	Parts confirmation, ordering and returns	Billing
Service & parts catalog	Service ticket handling	Social collaboration and real-time communications	Planned tasks and checklists	Van stock and parts catalog	Cost allocation and revenue recognition
Manage service contracts and maintenance plans	Knowledge management	Predictive maintenance and service	Advance shipment of parts	Time recording and expenses	Parts logistics
	Approval workflow		Optimize schedule and resource assignment	Counter readings	Real-time reporting and KPIs
	Warranty, contract and SLA determination			Work instructions	
				Visit reports and customer signature	

Figure 3.18 End-to-End Field Service Management

In the following sections, we'll review some of the key components of the field service capability in SAP Hybris Cloud for Customer.

Registered Products

Registered products include information about the customer and the products the customer has purchased. When a customer calls a contact center with an issue, the registered product information allows the service agents to identify the unique customer product and determine service entitlement for that customer. If a warranty exists on the product, the system links to the relevant warranty and automatically determines the warranty dates. With registered products in SAP Hybris Cloud for Customer, you can do the following field service operations:

- View and access registered products for customers and create new registered products with details shared by customers during product registration.
- View warranty details for the registered products and search for registered products with a warranty expiring soon.
- Export the list of all tickets created for registered products to Excel for further analysis.
- Create registered products with a minimum of information such as customer, product, and product serial number. After a product has been registered for a customer, you can view the same information in the **Account and Contact** screen under the **Registered Products** work center.
- Use the integrated map to view the geographical distribution of registered products, as shown in Figure 3.19.

Figure 3.19 List of Registered Products in Map View

- Generate a preview of registered products to display general data, address, notes, warranty information, and involved parties details.

- Get an overview of registered products and repairs performed on registered products, which is especially helpful for field technicians.
- Take and maintain measurements using measurement attributes with multiple readings for each attribute on registered products. These attributes can be used to drive warranty entitlements and maintenance plans.

Installed Base

In SAP Hybris Cloud for Customer, *installed base* is a structured arrangement of installation points as well as common information for these points such as business partners, addresses, products, and registered products. Installed base helps you keep track of all the assets installed at a customer site. It can assist customer service agents and field service technicians with information needed to successfully complete a service or support call. Some of the features of installed base in SAP Hybris Cloud for Customer are as follows:

- You can create installed base to capture notes, serial numbers, and other data associated with equipment installed at a customer location and keep track of all the assets installed at a customer site.
- You can create the hierarchy of installed base items (**Products**, **Registered Products**, **Texts**, etc.) with any number of levels as shown in Figure 3.20.

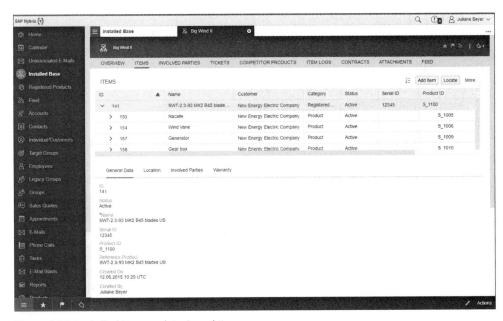

Figure 3.20 Installed Base and Assigned Items

- Installed base can be maintained in different statuses, such as **In Process**, **Active**, **Blocked**, or **Obsolete**.

- Through installed base, you can track multiple equipment records for an installation point and track multiple components (parts) for an equipment record.

- Installed base can also be created in SAP Hybris Cloud for Customer through replication of functional locations and equipment from SAP ERP.

- You can assign customer, primary contact, service technicians, employee responsible, and primary or preferred service technicians to the installed base header or items.

- You can track the service history on installed base and its components.

- You can assign one or more measurement logs to registered products and take measurement readings throughout the lifecycle.

- Service tickets can be created for an installed base header or any item depending on the identified issues or issues reported by customers.

- Installed base can be added as a covered object in a contract to accurately define the scope of the contract terms and entitlements.

- If needed, installed base can be changed from one customer to another, and, during reassignment, all the subitems under installed base are automatically reassigned to the new customer.

- You can enable access authorization for installed base based on various attributes to make sure details aren't visible to everyone in the organization. Some of these authorization attributes are employees, assigned territories, assigned service organization, and so on.

Warranty Management

SAP Hybris Cloud for Customer functionality supports time-based warranties for registered products. Any ticket created for a registered product will automatically include warranty information for that product. If needed, a warranty can also be manually associated with a ticket or removed from a ticket. Warranties can also be restricted to a specific subset of incident categories. In that case, if an incident is created in that category, the warranty will be automatically removed even if the incident was created for registered products under warranty. Warranties can be created, activated, and assigned to registered products as needed. When a service agent creates a ticket for this registered product, the warranty is automatically determined. As a part of defining a warranty, you can identify the incident categories that shouldn't be covered. Warranties are assigned to registered products for a specific period of time.

Service Contracts

The integrated service contracts functionality in SAP Hybris Cloud for Customer lets you manage the process from opportunity to contract and from contract to opportunity as follow-up transactions to enable the service organization to operate as a revenue center and not a cost center. Contracts can be created as templates to allow subsequent contracts to copy standard and extension fields. Contracts can be priced using an external pricing functionality from the SAP backend system. Through the request external pricing functionality, the system pulls the pricing data from the SAP ERP system per the pricing maintained in the source system. Pricing can be maintained for the header as well as individual items in a contract.

If a contract is cancelled, an agent can maintain rejection reasons on contracts for future reference and review. Using the **Transfer** action, service contracts in SAP Hybris Cloud for Customer can be transferred to the SAP backend system. After a contract is created in SAP ERP successfully, the SAP ERP contract ID is updated in SAP Hybris Cloud for Customer. To keep the links to the preceding and follow-up documents from contracts, the document flow view in contracts allows you to see the document flow graphically. To follow up on contracts due for renewal, you can configure the workflow to automatically create an opportunity from a contract per workflow rules. Figure 3.21 shows the **OVERVIEW** screen of a contract in SAP Hybris Cloud for Customer.

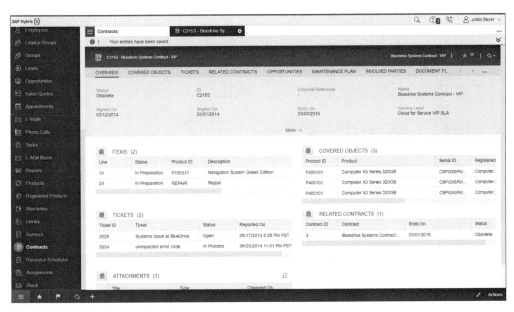

Figure 3.21 Contract Overview Screen

Maintenance Plans

Using maintenance plans in SAP Hybris Cloud for Customer, service organizations can plan and execute preventive maintenance scenarios by creating work tickets based on the predefined maintenance schedule for registered products or installed base. A maintenance plan can have counter-based schedule conditions only, time-based schedule conditions only, and both counter-based and time-based schedule conditions. The schedule type for a maintenance plan can be cyclical, fixed, one time, one time with no conditions, and absolute. To support a recall scenario, the schedule type **One Time – No Conditions** is provided. In this case, tickets are automatically generated without any conditions.

If more than one registered product is to be covered in a maintenance plan, then all those registered products are added as maintenance items in the maintenance plan. Contract information can be added for the maintenance item. Ticket templates can be used to populate fields in service tickets automatically generated by the maintenance plan. Figure 3.22 shows the **OVERVIEW** screen for a maintenance plan in SAP Hybris Cloud for Customer.

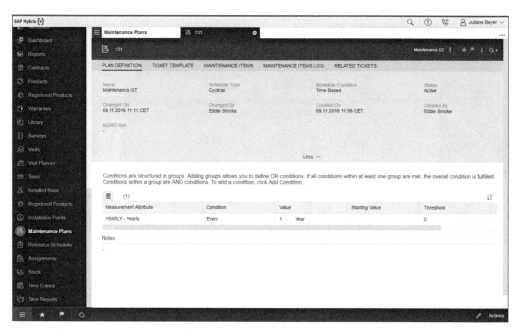

Figure 3.22 Maintenance Plan Overview

The maintenance plan also includes a **Delay** functionality to enable creation of a service ticket based on a time difference between two tickets. For example, with the **Delay** functionality, the next ticket creation is decided based on the resolved-on date of the previous ticket. For each maintenance object, you can see when the next trigger is for satisfying the conditions at which the creation of the next ticket becomes eligible. You can also see for the maintained item whether there are any outstanding tickets. If needed, registered products can be added as maintenance items in the maintenance plan in bulk based on a reference product. The maintenance plans can be viewed on registered products as well as contracts.

Resource Scheduling

Resource scheduling in SAP Hybris Cloud for Customer can be done either using the native Resource Scheduler functionality or using external scheduling tools such as SAP Multiresource Scheduling (MRS) and ClickSoftware. Integration between SAP Hybris Cloud for Customer and SAP MRS allows work items from SAP Hybris Cloud for Customer to be replicated as demands to SAP MRS. Resource assignments created in SAP MRS are replicated to work items in SAP Hybris Cloud for Customer and updated with technician, as well as requested start date/time and end date/time information. Using scheduling relevance flags on service items, you can control which service demands the planner needs to work on. The service relevance flag, along with the requested start and end date and time, defines the time constraint for the planning phase. The expected duration for a job is calculated from the planned quantity of the service item.

Figure 3.23 shows the **Resource Scheduler** view in SAP Hybris Cloud for Customer. Every ticket item relevant for service scheduling appears on the **Resource Scheduler** chart. Using drag and drop, the scheduler can assign resources to the open demands. After resource assignment is done, the demand disappears from the list. The Gantt chart in Figure 3.23 shows color-coded assigned demands for every employee. After assignments are completed, they show up on the service technician's calendar. Using SAP MRS or ClickSoftware with SAP Hybris Cloud for Customer, you can automate and optimize complex scheduling processes to maximize resource utilization. Assignments can also be rescheduled and adjusted in real time to meet changing service demands from customers.

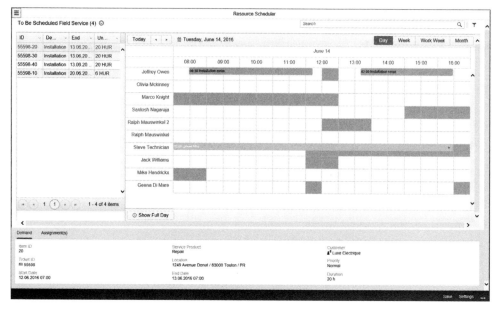

Figure 3.23 Resource Scheduler View

Time Recording

To keep track of time worked by service technicians on work tickets, you can leverage the time recording capabilities in SAP Hybris Cloud for Customer. Using time recording, field service technicians can record and manage time data for all the activities performed, including travel time, customer on-site time, or wait time. Time can be entered either manually by technicians in SAP Hybris Cloud for Customer using the time entry screen or automatically using the **Start/Stop** button available on different screens such as **Visits**, **Appointments**, and so on. Employees can enter time along with additional details such as activity type, travel time, billable time, nonbillable time, and so on, and then submit for approval. Managers can view all the time entries recorded to approve or reject. SAP Hybris Cloud for Customer allows you to define several approval steps with different approvers and conditions for approval and rejection of time sheets. The approved time sheets can be released to SAP ERP or Cross-Application Time Sheet (CATS) by managers.

Mobile Field Service Execution

Field service technicians can use SAP Hybris Cloud for Customer application from their mobile devices (iPhone, iPad, Android, Windows tablets and phone). The responsive offline mobile capability allows field technicians to perform their job even when they aren't connected to network. Field technicians can perform all the tasks such as view and update work tickets, time entry, service confirmation, parts consumption, access knowledge management, display installed base, view customer and service history, and so on from their mobile devices.

Service Logistics and Finance Integration

SAP Hybris Cloud for Customer integration with core systems like SAP S/4HANA and backend SAP ERP enables you to use controlling elements in SAP ERP to account for time spent by field technicians and parts used during service performance, and then finally bill the customer for the completed work tickets. This business scenario supports single object controlling via an internal order per work ticket. The actual working time and effort in the work ticket are used to create the internal order, billing request, invoice, goods movement, and time sheets. To arrange for the parts required to complete the work ticket, advance shipment of parts can be planned. If parts are consumed from technician stock, then such consumptions are accounted for in the internal order as a cost collector through service confirmation. Technicians can maintain van stock for frequently used parts as shown in Figure 3.24. Service technicians can also initiate service parts returns from the customer.

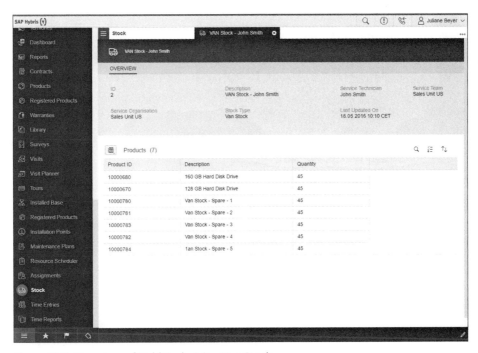

Figure 3.24 Overview of Field Technician Van Stock

The scenario for SAP ERP integration can start with the creation of a service ticket in SAP Hybris Cloud for Customer with the **Required Work** flag selected. As the service agents add services and parts needed, the type of parts will determine how integration is triggered with SAP ERP. If the item type is **Part,** then a goods movement is issued on SAP ERP for the used part. If the type **Service** is used, then automatic time recording is integrated with SAP ERP. A billing request for the parts and services is created in SAP ERP.

3.4   Reporting and Analytics

SAP Hybris Cloud for Customer includes standard out-of-the-box service KPIs, dashboards, and reports for both SAP Hybris Cloud for Customer and SAP Hybris Service Engagement Center supported by drilldowns and advanced analytics by business users. Using intuitive report and KPI design tools, business users can create additional reports and KPIs as needed. Figure 3.25 shows an example of a dashboard displaying the average handle time (AHT) for a call center.

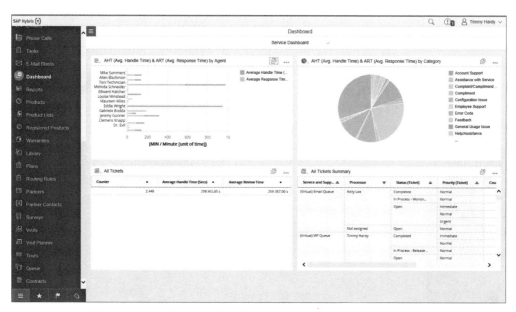

Figure 3.25 Service Dashboard with AHT

The following lists a small selection of the standard real-time service reports available out of the box with SAP Hybris Cloud for Customer:

- All Tickets
- All Tickets with All Interactions
- Tickets Backlog
- Unassigned Tickets by Age
- Agent Workload
- Response Times by Day, Hour, YTD

Examples of these reports are shown in Figure 3.26, Figure 3.27, and Figure 3.28.

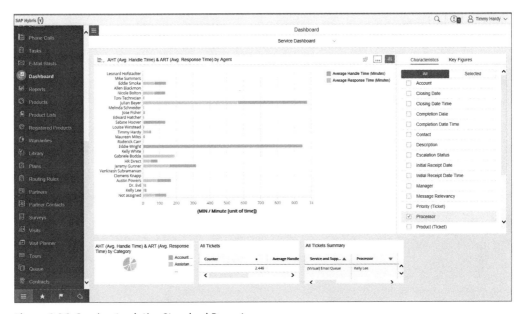

Figure 3.26 Service Analytics Standard Reports

Figure 3.27 Service Dashboard

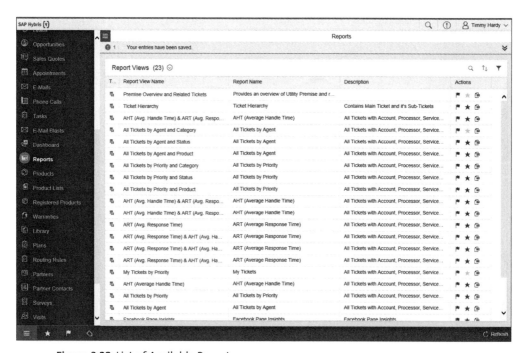

Figure 3.28 List of Available Report

To view historical data or trends, some of the standard service reports available in SAP Hybris Cloud for Customer are as follows:

- Daily Average Ticket Backlog by Service Organization
- Tickets Created vs. Completed (Last 7 Days)
- Ticket Backlog (Last 7 Days)
- Tickets Created This Month vs. Last Month
- Tickets Created This Week vs. Last Week
- Top 10 Agents by the Number of Tickets Completed

Figure 3.29 shows an example of displaying tickets based on their priority.

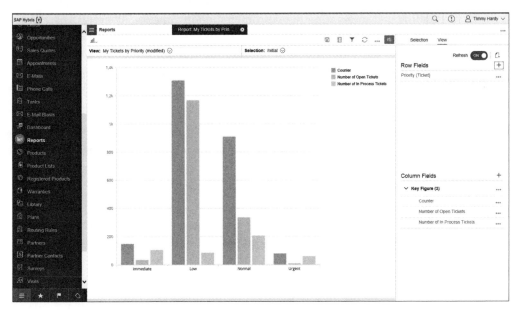

Figure 3.29 Tickets by Priority Report

3.5   Integrating with Other SAP Hybris Front-Office Solutions

As discussed in Chapter 2, SAP Hybris Cloud for Customer is the foundation for both SAP Hybris Sales Cloud and SAP Hybris Service Cloud. They both share a common database and are built for the public cloud on SAP HANA. No further integration is necessary to connect the two.

In the following, we'll review how SAP Hybris Cloud for Customer integrates with SAP Hybris Service Engagement Center and SAP Hybris Commerce:

- **Integrated SAP Hybris Service Engagement Center and SAP Hybris Cloud for Customer**
  We covered earlier that SAP Hybris Service Engagement Center solutions are available as SAP Hybris as a Service. Both SAP Hybris Cloud for Customer and SAP Hybris Service Engagement Center Solution are available in the cloud, and customers can pick and choose components of these solutions to implement desired business processes. For details on available SAP Hybris services in the SAP Hybris as a Service marketplace, visit *https://market.yaas.io*.

- **SAP Hybris Cloud for Customer integration with SAP Hybris Commerce**
  Extending and integrating the customer support functionality with SAP Hybris Cloud for Customer and SAP Hybris Commerce enables enhanced sales and service support to online customers. The out-of-the-box integration between SAP Hybris Commerce and SAP Hybris Cloud for Customer enables the following processes:

  - **Customer data integration**
    The integration with SAP Hybris Commerce Cloud uses the SAP Hybris Commerce Cloud data hub to replicate customer profiles and address information to SAP Hybris Cloud for Customer.

  - **Customer ticketing system**
    Customers can create, list, and update support request tickets from the SAP Hybris Commerce storefront to connect customers with SAP Hybris Cloud for Customer. The tickets created from SAP Hybris Commerce are transferred to the customer service agent.

  - **Single sign-on (SSO) functionality**
    This functionality enables seamless operation between SAP Hybris Commerce and SAP Hybris Cloud for Customer. It allows SAP Hybris Cloud for Customer service agents to sign in to the SAP identity service to gain access to the Assisted Service Module (ASM) and storefront from SAP Hybris Cloud for Customer without having to log on each time between systems. The SSO functionality in SAP Hybris is based on SAML2 open standard.

  - **ASM integration**
    With integrated ASM, a customer service agent can log in to an SAP Hybris storefront as a customer is browsing through the catalog and shopping cart, and

then help that customer with interactive sales and service support, as shown in Figure 3.30.

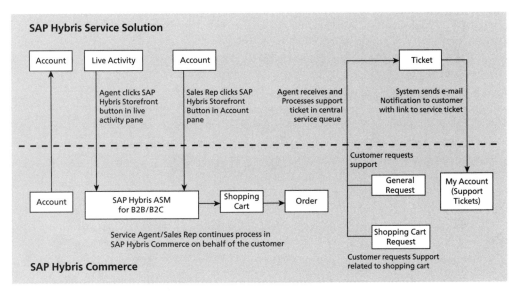

Figure 3.30 SAP Hybris Service Integration with SAP Hybris Commerce

3.6 Integrating with SAP S/4HANA and SAP ERP

In Chapter 2, you learned about the standard integration between SAP Hybris Cloud for Customer and SAP S/4HANA or SAP ERP using SAP Cloud Platform Integration. SAP has delivered standard iFlows that can be leveraged to enable work ticket integration between SAP Hybris Cloud for Customer and SAP S/4HANA and SAP ERP. The SAP backend can be used to perform billing for services and collect costs from labor and parts used by field service technicians while performing the services. The actual working time and effort in the work ticket are used to create the internal order, billing request, invoice, goods movement, and time sheets.

Figure 3.31 shows the integration between SAP Hybris Cloud for Customer and the SAP backend system to enable all the back-office processes for work tickets.

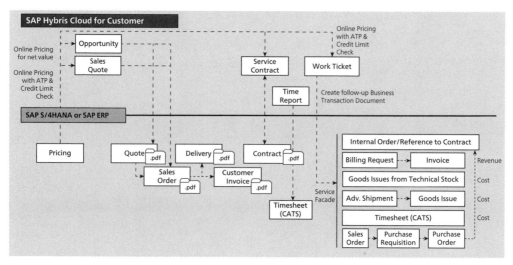

Figure 3.31 SAP Hybris Cloud for Customer Integration with the SAP Backend

3.7   Integrating with SAP Customer Relationship Management

Similar to SAP ERP, you saw in Chapter 2 that SAP CRM can be integrated with SAP Hybris Cloud for Customer using SAP Cloud Platform Integration. For SAP Hybris Service Cloud, you can replicate service tickets as well as work tickets between SAP Hybris Cloud for Customer and SAP CRM. You can replicate master data such as customers, products, pricing, and installed base between SAP CRM and SAP Hybris Cloud for Customer. Integrating with SAP CRM protects investments and at the same time allows users to leverage the new service processes available in SAP Hybris Service Cloud.

3.8   Summary

In this chapter, you've seen that the SAP Hybris Service Cloud includes SAP Hybris Service Engagement Center, SAP Jam Communities, and SAP Hybris Cloud for Customer. These solutions cover end-to-end service processes, from low-touch, high volume self-service to high-touch, low-volume field service. SAP Hybris Service solutions are integrated with SAP Hybris front-office solutions such as SAP Hybris Commerce Cloud, as well as SAP backend solutions such as SAP S/4HANA, SAP ERP, and SAP CRM. In the next chapter, you'll learn about the next important component of the SAP Hybris solution: SAP Hybris Commerce Cloud.

Chapter 4

Commerce

In omnichannel business, only context makes the difference. SAP Hybris Commerce delivers contextual, consistent, and relevant experiences to attract, convert, and engage customers regardless of the channel or device.

Commerce is one of the critical components of customer engagement. More and more brick-and-mortar businesses are being replaced by online storefronts. Online customers have more choices to buy better and cheaper products online than ever. Customers are expecting more from online storefronts, and it's becoming increasingly difficult for businesses to keep these online shoppers engaged. Customers are connected constantly through various channels such as online storefronts, social media, mobile apps, online communities, and so on.

Businesses need next-generation commerce applications backed with omnichannel capabilities to attract, convert, and retain customers. In this chapter, you'll learn about the SAP Hybris strategy for commerce and about the key components and capabilities of SAP Hybris Commerce. We'll review the unique capabilities of the SAP Hybris industry accelerators; SAP Hybris Commerce Cloud capabilities; business benefits of critical components such as SAP Hybris Customer Experience, product content management (PCM), order management, and configure, price, and quote (CPQ); and embedded commerce on SAP Hybris as a Service. We'll cover SAP Hybris Commerce Cloud integration with other SAP Hybris front-office solutions such as SAP Hybris Marketing Cloud, SAP Hybris Service Cloud and SAP Hybris as a Service, as well as SAP backend integration with SAP S/4HANA, SAP ERP, and SAP Customer Relationship Management (SAP CRM). In this chapter, we've also reviewed some options and scenarios for synchronous and asynchronous integration between SAP Hybris and SAP backend systems.

4.1 Strategy for Commerce with SAP Hybris

SAP's strategy for commerce is driven primarily by an ever-changing customer landscape powered by digital transformation. SAP Hybris Commerce Cloud helps companies transform their business by focusing on the following three areas:

- **Become an omnichannel business**
  SAP Hybris Commerce Cloud offers omnichannel commerce capabilities to customers. Whether a customer is buying online or calling a customer service agent about issues of placing an offline or online order, the experience for the customer has to be consistent. Sales and service agents—whether in a call center, an in-store environment, or in the field—can use SAP Hybris Commerce Cloud to collaborate with customers on the same storefront, guide them through their online experience, and finally help them achieve their goals. Additionally, as the number of customer touch points is exploding, innovation and agility are critical factors for business success. SAP Hybris Commerce Cloud lets you sell and communicate consistently across online stores, smartphones, tablets, social networks, and any Internet-enabled device.

- **Deliver a contextual customer experience**
  As a next-generation content management system, SAP Hybris Commerce Cloud enables streamlined and intuitive content management. The auto-optimized mix of products based on business goals and contexts delivers unmatched merchandising capabilities to customers with SAP Hybris Commerce Cloud. The ability to measure, learn, and improve helps you consistently deliver exceptional customer experiences. Contextual and personalized experiences are key to driving customer satisfaction and loyalty.

- **Unify the customer process**
  SAP Hybris Commerce Cloud is integrated with SAP Hybris front-office and SAP back-office processes to provide a unified customer experience. From marketing to the online shopping experience, customer information is shared across the processes to deliver accurate, transparent, and timely information to customers when they want it.

In subsequent sections in this chapter, we'll review how the unique capabilities of SAP Hybris Commerce Cloud align with SAP's strategy for a next-generation commerce solution.

4.2   SAP Hybris Commerce Cloud

SAP Hybris Commerce Cloud provides everything you need to deliver the ultimate multichannel experience that is both global and highly personalized to customers, prospects, suppliers, and partners—ensuring they are always able to engage with you and vice versa, wherever they sit and via whatever medium they choose. Most importantly, SAP Hybris Commerce Cloud guarantees a consistent customer experience, giving you the confidence that every customer and partner transaction is positive and profitable.

In the following sections, we'll begin by outlining the core commerce functionality provided by SAP Hybris Commerce Cloud before diving into specific business processes and offerings.

4.2.1   Core Commerce Functionality

The key components of SAP Hybris Commerce Cloud and their benefits are as follows:

- **Search and navigation**
  Before a customer can make a purchase, he needs to find what he is looking for. Poorly organized search results and unintuitive information architecture can create usability problems, frustrate customers, and, most importantly, result in lost sales. The search and navigation module helps your costumers browse through the pages of your web stores. This can contribute to higher conversions, larger orders, more page views, and fewer complaints from people who use the search and navigation. The module capabilities are seamlessly integrated with the system. They are built on the Apache Solr server, which makes the framework easy to expand.

- **Rule engine**
  The rule engine converts business objects to be used in rule conditions and actions. To enable businesses to manage rules easily, the rule engine provides a generic user interface (UI) called the rule builder. With this, the module provides the following advantages:

  - A configurable system based on rules
  - A system that is capable of separating data and logic
  - A fast and scalable system that provides an efficient way of matching rules and data
  - A centralized repository of executable and readable rules
  - Integration with a UI to manage rules and display results

  The rule engine is built to be extensible and generic. Across the SP Hybris Commerce platform, you can use it for bundle rules, order management for SAP Hybris Commerce warehouse and sourcing rules, and order change management rules.

The perfect sample implementation is the promotion engine, which allows businesses to create and manage promotions and runs on top of the rule engine.

- **Promotion engine**

  The promotion engine allows businesses to create and manage dynamic and individualized promotions. With the promotion engine, businesses are able to offer promotions on the fly and control the results throughout the customer's journey. It provides the following benefits:

  - Improved customer engagement and retention through highly targeted promotions

  - Easy-to-use and intuitive business tools for faster creation and publishing of promotions, as shown in Figure 4.1 and Figure 4.2

  - An omnichannel strategy for promotion management to boost sales and customer loyalty across all touch points

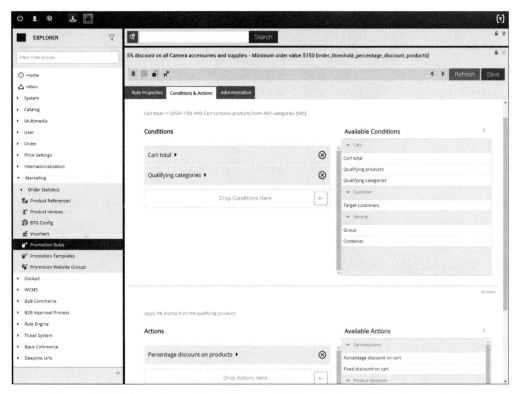

Figure 4.1 Defining Rules with Conditions and Actions for Promotions (Promotion Manager View)

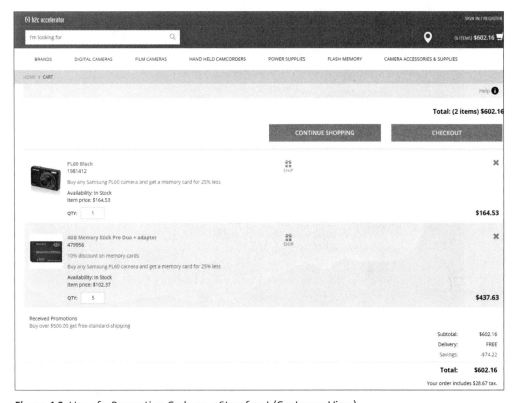

Figure 4.2 Use of a Promotion Code on a Storefront (Customer View)

- **Payment**

  The payment module (see Figure 4.3) answers the customer's expectations for a flexible and modular solution that is able to support the complexity of online payment processing. Its main purpose is to help the large number of merchants that are integrating with payment service providers (PSP) to map their commerce applications to the existing payment networks. This is necessary to reduce dependency on financial institutions and eliminate the need to establish individual connections directly. The payment module is ready to coordinate the flow of transactions among a complex network of financial institutions and processors. The module supports integrating payment gateways into SAP Hybris Commerce Cloud by grouping the adapters supporting the cooperation with external PSP.

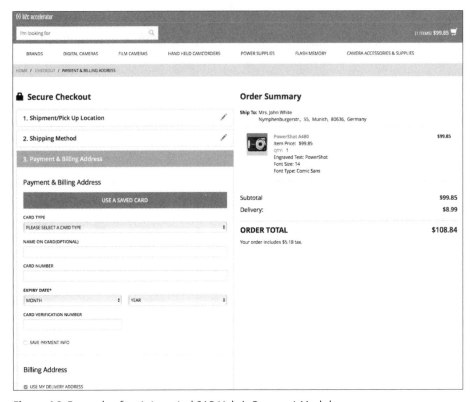

Figure 4.3 Example of an Integrated SAP Hybris Payment Module

■ **Bundling**

The bundling module (see Figure 4.4) provides the following functionality to personas who are acting in different areas of digital product marketing:

– Managing the combined sale of physical and digital goods to appropriately route and fulfill the physical and digital pieces separately

– Creating complex product offerings and personalized bundles that deliver multiple packages of digital goods such as a sports media package in the case of an IPTV provider, or a magazine package for a publisher

– Enabling businesses that sell digital goods to continually sell to their customers via commerce application programming interfaces (APIs), for example, in-app purchases, guided selling, and up-selling

The bundling feature lets you define different pricing for a product depending on whether it's sold individually or in a bundle of multiple quantities. Figure 4.5 shows phone and plan product bundles available in a storefront for selection.

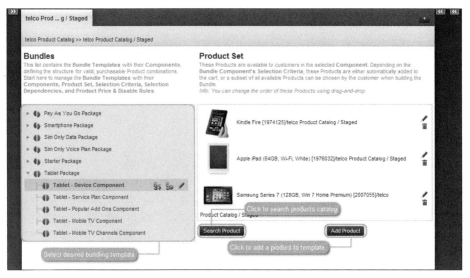

Figure 4.4 Setting Up Product Bundles in the Bundling Module

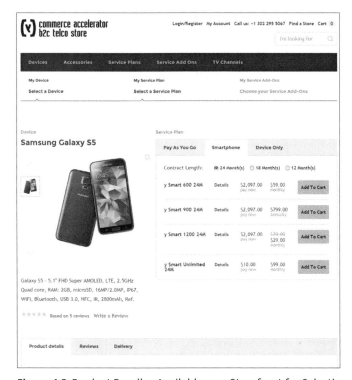

Figure 4.5 Product Bundles Available on a Storefront for Selection

- **Subscriptions**

  This module is specially designed to support businesses with a subscription-based sales model. SAP Hybris Commerce Cloud with the subscription module allows you to manage frequency, length, renewals, and other attributes unique to the subscription-based business models. Using this tool, business users can easily set up subscription-based pricing, pricing periods, subscription terms and conditions, entitlements and metering, and so on.

- **Assisted Service Module (ASM)**

  ASM allows customer sales and service personnel to provide real-time sales and service support to customers using the same storefront the customer is interacting with across the omnichannel framework. Whether the customer is buying online or in store, B2C/B2B sales reps or customer service agents can share the same buying experience and can even check out on behalf of the customer. Additional relevant customer information such as buying preferences, alternative product recommendations, or up-sell cross-sell propositions help those sales and service agents drive customer satisfaction and conversion.

  Figure 4.6 and Figure 4.7 show examples of ASM in the SAP Hybris Commerce Accelerator for B2C storefront.

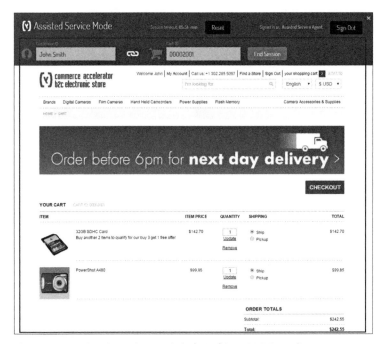

Figure 4.6 Assisted Service Module (ASM) in a B2C Storefront

Figure 4.7 ASM Unified Customer View

- **Commerce infrastructure services**

  The SAP Hybris Commerce Cloud infrastructure services deployment consists of a number of web applications for accessing third-party services such as shipping, tax calculation, payment, fraud detection, address verification services, and so on. Ready-to-use services based on SAP Hybris Commerce Cloud infrastructure services are available for certain third-party providers through the SAP Hybris marketplace.

- **Omni-Commerce Connect (OCC)**

  OCC is a commerce API offering a broad set of commerce and data services that enable you to use and leverage the complete SAP Hybris Commerce Cloud functionality anywhere in your existing application landscape. Its main benefits are as follows:

  - Customers can enable new touch points and channels quickly without lengthy and costly IT cycles.

  - Commerce processes and data can be reused easily across all touch points, increasing the speed and lowering the costs of providing new transactional interfaces.

– It isn't restricted to human UIs; you can easily integrate with other systems and even provide interfaces to partners and other organizations.

Figure 4.8 describes a variety of components which can be connected to SAP Hybris Commerce via OCC.

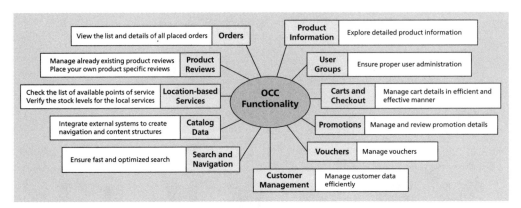

Figure 4.8 SAP Hybris Commerce Cloud Functionality to API Clients via OCC

- **Native mobile app and mobile SDK**
  SAP Hybris delivers native iOS and Android apps for B2B and B2C scenarios, as shown in Figure 4.9.

Figure 4.9 SAP Hybris Native Mobile App

Using mobile SDK delivered by SAP Hybris, as shown in Figure 4.10, custom mobile apps can be built for providing unique shopping experiences to both B2B and B2C customers.

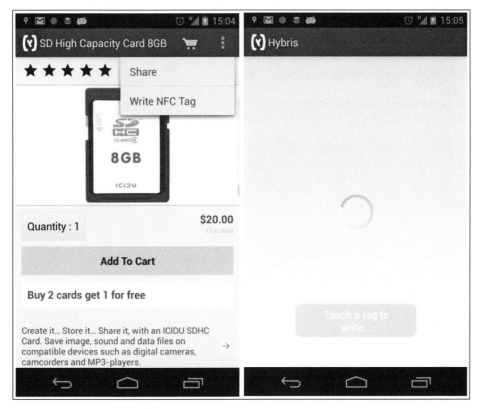

Figure 4.10 Mobile App SDK for iOS and Android

4.2.2   Business-to-Business and Business-to-Consumer

SAP Hybris Commerce Cloud includes ready-to-use SAP Hybris Commerce Accelerators for B2B and B2C that can be set up in as few as 50 days and get up and running with online storefronts as needed. Ready-to-use content, templates, shopping cart, and backend integration are some of the key functionalities delivered with these accelerators. The objective of accelerators is to reduce the time to value and lower the total cost of implementation. We strongly recommend that you evaluate these accelerators before embarking on an implementation. The details of these accelerators are as follows:

- **SAP Hybris Commerce Accelerator for B2C**

  The SAP Hybris Commerce Accelerator for B2C expedites value realization by providing a fully integrated and working storefront with delivered content. It includes multiple B2C storefront templates to choose from to meet storefront requirements. Some of the key requirements for B2C, such as PCM, business tools, touch point integrations, order management, search, and navigation, are delivered out of the box with the SAP Hybris Commerce Accelerator for B2C. Unlike B2B, visitors can browse B2C storefronts without registration, as shown in Figure 4.11.

Figure 4.11 Example of the B2C Storefront

Key features included in the SAP Hybris Commerce Accelerator for B2C are as follows:

- Web content management for easy creation and deployment of content in storefronts

- Merchandizing, data import, and attribute-rich product details in storefronts
- Intuitive product search based on product attributes and catalog navigation with internationalization support
- Store locator functionality based on various search criteria such as postal code, city, state, and so on
- Integration for user-generated content through social media augmented product ratings and content to boost sales
- Shopping cart, checkout, and payment functionality support out of the box
- Order management, fraud detection, and customer account management
- Native mobile applications for B2C to offer consistent shopping experience across multiple channels
- Express check-out functionality

- **SAP Hybris Commerce Accelerator for B2B**
  SAP Hybris Commerce Accelerator for B2B is a ready-to-use add-on that provides quicker and easier delivery of the B2B omnichannel commerce functionality by taking advantage of the unique flexibility and capabilities of SAP Hybris Commerce Cloud (see Figure 4.12).

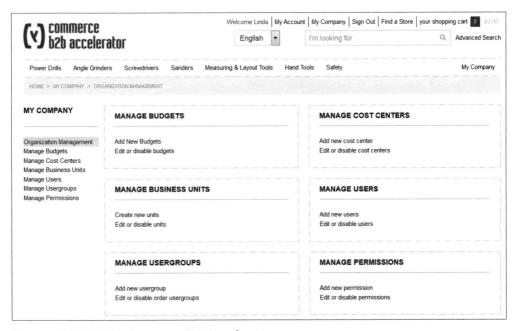

Figure 4.12 SAP Hybris Commerce B2B Storefront

The omnichannel commerce SAP Hybris Commerce Accelerator for B2B includes B2B storefront templates, PCM, business tools, self-service tools, B2B account management, order management, product configuration, and punchout services. An enterprise business customer's contact can log in to the storefront, browse through the product catalog, and add products to the shopping cart, as shown in Figure 4.13.

Figure 4.13 Example of a User Logged into an SAP Hybris Commerce Accelerator for B2B Storefront

The key features delivered by SAP Hybris Commerce Accelerator for B2B are as follows:

- **Self-service account management**
  Customer administrators can set up employees as users, assign required access rights, and set up individual purchasing units within the organization. They can also leverage built-in rules and workflows to configure and set approval rules for purchasing limits for individual users or purchasing units. Customer administrators can easily manage cost centers and budgets for all the purchases through the B2B shop by using the self-service account management capability.

- **Online ordering**
  In B2B, users can browse product catalogs and place orders online. They can also schedule orders that are replenished automatically if they represent recurring demands. The orders can be set up to go through an internal and external merchant-approval process. Orders can also be tracked online for their exact status such as shipping details.

- **Custom catalogs**
  B2B merchants can offer customized product catalogs for specific customers. For example, they can customize product lists and product search pages for specific organizations, departments, and customers as required.

- **Custom pricing**
  SAP Hybris Commerce Accelerator for B2B supports complex pricing models, which can be set up either in the SAP backend system and replicated to SAP Hybris Commerce Cloud or set up natively within the commerce platform.

- **Price quote request**
  Purchasers can submit a quote request to the merchant to negotiate the price for a sales order. Such quotes can be restricted to a minimum order quantity.

- **Credit management**
  Merchants can define credit limits based on various criteria such as currency, date range, order value, and so on.

- **Multidimensional products**
  Products can be defined based on various attributes such as size, color, fit, and so on.

- **Advanced product search**
  Users can search for products based on product attributes such as product code, bar code, text description, and so on.

- **Punchout support**
  An SAP Hybris Commerce B2B site can be integrated with a customer procurement system such as SAP Ariba. Orders placed on the B2B site can be automatically converted to purchase requisitions and saved in the customer's procurement system.
- **SAP backend integration**
  Integration with the back office enables streamlined order fulfillment processes for orders placed through B2B sites.

4.2.3   SAP Hybris Commerce Industry Accelerators

In addition to SAP Hybris Commerce Accelerators for B2B and B2C, SAP Hybris has a growing list of industry accelerators. SAP Hybris Commerce industry accelerators allow you to deploy a fully integrated and truly omnichannel commerce solution for specific industries such as telcos (telecommunication companies), financial services, and travel. These accelerators enable the unique shopping experiences customers demand and expect from merchants. These accelerators deliver fully integrated and working storefronts out of the box with a set of required business tools incorporating industry-recognized best practices and innovations. Hence, you have everything ready to go live faster because you only need to change the layout to reflect your branding and perform essential integration activities with your order fulfillment system and PSPs.

New industry-specific accelerators are being added to the SAP Hybris Commerce portfolio on a regular basis. In the following subsections, we'll look at some of the currently available accelerators.

SAP Hybris Commerce Telco Accelerator

Most commerce solutions are only centered on retail. However, below the surface of "a transactional website" a telco's business requirements differ hugely from a retailer's (e.g., subscriptions, add-ons, bundles, different promotions, unique checkout flows, upgrades, contracts, combining service and sales, etc.). Only SAP Hybris delivers a commerce platform specially designed to help telcos sell more online and in store, maximize average revenue per user (ARPU), and deliver an omnichannel customer experience that streamlines complex purchase processes. Using SAP Hybris Commerce Telco Accelerator, businesses can go to market in as little as 50 days with a fully featured omnichannel commerce solution, including Telco storefront templates, PCM, business tools, touch point integrations, bundling capabilities, order management, subscription capabilities, and guided selling. Figure 4.14 shows the standard storefront delivered with the B2C SAP Hybris Commerce Telco Accelerator.

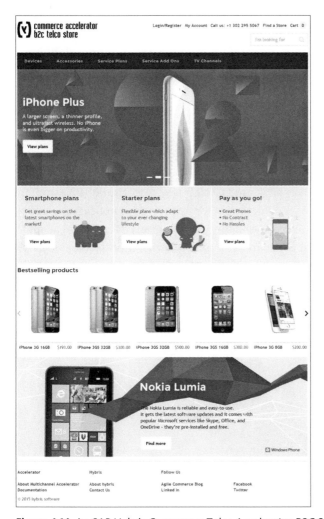

Figure 4.14 An SAP Hybris Commerce Telco Accelerator B2C Storefront Template

Some of the key features of the SAP Hybris Commerce Telco Accelerator are as follows:

- Provides a complete storefront for products and services with management of digital and physical goods packages

- Enables complete management of selling devices, contents, and changing devices
- Allows bundling of products and services, including rule-based discounts, bundles, and promotions
- Supports initial subscription data to customer invoicing with possible different scenarios such as upgrading a customer account and using a prepaid system
- Fully integrates with omnichannels
- Enables automatic cross-selling and up-selling of compatible accessories

SAP Hybris Commerce Financial Services Accelerator

SAP Hybris Commerce Financial Services Accelerator includes preconfigured reference integrations and storefront templates for property, travel, and event insurance policies. It can also be easily customized and extended to meet the needs of other financial service providers such as banks and retail financial institutions. Customers are guided through each step of the quote process, with various policies and added options, and they can enter all relevant data through customized forms that adapt to their answers. You can easily set up insurance bundles consisting of plans, associated options, and payment methods in the product cockpit. You can also provide customers with a summary of their choices, and the option to request a quote, issue a policy on the spot, or save for later review, as shown in Figure 4.15.

Figure 4.15 SAP Hybris Commerce Financial Services Accelerator Storefront for Insurance

The SAP Hybris Commerce Financial Services Accelerator also includes an ASM solution that enables agents to take over a customer's online frontends and quotes, offer product support on the spot, or simply complete an order on a customer's behalf. Some of the key components included with this accelerator are financial services storefront templates; PCM; business tools; touch point integrations; dynamic online forms; support for homeowner, renter, auto, life, and event insurances; bundling capabilities; ASM; and subscription capabilities. Consumers can easily request insurance quotes by entering their details in the **Financial Services** accelerator storefront, as shown in Figure 4.16.

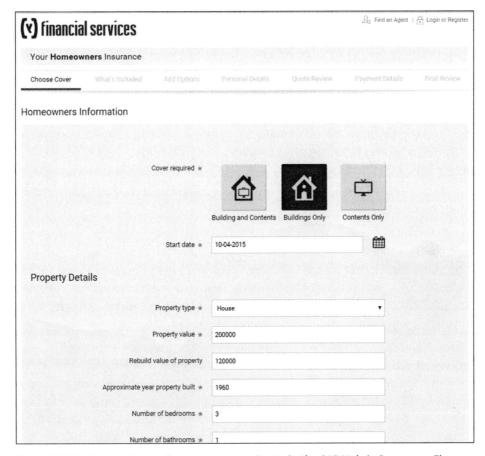

Figure 4.16 Customer Requesting an Insurance Quote in the SAP Hybris Commerce Financial Services Accelerator Storefront

Some of the key features of SAP Hybris Commerce Financial Services Accelerator are as follows:

- Tailor-made omnichannel solutions for financial service providers
- Customer portals for improved selling and integrated forms for customers to fill in all relevant data via yForms
- Ability to retrieve, save, and review quotes in the checkout process
- Preintegrated homeowners, renters, travel, and event insurance storefronts
- Customizable prices and additional policy options
- Guided selling options included to guide customers through the ordering process, including the ability to compare different insurance plans
- Support of dynamic forms for complex insurance policy types
- Easy configuration of bundling options for insurance plans with associated options
- Ability to offer flexible customer payment options, for example, monthly, quarterly or yearly
- Integration with ASM to offer product support in completing the transactions for complex policies by taking over customers' storefront experience
- Supports find agent functionality, enabling customers to find experts quickly in a financial-related field of interest and communicate directly with agents of their choice

SAP Hybris Commerce Utilities Accelerator

The utilities accelerator for the SAP Hybris Commerce Cloud enables utilities to offer an online sales process from order to billing through integration with the SAP Industry Solution for Utilities (SAP IS-U). Energy products, such as gas and electricity can be offered together with nonenergy products and services.

Product content and catalog functionality from SAP Hybris Commerce has been enhanced with energy products and attributes to be used as templates for adding new product offers to the market and reacting quickly to customer demand. A predefined and guided sales process selects valid products based on given customer information such as region and consumption. Through the sales process, energy prices are automatically retrieved from the backend system. In the checkout process, the customer information is collected and transferred to SAP IS-U. Further solution capabilities allow the integration to SAP IS-U tariffs and the mapping to SAP Hybris Commerce products. Customer master data are transferred and ready for the forthcoming processes.

With SAP Hybris Commerce Utilities Accelerator (see Figure 4.17), you can easily set up an order-to-cash process for energy and nonenergy products. As a result, the new solution helps utilities accelerate the time to market with any product and service while reducing the cost to serve their customers.

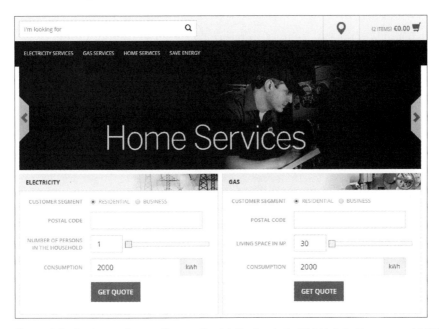

Figure 4.17 Customer Requesting an Electricity Quote in SAP Hybris Commerce Utilities Accelerator

SAP Hybris Commerce Travel Accelerator

The SAP Hybris Commerce Travel Accelerator enables travel companies to deliver their omnichannel strategies through SAP Hybris Commerce, providing market-leading retail capabilities to meet modern travel business demands.

The core of the SAP Hybris Commerce Travel Accelerator is the data model, which is designed specifically to provide a reference model that can be extended and adapted to meet the needs of customer implementations. Based on the Open Travel Alliance (OTA) industry standard, it encompasses the main data objects for transport providers: air, rail, bus, cruise, and ferry.

The SAP Hybris Commerce Travel Accelerator provides a preconfigured storefront based on an airline B2C model, containing pages and components that deliver a responsive UI design as well as a complete booking funnel for flights and related products. It provides a suite of business services that can be exposed through any channel to deliver a complete end-to-end customer experience.

The underlying integration capability of the SAP Hybris Commerce platform enables customers to develop connectors to a range of industry reservation and inventory systems.

The main features of the SAP Hybris Commerce Travel Accelerator are as follows:

- Fully responsive storefront featuring a landing page, travel search, fare selection, ancillaries, customer login, passenger details, payment, booking management, flight status, trip finder, and customer login/registration
- Fare selection page with search results and a dynamically updating itinerary basket
- Ancillary selection page with the ability to add supplementary products (flight meal options, seat selector, lounge access, fare upgrades, etc.) to the itinerary
- Ability for customers to log in or create an account with a passenger profile complete with preferences
- Ability for customers to manage their bookings, check flight status, search for past or upcoming bookings, and update their profile
- Integrated ASM so customer service agents can offer product support and help complete transactions for customers directly from their basket
- Back-office cockpits with business administration interfaces for creating and managing products, flight schedules, bundles, promotions, and business rules

SAP Hybris Commerce Citizen Engagement Accelerator

The citizen engagement accelerator helps bring services to citizens through a single, unified UI which resides in users' personal accounts. It provides ease of use in document handling, requests, payments, permits, and registrations in areas such as:

- Civic services to deliver public services online, such as applying for an ID, visa, or parking permit, and filing public grievances
- Social services to support financial or medical assistance, child care assistance, and unemployment benefits
- Tax and revenue management including online taxpayer services or using omnichannel capabilities across all devices and channels, allowing agencies, citizens, and governments to exchange information and minimizing the need for "double-touch" interactions
- Grantor requests to allow, e.g., schools to easily request and track grants for modernization projects, such as new building insulation

4.2.4   SAP Hybris Customer Experience

The traditional approaches to engaging customers with mass-segmentation and boilerplate-driven content aren't sufficient to attract and retain digital customers. The expectation is increasing for improved customer experience with each passing moment. Organizations need to fine-tune their customer experience constantly to win and retain online customers. Customers are constantly looking for new contextual experiences based on personalized contents.

SAP Hybris Commerce Cloud enables businesses to provide contextual experiences to their customers. It delivers dynamic, consistent, and targeted content, as well as personalized offers, to online customers across the touch points. SAP Hybris Customer Experience is integrated fully with SAP Hybris Commerce Cloud, SAP Hybris Merchandising, and Digital Asset Management to provide a 360-degree perspective of customers and present relevant content dynamically based on customer context.

SAP Hybris Customer Experience is based on a three-pronged methodology as follows:

- **Understand customers**
  Before offering any engaging experience, it's absolutely critical that you understand your customers and their journey, uncover their needs, and record their transactions, events, interactions, contexts, and behaviors.

- **Create experiences**
  Based on customer profiles, you craft customer experiences by personalizing content, merchandising, and commerce behavior. Using customer preferences, interactions, predictive analytics, and business rules, you create exceptional and contextual omnichannel customer experiences and deliver relevant and timely offers that are effective in shaping the customer journey from discovery to advocacy.

- **Deliver and optimize**
  Deliver the customer experience, measure results, and fine-tune as needed to improve the business results. You need to measure performance based on certain key performance indicators (KPIs) such as conversion rate, customer lifetime value, cost per acquisition, shopping cart abandonment rate, bounce rate, and so on.

Businesses can execute on this methodology to create value and attract, convert, and retain customers. Through optimized websites, streamlined marketing, and branded experiences, businesses can attract new customers to their storefronts. Attracting customers to storefronts is just one side of the equation unless you convert them to actual buyers. Without conversion, it's as good as not having those customers at all. Converting visiting customers to buyers requires offering personalized search and merchandising for relevant products with tailored contents and promotions, and, finally, retaining the customers to create stronger brand loyalty through optimized customer experiences and cross-channel consistency. The contextual customer experience is possible through the SAP Hybris web content management system (WCMS). WCMS is a marketing and publishing tool that offers web content management capabilities for all channels and devices, as shown in Figure 4.18.

Figure 4.18 Consistent Content across All Devices

It's integrated fully with PCM and SAP Hybris Commerce Cloud. WCMS enables you to easily manage contents across channels, including online, mobile, and rich Internet applications, from a single interface.

You can effectively create, manage, and drive customer experiences across all touch points. WCMS supports comprehensive preview capabilities for both desktop and mobile devices with the ability to make changes to product contents by live edits; drag and drop; synchronization of single components, whole sections, and entire pages; responsive image management; and on the fly. These functionalities enable businesses to easily place and reuse cross-channel marketing campaigns, as shown in Figure 4.19.

With WCMS, you can make content easily available across all output channels, enable fast and easy creation of first-class multifunctional sites, manage responsive sites from a single business UI, and ultimately create a seamless omnichannel customer experience. Some of the key compelling features of WCMS are as follows:

- **SmartEdit**

  You can design intuitive content management and navigation using world-class SmartEdit capabilities. It allows you to manage websites with versions and edit content contextually with options to preview and synchronize with catalogs. It allows you to expedite content management through consumer-grade interactions by editing directly on the website using drag and drop, as shown in Figure 4.20. WCMS web services allow the reuse of content and integrations. SAP Hybris Customer Experience and SmartEdit enable exceptional and contextual customer experiences from a single business tool.

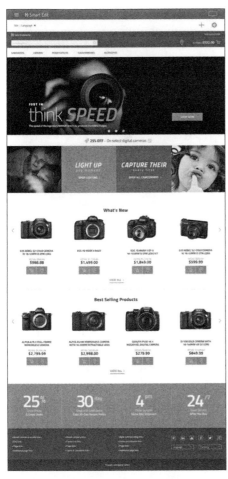

Figure 4.19 Example of a Campaign on a Storefront with a Special Offer

Figure 4.20 SmartEdit Capability in SAP Hybris Commerce WCMS

SAP Hybris Customer Experience helps you provide consistent, dynamic, and contextual content across all touch points and devices with responsive templates and powerful capabilities, including SmartEdit, test, and preview. Most importantly, it has lower implementation times and requires no extra integration costs. SmartEdit provides a framework for managing merchandising, personalization, optimization, and other commerce-related functionality in one tool, as shown in Figure 4.21.

Figure 4.21 Personalization with SmartEdit

- **Contextual merchandising**
  SAP Hybris Customer Experience can be enhanced with contextual merchandising to drive real-time business metrics, which helps to place hot products for customers to easily see and buy, as shown in Figure 4.22.

  Hot products are more likely to drive conversion. You can push products to the storefront that need to be sold sooner by synchronizing merchandising with the promotional calendar to drive more sales of promoted products. You can also drive conversion by personalizing merchandise to individual customers and showing products that are relevant to them. Customer conversion is highly volatile and depends on many factors such as time of day, weather, availability, promotions, competitors' promotions, press reviews, social trends, and so on. The static merchandising rules aren't sufficient to keep up with these factors. Merchandising has to be contextual and data driven. Using internal and external data sources, you need to adjust the merchandising mix continuously to leverage the real-time changes in customer conversion, as shown Figure 4.23.

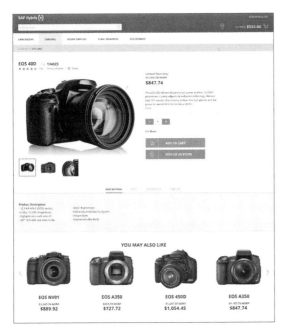

Figure 4.22 Contextual Placement of Merchandise in a Storefront

Figure 4.23 Example of a Merchandise Mix in SAP Hybris Merchandising

Figure 4.24 shows how SAP Hybris Merchandising business users can easily drag and drop the products to change the merchandising mix.

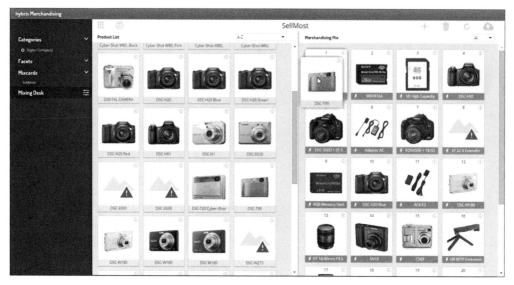

Figure 4.24 Dragging and Dropping Products to Change the Merchandise Mix

You can also personalize the experience for each storefront visitor automatically by proposing one-on-one merchandising recommendations.

To implement contextual merchandising effectively, you can leverage data continuously updated from the storefront in real time to track metrics such as best sellers, top converters, top trending, or most profitable products. Merchandisers can preview product mixes suggested by the system based on metrics for different contexts and adjust the priority of metrics to meet business and merchandising goals. Product mixes can be adjusted in real-time to show an up-to-date and contextually relevant product mix to the customer. Figure 4.25 shows how merchandisers can adjust the merchandising mix using business metrics, manually dragging and dropping products to components slots, and adding personalization rules to component slots for targeted product results as needed.

SAP Hybris Merchandising enables higher customer satisfaction with personalized buying experiences and offers business users the unique ability to quickly respond to trends—what is selling now as shown in Figure 4.26—to move products in the storefront more efficiently. It provides businesses better control over the dynamic commerce experience.

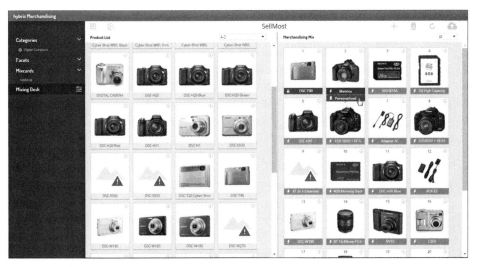

Figure 4.25 Adjusting the Merchandise Mix Using Business Metrics

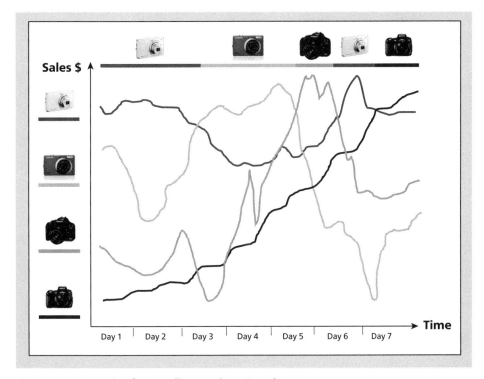

Figure 4.26 Example of Best-Selling Products Trends

- **Superior search experience**

The search and navigation module under SAP Hybris Customer Experience offers faceted navigation as well as free-text search, integrated in a single interface. With type-ahead keyword suggestions and clues, users can fine-tune their searches. With spell check enabled, products appear in the search results even if keywords are misspelled by the customer. Faceted browsing enables you to display your offerings based on specific combinations of attributes that are important to customers. Customers can combine attributes dynamically to quickly browse huge product categories and easily find relevant product details, as shown in Figure 4.27.

Figure 4.27 SAP Hybris Commerce Search Based on Attributes

The module also enables you to proactively manage the search experience with synonyms and stop words to adapt searches to reflect the real world. Shoppers can find what they are looking for with a wide range of related words. SAP Hybris Commerce Cloud also supports searchandising with keyword redirects, which allows you to define specific keywords that redirect shoppers to a specific landing page when they search for that term. This helps you manage content for certain products to maximize conversions, as well as up-sell and cross-sell opportunities, through carefully merchandised landing pages.

You can easily promote specific products, vendors, and product categories by placing them at the top of the search results, as shown in Figure 4.28.

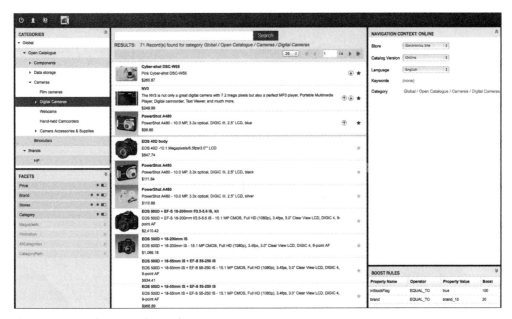

Figure 4.28 Product Search Results

The SAP Hybris Commerce Search Cockpit empowers even nontechnical business users to manage and maintain search and facet preferences with its user-friendly interface. In the Commerce Search Cockpit, you can promote "hero products" to the very top of search results by just clicking the star symbol next to the product. Facets can be turned on and off, and the order of facets can be changed as well. Boost and bury functionality allows you to prioritize certain products or product categories in search results based on business needs, pushing them higher or lower on the list.

The SAP Hybris search functionality offers direct access to Apache Solr queries, including advanced Solr features such as field collapsing, geospatial search, simplified updating of search results with automatic updates through real-time synchronization of catalog changes, and custom mapping of Solr search results.

Faceted browsing in the SAP Hybris search functionality offers a range of sorting and browsing options to allow you to narrow and broaden the criteria by facets such as price, brand, product type, product color, product size, and so on. It includes support for multilanguage, multicatalog, and multistore search capabilities.

- **New personalization**
  SmartEdit-based personalization capabilities work across both content and commerce in an integrated way, so that you can build customer experiences consistently across channels and functionality. Using SmartEdit for SAP Hybris Customer Experience, you can see the end-customer experience as you build it, all the while working in one set of tools.

  The new personalization functionality comes with the following benefits:

  - Easy targeting of content with the help of SmartEdit
  - Creating customizations and managing how they interact for a complete user experience
  - Observing changes in the correct context as you work using a dedicated preview
  - Delivering a personalized experience to customers through the accelerator storefronts

  The personalization mode available in SmartEdit helps you easily organize and customize the content displayed to particular users based on their allocation to user segments.

  The personalization mode allows you to do the following:

  - Manage targeting of content from within SmartEdit.
  - Create new customizations and manage how they layer and interact to build a complete user experience.
  - See changes in the correct context as you work.
  - Preview the customizations from the context of different customers.

You can create your customizations using the SmartEdit UI. After the particular customization is ready, you can preview it to see how the customization works for a particular target group.

4.2.5   Product Content Management

Businesses today sell across multiple brands, channels, and business models. More often, product contents and business information are scattered across the organizations and systems. It becomes increasingly difficult to assimilate information from various sources to offer consistent branding and execute effective marketing campaigns. Traditional product information management (PIM) solutions are limited by their capability to only manage structured product content such as product number, name, price, and so on.

By consolidating the management of product content and business data on a single platform, PCM enables organizations to ensure consistency and increase efficiency across channels, systems, and line of businesses. It has been designed to enable customers to bring all customer-facing content, structured and unstructured, into a common repository—creating a golden record for product-related content—to allow business users to easily edit and maintain the contents. PCM is a strategic component to enable omnichannel customer experiences not only for touch points managed with SAP Hybris Commerce Cloud, but any kind of marketing-related communication to customers such as email, mobile apps, search engines, and third-party marketplaces. It complements classical MDM solutions, which generally focus on managing product master data to ensure backend process execution, while PCM defines data for customer experiences. PCM is normally owned by the line of business to develop relevant product content and to sell brands and relationships to power cross-selling and up-selling. The key features of PCM are as follows:

- **Creating a single truth of product content**
  PCM absorbs data from disparate sources (e.g., users, internal and external data sources, offline channels, online channels, etc.), ensures that consistent product information is available across all the channels and touch points, and then presents a uniform view to users, devices, and channels. The flexibility and agility of PCM makes it suitable for B2C, but B2B companies also can use PCM to develop a consistent product content repository. For example, you can see how PCM supports the management of base products and their product variants in Figure 4.29.

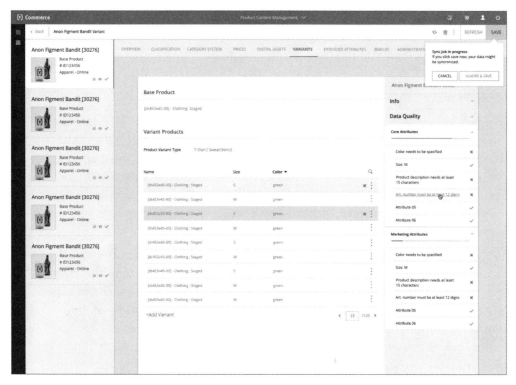

Figure 4.29 Managing Product Variants in PCM

- **UI for product managers and marketers**
  The SAP Hybris product cockpit is the central business tool to create and manage all product content in PCM. The highly configurable graphical UI makes product data management more efficient, process oriented, and user friendly. The Product Cockpit can be configured to display role-based sets of UI elements and provide guided procedures to ensure that all relevant information is maintained. It supports mass data management capabilities, simplified workflows, and synchronization. As a preconfigured solution, Figure 4.30 shows that you can easily browse catalogs, navigate product content, and edit product attributes as needed. It's an ideal product data management solution to deliver excellent usability and cost savings.

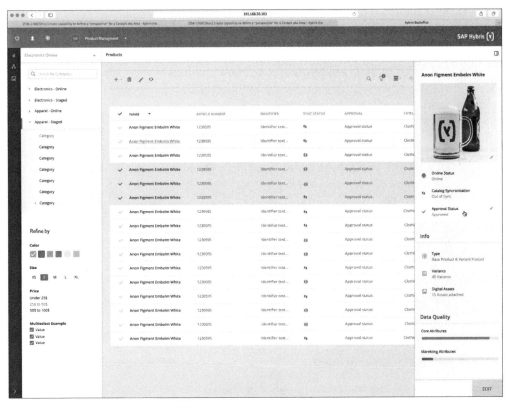

Figure 4.30 Product Cockpit in SAP Hybris Commerce

- **Effectively managing multiple catalogs**
  To ensure proper display of products, organizations must be able to manage product information as a hierarchically structured catalog. PCM enables organizations to define a catalog structure, create a master taxonomy, classify and categorize products, manage catalog versions, and import multiple supplier catalogs.

- **Product data syndication**
  Apart from aggregating master data from your own data sources, such as SAP ERP, Digital Asset Management, or other databases, PCM allows you also to connect with suppliers, who can easily upload, map, and import their product data. This helps you standardize the upload process of your suppliers, while the validation engine ensures that the data are delivered in high quality. As it's also important to distribute product data to third-party channels such as marketplaces or partners,

PCM allows you to map, sync, and optimize your product data to the different target channels.

- **International support**
PCM is built for global businesses with international support, including multiple languages, currencies, and brands; and region-specific payment services, address forms, fulfillment processes, and tax calculations. It allows you to configure and synchronize multiple catalogs in multiple languages and local touch points.

- **Ready to leverage SAP Master Data Governance (SAP MDG)**
PCM provides out-of-the-box integration with SAP MDG, which is the key solution for master data management. SAP MDG supports companies in consolidating master data from any SAP and non-SAP system and creating a single record, centrally creating and maintaining master data across heterogeneous systems in the enterprise, and providing a verifiable audit trail of when, why, and by whom master data were changed.

SAP MDG and PCM complement each other to support end-to-end product data management and provide governance, control, and data quality, enabling consistent product experiences through the customer lifecycle.

4.2.6   Order Management

The order management functionality in SAP Hybris Commerce Cloud is the bridge between the frontend and backend. Customers view order management and commerce as one. The order management functionality bridges the gap between commerce and downstream systems to enable consistent order capture, accurate price and availability information, reliable insight into order status with visibility across channels, optimal order allocation between various fulfillment systems and harmonious orchestration across front-office and back-office processes, and hiding the complexity from customers. Omnichannel orders coming in from anywhere using a single view of inventory can be fulfilled from anywhere internally or externally using multiple backend systems. SAP Hybris Commerce Cloud provides cross-industry order management for resellers and other e-commerce providers as a centralized hub to integrate all the order processes from different channels, as shown in Figure 4.31.

The order management system provides tools to handle all order-related activities such as creating new sales orders, changing or canceling orders, creating returns and refunds, and checking availability of products on the fly. You can also update delivery and shipping information, check the order status, and see the total cost of ordered goods, including shipment cost and taxes, based on the delivery address and delivery method. The system supports multiple methods of payment that are extensible and customizable.

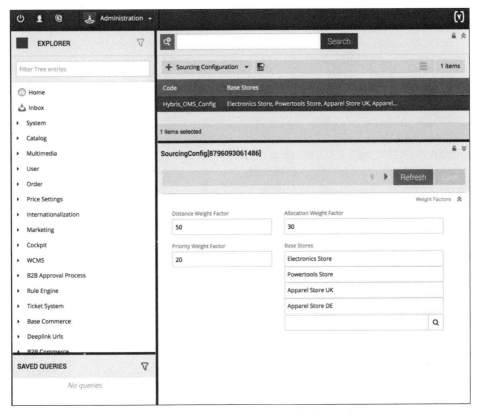

Figure 4.31 SAP Hybris Commerce Order Management Administration

The benefits of using order management are reflected in the ability to offer consistent customer experiences across channels. Customers can research products in one channel, buy in yet another channel, and check the order status in another channel. For example, customers can research products on a web storefront, place the order by calling a service agent in a customer contact center, and then finally check the status of their order in a mobile app. The centralized processing and controlling of all the orders in an organization provides an aggregate view of all the orders placed by customers irrespective of channel.

The key components of the order management functionality are as follows:

- **Order process workflow**

  The order process workflow, also known as order controller, manages and controls customer orders as they pass through various stages. When an order is placed, controller understands the current status of the order and what stage it has to go to next. The order updates can be leveraged by third-party system integration to react to status changes such as if the order is canceled, put on block for delivery, and so on.

- **Order versioning**

  During the different stages of order processing, the order status can change many times. The order status can be changed for various reasons such as items not available in stock, items on backorder, order partially or fully shipped, payment declined, or potential fraud detected. The order server records such changes to orders and prepares a log of the order version history. The order status changes are logged for orders as well as each for consignment of an order. This order versioning provides greater visibility of order status to both customers and service agents.

- **Distributed order management**

  Customer orders may include items from multiple sources, and individual items may need to ship to different addresses or may require different shipping methods. In such scenarios, orders are split into multiple consignments. Such consignments need to be shipped to separate addresses. Orders may also get split if all items aren't available for immediate shipment (e.g., a back order or partial shipment). Distributed order management also splits orders to allow a vendor to fulfill orders from different physical locations. The optimized sourcing can meet specific business requirements such as fewest shipments, closest location, or overstocked locations. Order management supports order splitting and routing to different back-office systems based on business rules. It also supports back-order and pre-sales campaign scenarios.

- **Order cancellation**

  Order management allows cancellation of orders before cut-off times or cancellation of parts of an order prior to dispatch. The cancellation changes can be applied automatically on such orders based on business rules. Sellers can define such rules for the customer to get a complete or partial refund for the order cancellation.

- **Hub for warehouses**

  Because order management works as a centralized hub for processing, routing, and controlling orders, warehousing can integrate with the order management module and fetch orders or parts of orders and report back stock levels and availability of items to the system. Warehouses can also provide additional information on order shipments such as carrier details and tracking details if items have been shipped. Order management also provides interfaces to query information such as stock levels, availability, expected to be in stock, tracking details, and so on to display information on the website or when required. Email notifications can be sent when an item becomes available in stock, and items may be marked as presales items or always being in stock.

- **Hub for fraud service providers**
  The order management module can be used to detect fraud attempts on orders via fraud checks, followed by additional and more sophisticated fraud detection using a third-party integrated solution. If a fraudulent order is detected, the order is placed on hold and placed in the fraud queue for customer service agents to review. It prevents an order from being processed further unless service agents have reviewed the order and removed the fraud block. The interface with order management allows you to query why an order has been flagged for fraud so that you can determine the fraud judgment criteria.

- **Stock information**
  With the stock service in order management, you can display product inventory stock levels as a net of reservations and sales, and so on. By leveraging integrated available-to-promise (ATP) functionality, you can also display delivery lead times for various delivery conditions and manage stock information. You can also configure important thresholds, such as allowed overselling quantities and always in stock or always out of stock quantities, and easily integrate with existing warehouse management systems to control these quantities in source systems. Order management delivers out-of-the-box functionality for strategies to deal with product availability-based order splitting and stock level check during order creation.

- **Returns and refunds**
  Order management allows you to create customer returns from the back office or to enable a self-service return request for end customers. This offers end customers the flexibility to initiate return and refund requests from the web storefront and check the status of their requests online using the self-service functionality. They can also call a customer service agent to initiate the process directly in the back-office system.

- **Store fulfillment**
  Order management offers pick, pack, and ship; buy online pickup in store (BOPIS); and buy online return in store (BORIS) capabilities. End customers have comprehensive and streamlined shopping experiences across the channels (online, mobile app, or in store).

4.2.7   SAP Hybris Commerce as a Service

SAP Hybris as a Service is a technology and business strategy for SAP Hybris (for more information on SAP Hybris as a Service, see Chapter 7), as well as a workbench and a marketplace, as described here:

- A workbench for building and assembling data-driven front-office microservices and software-as-a-service (SaaS) applications to enable new commercial models and digital products and services

- A marketplace for the commercialization and consumption of prepackaged front-office microservices

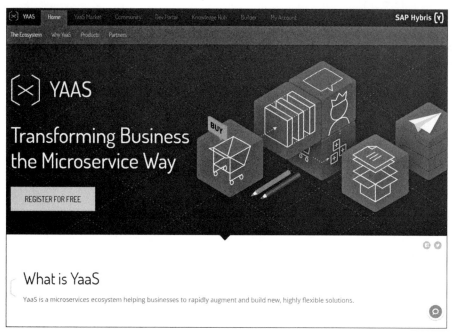

Figure 4.32 SAP Hybris as a Servce Homepage

Microservices from the SAP Hybris as a Service marketplace (*http://www.yaas.io*) can be leveraged by anyone to develop and extend microservices and applications online. Each of these microservices delivers only one self-contained functionality, which can be consumed by any other microservice or application. Integration with and to other microservices is established via RESTful application programming interfaces (APIs), which make it easy to connect and embed existing and newly built services to customer-specific, innovative business applications.

SAP Hybris Commerce as a Service does the "heavy lifting" for its clients by developing the most important base components that are required for enabling transactional commerce scenarios. Customers as well as partners can subscribe to these services, connect, and extend them for a variety of use cases ranging from short-term promotional sites; adding new channels by embedding commerce into media; entering new, smaller geographies; and innovation projects such as conversational commerce, testing same day delivery, and so on.

Here are some examples of already existing microservices:

- **Product Content**
  Used for managing products, variants, and related media.

- **Customer Accounts**
  Used to let customers sign in via email and social media.

- **Cart/Checkout**
  Used for customers to place an order with items in a cart.

- **Order Management**
  Used for collecting orders from the Cart and Checkout microservice.

- **Site Management**
  Used for administering sites, sales tax, and shipping.

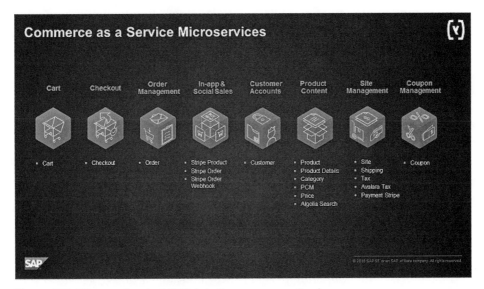

Figure 4.33 Microservices in SAP Hybris Commerce as a Service

4.2.8   Data Integration in SAP Hybris Commerce Cloud

The data integration capabilities of SAP Hybris Commerce Cloud allows you to easily and efficiently import, export, and synchronize data between SAP Hybris Commerce Cloud and other systems. You can leverage the following tools to handle any data exchange activity with SAP Hybris Commerce Cloud:

- **SAP Hybris Commerce Cloud, data hub**
  SAP Hybris Commerce Cloud, data hub is a powerful data staging and data integration platform to enable the loading of large amounts of data from many sources. These data can be processed based on various rules and then prepared to be delivered to any number of target systems. One of the key advantages of SAP Hybris Commerce Cloud data hub is that it stores information in a canonical form, or standard state, independent of source or target systems. After processing, the data can be ultimately transformed to a format the target system accepts.

- **ImpEx**
  ImpEx is a text-based import and export functionality available with SAP Hybris Commerce Cloud. The ImpEx engine allows you to create, update, remove, and export platform items such as customers, products, or sales orders data from comma-separated value (CSV) data files, both during runtime and during the initialization or update process.

- **Import cockpit**
  To provide complete and accurate information about products to online customers, you need to aggregate information from various sources. Importing data from multiple sources into a central application is a complex, time-consuming, and error-prone process. The import cockpit is designed to reduce import complexity and enable business users to create import mappings within an intuitive graphical user interface (GUI) tool. It allows users to import data into SAP Hybris Commerce using a CSV source file, without the need to specify an ImpEx import script. You can consolidate and validate heterogeneous data to improve the overall quality of data sets. Using the import cockpit module, you can create and edit import jobs, create and edit mappings of imported files, and create concurrent Cron jobs.

- **SAP Hybris to SAP Hybris synchronization**
  Known informally as y2ysync, SAP Hybris to SAP Hybris synchronization allows you to synchronize data from one SAP Hybris Commerce Cloud instance to another. The synchronization of data between the source and target systems of two installations, for example, is carried out using SAP Hybris Commerce Cloud data hub.

4.2.9   Configure, Price, and Quote

Configure, price, and quote (CPQ) for product configuration provides a comprehensive solution to manage personalized and configurable products in SAP Hybris Commerce Cloud. The CPQ solution allows you to model the configurable products in the back office so that end customers are able to configure products in the online storefront, as shown in Figure 4.34.

Figure 4.34 Product Configuration in SAP Hybris CPQ

Because companies can expose the variant and product configuration capabilities to customers, they can sell configurable products in online stores where customers can choose various product options interactively and then place an order. CPQ supports both single-level and multilevel product configuration, as well as 3D visualization for products in storefronts (see Figure 4.35).

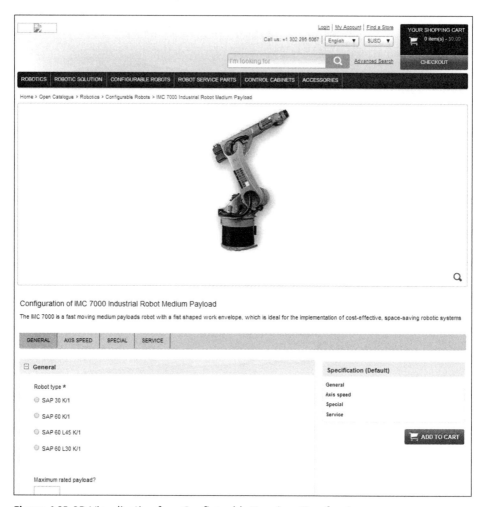

Figure 4.35 3D Visualization for a Configurable Item in a Storefront

When you set up the configurable products to be sold through the online store, you can do so through modeling, replication, and enrichment. The modeling exercise is carried out in SAP ERP. After modeling, you create the knowledge base and import it into SAP Hybris Commerce Cloud along with the product master using the data loader. Finally, you enrich the product data using PCM.

The key features of CPQ product configuration are as follows:

- **Online store support**
  SAP Hybris Commerce Cloud provides guided selling for configurable products so that customers can interactively configure products while the system ensures that only valid options are displayed for selection (providing suggestions for conflict resolution) and only relevant information is requested by the customer. Product configurations started but not completed by customers are retained even if customers navigate away from the configuration page. Customers can add configured products to the shopping cart even if the configuration is incomplete or has conflicting characteristic values. Using WCMS integration, business users can configure the configuration page in SAP Hybris Commerce.

- **Local configuration runtime engine**
  The product configuration is based on a fully featured runtime engine that runs locally in SAP Hybris Commerce Cloud. Hence, customers can easily configure products online without needing an active connection with the SAP backend system. Currently, configuration is provided by the Solution Sales Configurator engine; however, SAP is working on replacing this engine with a cloud-based Internet Pricing Configurator (IPC) engine in late 2017. The product configuration in SAP Hybris Commerce Cloud is in complete sync with product models in the SAP backend system. A fully compatible configuration runtime engine based on original master data from the SAP backend system ensures smooth integration with SAP's fulfillment capabilities.

- **SAP integration**
  CPQ supports both synchronous and asynchronous order management scenarios. Hence, for both order management scenarios, configuration results are sent to the SAP backend system for further processing

4.3   Integrating with Other SAP Hybris Front-Office Solutions

SAP Hybris Commerce Cloud integrates with other SAP Hybris solutions to enable simplified front-office processes. We've already covered some of the SAP Hybris Commerce Cloud integration scenarios with SAP Hybris Sales Cloud and SAP Hybris Service Cloud in Chapter 2 and Chapter 3. Let's review some of the key front-office integration scenarios with SAP Hybris Commerce in this section.

4.3.1   Integration with SAP Hybris Marketing

The integration between SAP Hybris Commerce Cloud and SAP Hybris Marketing Cloud enables you to identify and target customers with personalized offerings. You can maintain omnichannel profiles to create target groups and execute targeted campaigns to extend personalized shopping experiences to all customers. The ability to track customers' interactions gives you the power to make intelligent product recommendations to your customers. Some of the advantages of using integration with SAP Hybris Commerce Cloud are as follows:

- **Customer segmentation**
  Marketers can segment customers based on different attributes using predictive analysis. They can create tactical customer segments in SAP Hybris Marketing Cloud segmentation and create a campaign for each segment. Customers can also be dropped into segments and corresponding campaigns as and when they are identified in the storefront.

- **Design personalization**
  Using SAP Hybris WCMS design personalization, you can define web shop personalization per customer segment and then assign those segments to the corresponding campaigns in SAP Hybris Marketing Cloud for personalized and targeted campaigns.

- **Personalized interaction**
  You can offer personalized shopping experiences to SAP Hybris Commerce Cloud storefront customers through the assignment of a login user to the customer segment and the corresponding campaign.

- **Track customer journey**
  Using SAP Hybris Marketing Cloud data management, you can track the customer journey and shopping behavior. You can leverage the shopping behavior to track cross-channel customer journeys and score and nurture customers through effective segmentation and optimized campaign execution.

- **Clickstream integration**
  Using SAP Hybris Commerce Cloud and clickstream integration, you can capture and detect a customer's interest in specific products, product categories, special offers, and so on. Clickstream feeds can be aggregated to create interaction in SAP Hybris Marketing Cloud. You can also record important events in the customer shopping journey, such as add to shopping cart, add to wish list, shopping cart abandonment, and so on, and then create interactions in SAP Hybris Marketing Cloud.

- **Real-time product recommendations**

  You can build a recommendation model using predictive capabilities to offer real-time product recommendations to web shop customers for cross-selling and up-selling using SAP Hybris Marketing Cloud. You can propose products in the form of "you might be interested in the following products."

4.3.2   Integration with SAP Hybris Cloud for Customer

SAP offers a ready-to-use integration framework between SAP Hybris Commerce Cloud and SAP Hybris Cloud for Customer. The integration enables organizations to go beyond customer relationship management (CRM) and combine SAP Hybris Sales Cloud and SAP Hybris Commerce Cloud. It allows sales agents to browse catalogs, configure products, and create orders directly from SAP Hybris Cloud for Customer environment for true interactive selling. SAP Hybris Commerce Cloud and SAP Hybris Cloud for Customer provide a standard integration between the market-leading omnichannel commerce and customer support solutions in the SAP product portfolio. It keeps the customer data synchronized between SAP Hybris Commerce Cloud and SAP Hybris Cloud for Customer, as well as service tickets between these two systems to connect customers with customer support agents. Customer service agents can resolve tickets through the SAP Hybris customer ticketing system or over the phone.

In addition, using Single Sign-On (SSO), customer service agents can open ASM on top of the commerce storefront to provide seamless interactive sales and service support to customers in real time. Sales agents can browse the commerce storefront, search the product catalog to look up product information, configure product bundles, add products to the cart, create quotes, or check carts out for customers on their behalf. If needed, they can also help customers with their account information such as payment details, existing orders, delivery details, and so on, enabling both sales and service teams to provide interactive selling and service to customers on the spot.

Integrated SAP Hybris Commerce Cloud and SAP Hybris Cloud for Customer allows businesses to provide integrated customer service and sales support across customer touch points. It enables the sales force to provide interactive and engaging selling experiences with customers throughout the sales process. Customer service agents are also able to provide exceptional service in all the channels, leading to increased sales and a loyal customer base.

4.3.3   SAP Hybris as a Service Connect

SAP Hybris as a Service Connect allows you to integrate SAP Hybris Commerce Cloud and SAP Hybris as a Service-based commerce sites (SAP Hybris Commerce as a Service) to enhance the native SAP Hybris Commerce Cloud platform capabilities with cloud-based microservices built on SAP Hybris as a Service. You can connect data between SAP Hybris Commerce Cloud and SAP Hybris as a Service on an SAP Cloud Platform instance asynchronously through the SAP Hybris Commerce Cloud, data hub. This may change in late 2017 with a combined SAP Cloud Platform Integration and SAP Hybris Commerce, data hub solution.

SAP Hybris as a Service Connect helps to moves data (e.g. products, prices, orders, stocks, etc.) between SAP Hybris Commerce Cloud and SAP Hybris Commerce as a Service. For example, an order placed in an SAP Hybris as a Service-based commerce site is transferred automatically to the SAP Hybris Commerce Cloud platform where subsequent order fulfillment will be carried out. At the same time, status updates are passed to the SAP Hybris as a Service storefront from SAP Hybris Commerce Cloud. SAP Hybris as a Service Connect can be used to provide comprehensive commerce scenarios between SAP Hybris Commerce Cloud and SAP Hybris Commerce as a Service.

4.4   Integrating with SAP S/4HANA and SAP ERP

SAP Hybris integration with SAP S/4HANA or SAP ERP provides a standardized, ready-to-use framework that connects SAP Hybris omnichannel commerce capabilities with the SAP backend. SAP customers and partners don't need to build complex integrations from scratch to connect SAP Hybris Commerce Cloud with SAP backend solutions. SAP Hybris Commerce supports orchestrating orders to multiple backend systems. This out-of-the-box integration allows you to connect SAP Hybris Commerce with both SAP ERP and SAP S/4HANA simultaneously. SAP Hybris Commerce Cloud can act as the omnichannel order capture and orchestration engine. The SAP backend remains the system of record for order fulfillment (shipping and billing). SAP Hybris Commerce Cloud integration with the SAP backend system supports the following scenarios:

- **SAP master data**
  You can replicate backend (SAP ERP and SAP CRM) master data such as customers (B2B), Customers per Day (CpD) or one-time customers, addresses, products, classification, pricing data (condition records), stock levels or inventory, installed

base, and business agreements (from SAP CRM only) to SAP Hybris Commerce Cloud.

- **Asynchronous order management (loosely coupled integration)**
  This type of integration between SAP Hybris Commerce Cloud and the SAP backend is developed for B2B and B2C scenarios. In these scenarios, communication between the SAP Hybris frontend and the SAP backend run in background, and customer interaction happens only through and within SAP Hybris Commerce Cloud. SAP Hybris remains independent of the SAP backend as far as data persistence and business process are concerned. In this case, sales orders are created and saved in SAP Hybris first and then replicated to the SAP backend asynchronously. The order fulfillment processes (delivery and billing) are done in the SAP backend, and order statuses for delivery, goods issue, billing and so on are exchanged with SAP Hybris.

- **Synchronous order management (tightly coupled integration)**
  This type of integration is preferred for B2B scenarios, and communication between SAP Hybris Commerce Cloud and the SAP backend is mainly synchronous. Although customer interactions are handled mostly through SAP Hybris Commerce Cloud, the data persistence and business processes reside in the SAP backend. In this case, calls to check out and view the order history are transferred directly to the SAP backend system, and they don't have any representation in the SAP Hybris system. It's possible to run both the synchronous as well as asynchronous scenarios at once. You can have one store integrated with asynchronous order management and another store in parallel with synchronous order management.

- **Synchronous pricing**
  You can use synchronous pricing between SAP Hybris Commerce Cloud and the SAP backend to enable the online store to read pricing information in real time from the SAP backend system. This functionality allows the latest prices to be shown, including complex pricing procedures, in store without any delays and can be used in different store areas such as catalog, product details, and cart.

- **Report to synchronize data**
  A report is provided to synchronize the foundational data between SAP Hybris Commerce and SAP backend systems such as currency codes, units of measurement, countries, plants/branches (to transfer plant data), regional taxes, price elements, data on material numbers conversion (transfers output format settings for product IDs), material groups (includes product price classes and product discount

classes), customer groups (includes customer price lists and customer discount groups), form of address keys, distribution channels, and divisions. In the report, you can specify the languages required to import into SAP Hybris Commerce.

- **SAP invoices**
  Customers (both B2B and B2C) can view their invoices online from their SAP Hybris storefront, although they were created in the SAP backend system.

4.5   Integrating with SAP Customer Relationship Management

Similar to SAP ERP, SAP Hybris Commerce Cloud can be integrated with SAP CRM to leverage powerful backend functionalities with commerce frontend capabilities. SAP CRM integration supports the following scenarios:

- **Master data**
  On the same line as SAP ERP, you can replicate customers (B2B), consumers (B2C), products, pricing, and installed base data from backend SAP CRM to SAP Hybris Commerce Cloud.

- **Asynchronous order management**
  Similar to SAP ERP, for B2B and B2C scenarios, sales orders can be saved and captured in SAP Hybris Commerce Cloud and replicated to SAP CRM for backend processing.

- **Synchronous order management**
  In this scenario, communication between SAP Hybris Commerce Cloud and SAP CRM is synchronous, and orders are created directly in SAP CRM.

- **Synchronous pricing**
  Using synchronized pricing, SAP Hybris Commerce directly reads pricing information from SAP CRM in real time. Hence, the storefront displays the most up-to-date pricing information for products.

- **SAP invoices**
  If you're using the SAP CRM billing functionality and integrating SAP Hybris Commerce Cloud and SAP CRM, you can allow B2B customers to view invoices originating from SAP CRM in online stores.

- **Service request management**
  Using this scenario, you can replicate service requests between SAP CRM and SAP Hybris Commerce Cloud.

- **Complaint management**
  Similar to service requests, you can replicate complaints between SAP CRM and SAP Hybris Commerce Cloud.

- **Service contract management**
  Using service contract integration, you can enable online customers to retrieve and display service contracts from SAP CRM in an online store. SAP CRM service contracts can also be renewed or terminated from the SAP Hybris Commerce Cloud storefront.

- **Service order management**
  You can replicate service orders created in SAP CRM to SAP Hybris Commerce Cloud to display in an online storefront. The service order can be created as a follow up from a service quotation, service contract, or service request, or it can stand alone.

- **SSO to ASM**
  You can integrate ASM to streamline the service process between SAP CRM and SAP Hybris Commerce Cloud to resolve customer issues quickly.

- **Product registration**
  This integration scenario enables customers to register the products they have purchased in an online B2C storefront for service entitlement.

- **Return orders**
  In this scenario, return orders can be initiated from the SAP Hybris Commerce Cloud storefront and replicated to SAP CRM for further processing. Returns can be initiated for B2B and B2C asynchronous orders, and the status is updated between SAP Hybris Commerce Cloud and SAP CRM at each step of the return process.

4.6   Summary

In this chapter, you've learned how SAP Hybris Commerce Cloud provides rich and modern commerce capabilities to attract, convert, and retain customers in the digital economy. Easy-to-use and extremely powerful tools and solutions such as the SAP Hybris Commerce industry accelerators, SAP Hybris Customer Experience component with WCMS capabilities, the PCM module, and finally the extensive order management features, including deep integration capabilities, enable companies to offer comprehensive omnichannel commerce capabilities.

In the next chapter, we'll discuss the SAP Hybris Marketing solution and how you can leverage it with other SAP Hybris solutions to grow a loyal and profitable customer base.

Chapter 5
Marketing

SAP Hybris Marketing fundamentally changes the way marketers attract, convert, and retain customers. Based on real-time customer contexts, SAP Hybris Marketing delivers highly engaging content and interactions across the channels to drive both customer growth and loyalty.

The digital economy offers unprecedented challenges and opportunities for marketers. Traditionally, marketers have relied on historical data to segment their target market and run marketing campaigns. The ineffectiveness of such campaigns is evident from facts such as 99.83% of online ads are ignored, only 5.9% of links in email campaigns are clicked by prospective email recipients, and, shockingly, the overall digital channel response rate is only 0.62%. Traditional approaches to marketing aren't working, especially in the era of empowered customers.

On the other hand, the new socially connected world offers enormous opportunities for marketers to engage with prospective customers and consumers in a whole new way. More data sources are available now than ever to learn about customers' behavior, their sentiments, browsing history, their likes and dislikes, and so forth. You have more channels and touch points now to engage with your target audience such as mobile apps, Facebook, Twitter, Snapchat, LinkedIn, text messages, online communities, and so on. The challenge lies in assimilating information from all these internal and external sources to draw meaningful and actionable marketing insights. On average, marketers use more than 10 siloed systems and sources to collect data on customers and prospects, excluding external sources. It's critical that the next-generation marketing tool is able to collect and organize both structured and unstructured data from all the sources and then allow marketing professionals to segment customers in real time, execute marketing campaign across channels, manage marketing resources, and offer predictive analytics and dashboards to measure various key performance indicators (KPIs). The answer is the SAP Hybris Marketing solution.

In this chapter, we'll discuss SAP's strategy for SAP Hybris Marketing and the deployment options for on-premise versus cloud applications. We'll review the key capabilities of the SAP Hybris Marketing solution such as consumer or customer profiles, segmentation and campaign management, marketing leads, commerce marketing, loyalty management, and analytics. In line with previous chapters, we have sections dedicated to integration scenarios for SAP Hybris Marketing with other SAP Hybris front-office solutions such as SAP Hybris Sales Cloud and SAP Hybris Commerce, and SAP back-office solutions such as SAP S/4HANA's core, SAP ERP, and SAP Customer Relationship Management (SAP CRM).

5.1   Strategy for SAP Hybris Marketing

SAP's strategy for SAP Hybris Marketing is very simple—offer a solution for today's businesses to transform their marketing organizations and deliver contextual marketing that is truly real-time and one-on-one. What exactly is contextual marketing? It's a customer's past history, current context, and what the customer is likely to do in the future. It blends together three types of customer information: past interactions (purchases, campaigns, orders, etc.), propensity scores (cross-sell/up-sell, retention), and the in-moment intentions. Then, based on this real-time insight, you can develop the full context of the customer at the point of engagement. Next you can determine the best offer, promotion, or reminder for customers based on your business objectives. Per a customer's response to these actions, you can fine-tune and make contextual marketing more effective.

SAP's objectives for SAP Hybris Marketing solutions can be summarized as follows:

- Gain real-time insights into customer's intent to enable contextual marketing by blending together both structured and unstructured data, including implicit and explicit customer behavior, into one unified view.
- Deliver contextual and relevant customer experiences by executing individualized 1:1 marketing offers and promotions based on real-time customer intents.
- Market with speed and agility by aligning marketing organizations with increased collaboration and real-time insights.

- Offer a single integrated marketing platform with open application programming interfaces (APIs) and flexible architecture that can easily fit into any environment and grow with the organization.

Although the SAP Hybris Marketing Cloud and SAP Hybris Marketing capabilities are more or less the same (as we'll cover in the next section), it's important to review the decision criteria and benefits for choosing one deployment option over the other so you can make an informed decision. Figure 5.1 shows that SAP Hybris Marketing Cloud has lower upfront costs and time to deployment but limited flexibility and extensibility. On the other hand, SAP Hybris Marketing has greater flexibility and extensibility but requires a higher upfront investment and a longer time to go-live. In addition, you need SAP HANA technical skill sets in the team, unlike for SAP Hybris Marketing Cloud.

SAP Hybris Marketing Cloud	Decision Criteria	SAP Hybris Marketing On-Premise/Private Cloud
⬇	Up front investment	⬆
⬇	Time to go-live	⬆
⬇	Technical skill sets required (HANA)	⬆
⬆	Speed of Innovation (adoption of new version)	⬇
⬇	Flexibility/Extensibility	⬆

Figure 5.1 Decision Criteria for Deployment Options

Note

SAP Hybris Marketing can be deployed either using the public cloud solution or the on-premise/private cloud solution. SAP Hybris Marketing Cloud is the public cloud option. SAP Hybris Marketing Cloud is available on a monthly subscription and is run on the SAP infrastructure as managed services. SAP Hybris Marketing can be deployed either on premise on the customer's IT infrastructure or in a private cloud using SAP HANA Enterprise Cloud.

5.2 SAP Hybris Marketing Cloud

As we discussed in the previous section, SAP Hybris Marketing is available on premise as well as via subscription in the public cloud. Both of these deployment options have similar functionalities, with the exception of loyalty management. Loyalty management is currently available through an SAP Hybris as a Service on SAP Cloud Platform subscription and requires additional licensing. Because the marketing capabilities available in both SAP Hybris Marketing and SAP Hybris Marketing Cloud are about the same, we'll review these key capabilities together. For consistency, we'll be using the term SAP Hybris Marketing Cloud and SAP Hybris Marketing interchangeably in describing their capabilities. However, before we go through these capabilities, let's review the key requirements of today's marketers and what they need to successfully do their jobs. It will be easier to appreciate the marketing capabilities with reference to the marketer's actual work.

The following seven scenarios represent a marketer's actual work:

- **Profile customers**
  The primary goal of marketers is to understand their customers, and real understanding comes from standardized and real-time profiling. The more they know about their customers, the better equipped they are to attract and engage with them. They must capture and enrich customer information to get a single view of a customer's interactions in real time.

- **Segment and target customers**
  Marketers need to segment their market based on various attributes and then target customers through various campaigns. The ability to effectively target customers is vital to growing both the customer base and market share. Marketers are required to identify a target audience for marketing campaigns and reach that audience at the right moment with personalized messages across multiple channels.

- **Commerce marketing**
  More and more customers are buying online, and commerce marketing has emerged as one of the top focus areas for marketers in the digital era. Marketers must extend customer information to the storefront to enable seamless customer experiences.

- **Marketing resource management**
  Marketers need to effectively orchestrate and optimize all the marketing resources. Organizing marketing resources can help in effective collaboration and execution of marketing campaigns.

- **Marketing analytics**
  Along with real-time analytics, predictive analytics is one of the most critical requirements to effectively respond to new marketing opportunities. Campaign performance needs to be monitored and measured to take corrective actions and align resources to ensure the success of marketing initiatives.

- **Marketing lead management**
  One of the success factors for marketers is measured by their ability to deliver quality leads to the sales team. Marketing solutions should enable nurturing of contacts to hand over qualified contacts as potential buyers to the sales team. They should be able to measure and monitor success to ensure effective collaboration between marketing and sales.

- **Loyalty management**
  Loyalty management has evolved beyond offering deals to customers. Marketers need to effectively enhance customer retention and lifetime value using next-generation loyalty management solutions. They should be able to offer enriched and engaging customer experiences and encourage advocacy and referrals. Mobile wallets need to support digital loyalty cards and coupons.

In the following sections, we'll look at the key capabilities of SAP Hybris Marketing Cloud and how these rich functionalities can be leveraged by today's marketers to most effectively achieve their marketing goals.

5.2.1   Consumer and Customer Profiling

Your ability to engage with customers is largely limited by your understanding of customers' behavior and their environment. It's all about understanding the customers and, at the same time, respecting their privacy. SAP Hybris Marketing Cloud offers consumer and customer profiling functionality to dynamically capture and enrich customer information or profiles across all sources into a single view, as shown in Figure 5.2, to help you gain insights into customers' real-time intents.

These intelligent and continually evolving profiles capture and analyze real-time customer interactions (see Figure 5.3), contexts, and behaviors. This information is shared across customer-facing applications to deliver consistent, relevant, and engaging customer experiences across all channels.

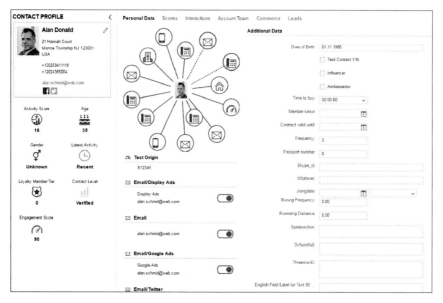

Figure 5.2 Example of Customer Profile in SAP Hybris Marketing

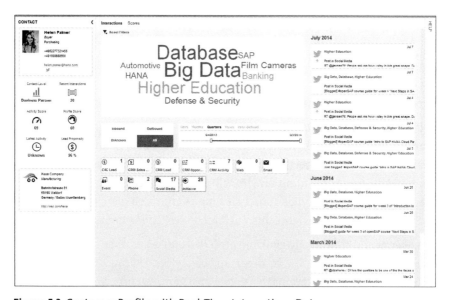

Figure 5.3 Customer Profile with Real-Time Interactions Data

The profile can be used for business-to-business (B2B) scenarios as well as to create customer profiles with contacts and other details, as shown in Figure 5.4.

Figure 5.4 Example of a B2B Customer Profile

The embedded analytics in profiles can be leveraged to get additional insights about B2B customers, as shown in Figure 5.5.

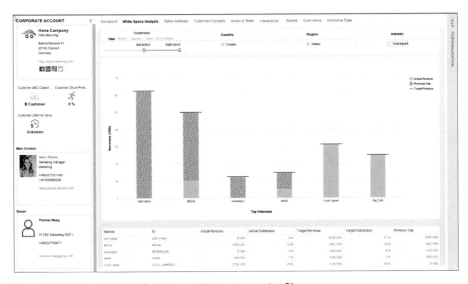

Figure 5.5 Embedded Analytics in a B2B Customer Profile

The key capabilities of consumer and customer profiling are as follow:

- You can uncover customer interest and create a 360-degree view of the customer across all channels, as shown in Figure 5.6 and Figure 5.7. Regardless of the channel, you can create unified profiles of customers that can be leveraged across all customer touch points to offer unique customer experiences.

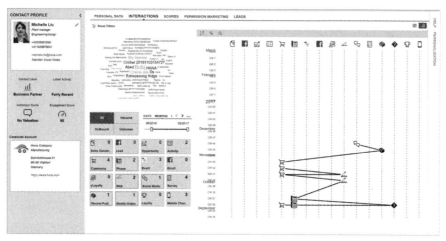

Figure 5.6 Customer Profile with Data from Across the Channels

Figure 5.7 Uncover a Customer's Browsing History

- You can develop and nurture anonymous contacts with additional information and offers and then convert them to high-value customers and brand advocates.

- Customer profiles are continuously enriched with real time information from internal and external data sources to keep it current. You're no longer limited by historic and obsolete customer information.

- Visual analysis and exploration tools available with SAP Hybris Marketing Cloud (see Figure 5.8) can be leveraged for fast insight into customer behavior and patterns based on customer profile information.

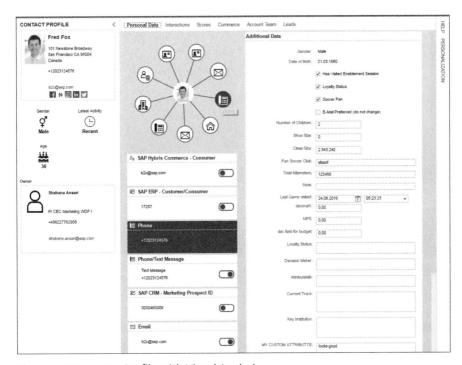

Figure 5.8 Customer Profile with Visual Analysis

- Predictive and advanced analytics are delivered out of the box with SAP Hybris for real-time customer insights, as shown in Figure 5.9.

- You can analyze structured and unstructured data associated with SAP Hybris Marketing Cloud customer profiles to extract customer sentiments, gain meaningful insights, and convert prospects to customers.

- You can gain insights into known and unknown customers using information available in customer profiles.

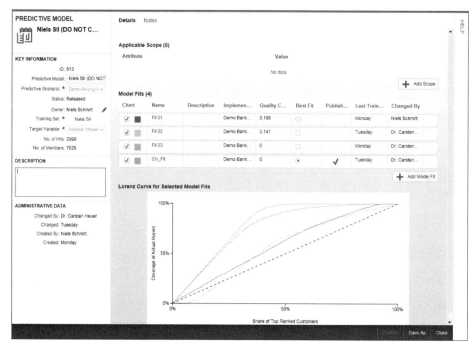

Figure 5.9 Predictive Analytics Delivered with SAP Hybris Marketing Cloud

- You can define your own scoring rules to score customer interactions, as shown in Figure 5.10. These scores can help you quantify and qualify target audiences for various marketing campaigns and offerings.

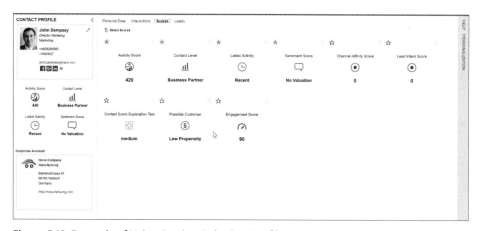

Figure 5.10 Example of Using Scoring Rules in a Profile

5.2.2   Segmentation and Campaign Management

The key capabilities of segmentation and campaign management in SAP Hybris Marketing Cloud are as follows:

- You can carry out high-performance customer targeting on big data in real time. You can take advantage of high-performance segmentation tools to react to a customer's context in real time to make sure communications are always targeted and relevant (see Figure 5.11).

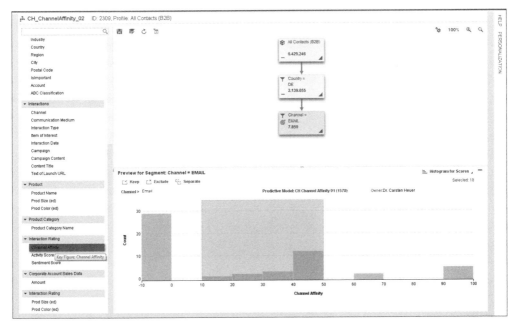

Figure 5.11 Example of Segmentation and Target Group

You can leverage high-volume segmentation and predictive capabilities to find the right audience for campaigns, as shown in Figure 5.12.

- Segmentation and campaign management in SAP Hybris Marketing Cloud enable you to deliver highly personalized and dynamic messages to targeted customers or consumers. Figure 5.13 shows customer's permissions that can help you offer personalized landing pages and subscription forms to customers based on their preferences or permissions and previous interactions.

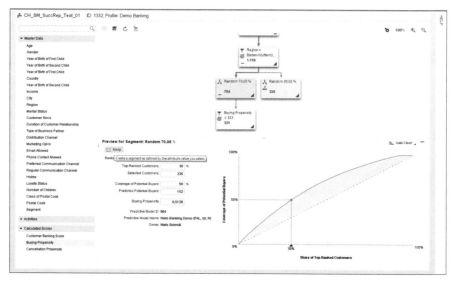

Figure 5.12 Predictive Analytics in Campaigns

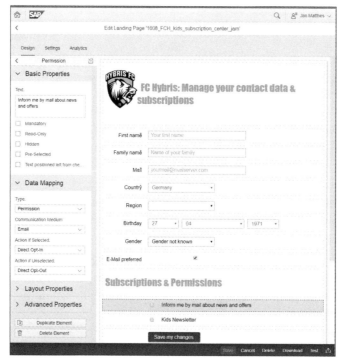

Figure 5.13 Marketing Permissions and Preferences

- Marketing permission and subscription management are available in real time and across channels. You can allow customers and consumers to manage their marketing permissions and subscriptions across the channels, as shown in Figure 5.14.

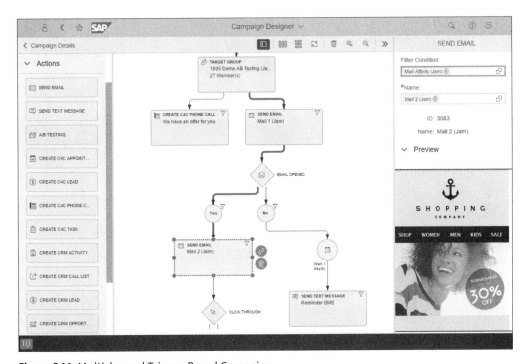

Figure 5.14 Multichannel Trigger-Based Campaign

- Multichannel and trigger-based marketing allows you to plan and execute marketing campaigns across channels. You can communicate with customers using the channels they prefer—from email to social media—for meaningful conversations. You can enable triggers and corresponding actions as part of campaigns, as shown in Figure 5.15; for example, clicking on a link in an email campaign triggers a personalized offer to be sent to the customer.

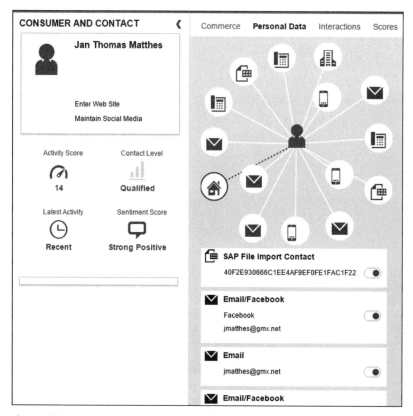

Figure 5.15 Marketing Subscriptions and Permissions as Set by the Customer

- Marketing campaign functionality available in SAP Hybris Marketing Cloud enables high-volume, multiwave campaign execution. You can set up multiwave, multi-channel, and trigger-based marketing campaigns. You can execute one-time as well as periodic marketing campaigns based on some predefined triggers or events. Marketers can get campaigns ready faster without involving IT by using simple visual exploration tools.

- A unified marketing calendar and campaign planning, execution, success, and cost analysis are all available in one application and platform.

5.2.3   Commerce Marketing

Commerce marketing helps you encourage your online customers to easily move from browsing to buying by understanding their needs and offering them a personalized shopping experience. You can increase the effectiveness of your omnichannel commerce strategy by leveraging the customer insights from marketing. Key capabilities of commerce marketing in SAP Hybris Marketing Cloud are as follows:

- Commerce marketing connects commerce and marketing together to define web shop personalization per customer segment as shown in Figure 5.16. By using accurate profiles and an in-depth understanding of customers, you can see what customers are looking for and use that information to tell them what additional products they may be interested in.

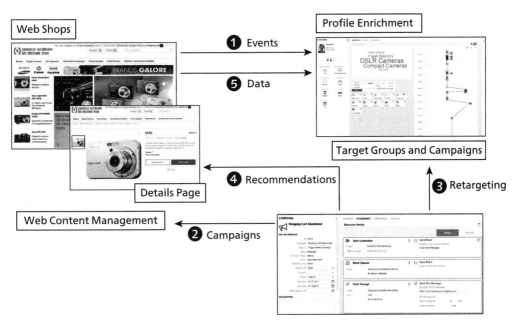

Figure 5.16 Commerce Marketing for Personalization per Customer Segment

- You can translate customer interests into conversion by providing real-time personalized recommendations also known as retargeting. If a customer abandons his shopping cart, you can use targeted campaigns to get the customer back to check out the shopping cart. You can deliver intelligent recommendations to customers with a self-learning solution that reads customer interactions to select and offer the best products, as shown in Figure 5.17.

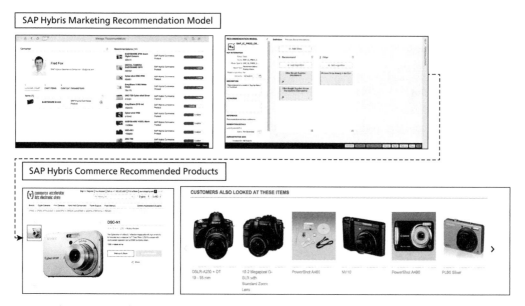

Figure 5.17 Real-Time Product Recommendations Based on a Model

- You can link customers with information from transactions, social media, click-streams, and point-of-sale data to build and enrich the online customer's full profile.

- Services are included to replicate customers, products, and orders to SAP Hybris Marketing Cloud for a unified and comprehensive view of customers across channels.

- Using customer profiles and insights, you can deliver personalized shopping experiences to targeted customers, as shown in Figure 5.18.

SAP Hybris Marketing Cloud also has standard out-of-the-box integration with SAP Hybris Commerce Cloud to make personalized recommendations to online shoppers (see Figure 5.19) using information from SAP Hybris Marketing Cloud to increase revenue and customer satisfaction.

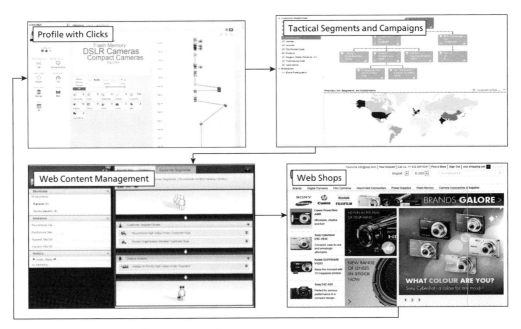

Figure 5.18 Personalized Shopping Experience

Figure 5.19 Personalized Offers and Product Recommendations

5.2.4   Marketing Resource Management

Marketers need to effectively manage all marketing activities to make sure they are on track, on budget, and working toward achieving their business goals. Key capabilities of SAP Hybris Marketing Cloud's resource management are as follows:

- **Marketing planning and financial management**
  With SAP Hybris Marketing Cloud's resource management, you can plan, budget, prepare marketing plans and campaigns, manage the marketing calendar, and manage marketing spends with integrated financials and collaboration. Marketing managers and marketing experts can use planning to plan budgets, programs, campaigns, and spends in a simple and intuitive way. In planning, you can use the budget plan application to allocate the budget for marketing activities and to plan budgets for dimensions such a brands, markets, or other dimensions based on your planning model (see Figure 5.20).

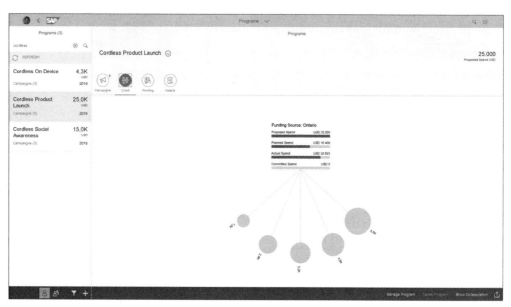

Figure 5.20 Example Campaign Planning and Budgeting

You can view, compare, and use various measures, such as **Planned Budget**, **Allocated Budget**, **Proposed Spend**, **Planned Spend**, and **Actual Spend**, as shown in Figure 5.21. You can also create programs and define proposed spends for them. You can view the proposed spend for a program and the planned spend for each campaign assigned to the program in a chart.

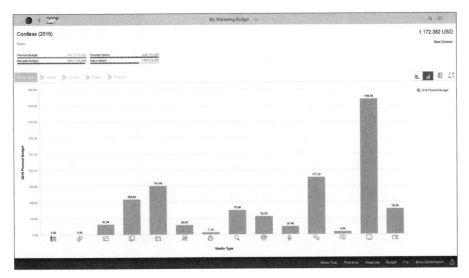

Figure 5.21 Analytics for Planned Budget and Spend

You can assign a funding source to a program (see Figure 5.22), which is a portion of the planned budget from a public plan that is used to finance a program.

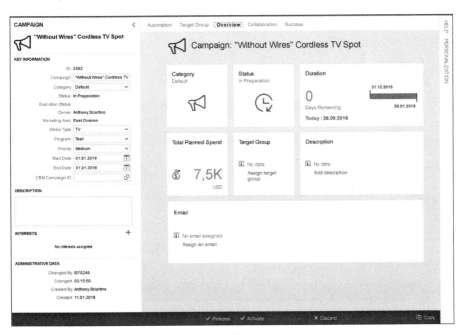

Figure 5.22 Campaign Details with Funding Source

- **Content and campaign development**

  You can create and manage content and campaigns with review and approval workflows so that campaigns aren't executed unless first reviewed and approved by responsible team members. You can also use campaign automation and collaboration to execute multistep and multiwave campaigns.

- **Spend management**

  To plan spend management, you have two applications: Quick Campaign Spend and Detailed Campaign Spend. When a campaign is created, you can assign a program with a proposed spend. You can select all programs that were defined during budget planning to fit the timeline of the campaign. If you can spend more or less than the originally planned spend for the campaign, you can adjust the value in the **Spend Amount** field to distribute the modified amount between the campaigns in relation to the spend that has already been planned (see Figure 5.23).

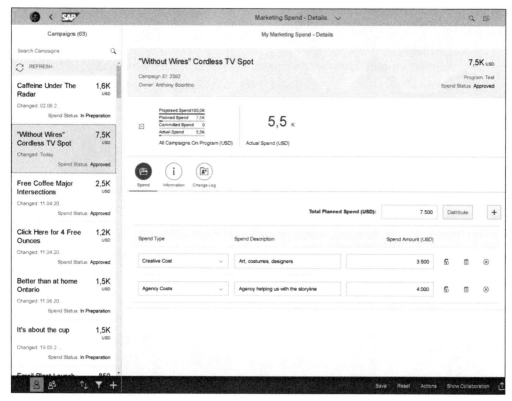

Figure 5.23 Example of Marketing Spend Details for a Campaign

After you've completed your planning, you can approve the spend assigned to a campaign individually or approve several spends collectively. For a detailed campaign spend, you can manage the spends for campaigns based on spend types such as printing costs or digital advertising costs. Figure 5.24 shows an example of a planned spend for a campaign.

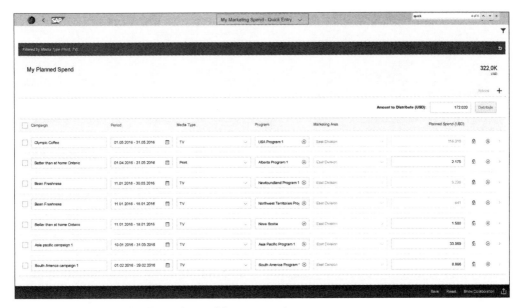

Figure 5.24 Example of a Planned Spend for a Campaign

- **Marketing calendar**
  You can use marketing calendars to get an overview of your campaigns for a specified time range, as shown in Figure 5.25. When you open the calendar, by default, the time range displayed is three months before the current date and three month after it. In the calendar view, the color in which campaigns are displayed indicates the status of the campaign.

  By clicking a campaign, you can see the details about the campaign, as shown in Figure 5.26. You can use the sliders to select different dates and the filter to restrict the campaigns by different criteria, such as category, priority, and media type.

Figure 5.25 Marketing Calendar for a Time Range

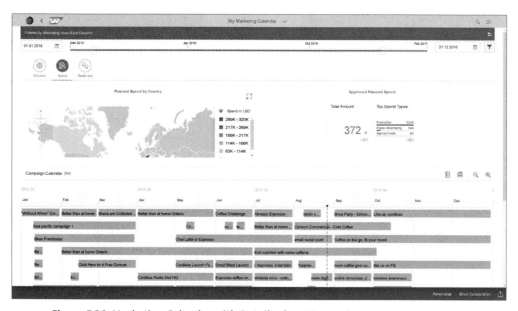

Figure 5.26 Marketing Calendar with Details about Campaigns

- **Marketing analytics and performance management**

  Using standard analytics and dashboards delivered with SAP Hybris Marketing Cloud, as shown in Figure 5.27, you can track budget, spend and actuals, and so on. You can also measure and track campaign performance with marketing executive dashboards. Administrators can build reports using custom analytical queries applications based on the marketing planned budget, committed, and actual spend composite view. Marketing managers can build reports using the query browser based on marketing planned budget, committed, and actual spend consumption view.

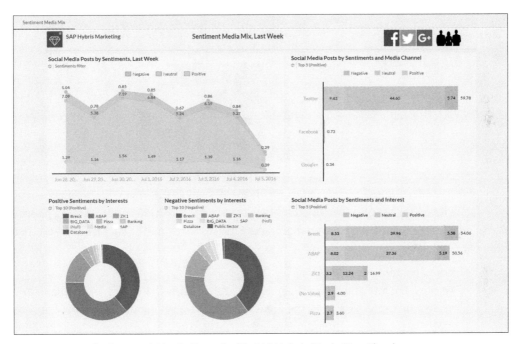

Figure 5.27 Marketing Analytics Delivered with SAP Hybris Marketing Cloud

5.2.5   Marketing Analytics

Making data accessible to marketers reduces or eliminates the burden on IT and builds greater agility in the marketing process. Marketing analytics is included in the **Marketing Executive Dashboard** screen to give an overview of marketing KPIs and benchmarks, as shown in Figure 5.28.

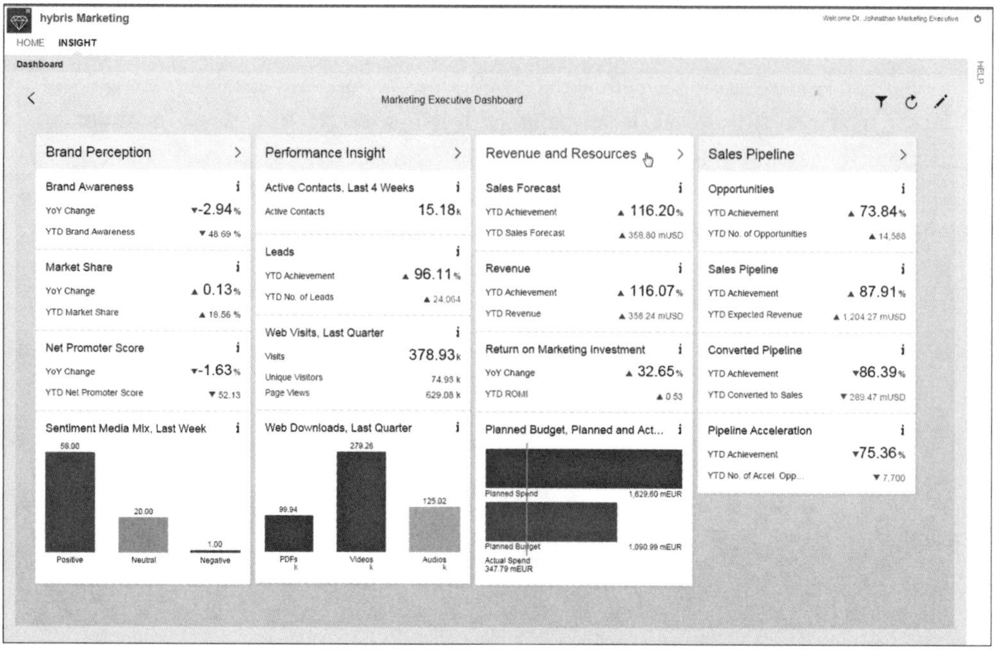

Figure 5.28 Marketing Executive Dashboard with Marketing KPIs

The following list provides a comprehensive overview of KPIs and marketing performance benchmarks to allow marketing executives to review the success of marketing investments:

- **Brand perception**
  To measure and track brand perception, KPIs and benchmarks are available for marketing professionals in the areas of brand awareness, market share, net promoter score, and sentiment media mix:
  - For brand awareness and market share, KPIs measure and display average brand awareness and market share year over year by comparing the current year values over last year. It's calculated as the average percentage and shows the trend for the year on year change. These KPIs also offer drilldowns for market share by country, market share by market, and market share by competitor.
  - The net promoter score is an index that measures the willingness of customers to recommend a company's product or services. The KPIs for net promoter score displays a year over year change to the average net promoter score by comparing current values with the previous year's values. It also provides a drilldown for net promoter score by country and market.

– The KPIs for sentiment media mix, as shown in Figure 5.29, monitor social media to determine the number of sentiments by channel and on the Internet in the past seven days and provides drilldowns for social media posts by interest, social media channels, and social media posts for last week. The KPIs enable marketing executives to review key performance figures to make decisions and come up with an appropriate plan of action.

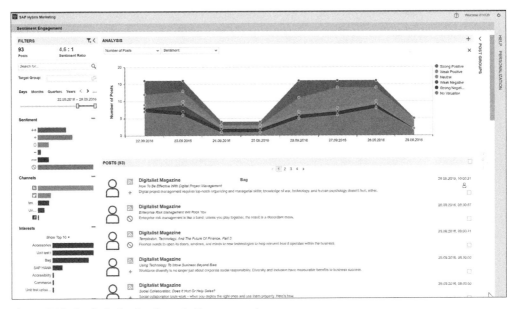

Figure 5.29 Analysis for Sentiments Engagement

- **Revenue and resources**
  To help marketers measure the effectiveness of marketing plans with reference to return on investments (ROIs), standard KPIs and metrics are available for sales forecast, revenue, return on marketing investment (ROMI), and, most importantly, planned budget, planned spend, and actual spend.

  – The KPI for sales forecast displays the sales forecast (achievement) in relation to the expected sales forecast (target) in a percentage for the current year as well as for last year. It helps you analyze the success of marketing investments to predict the sales forecast that can be gained from those investments. The KPIs help you analyze key figures such as YTD target achievement, YTD target, YTD sales forecast, and so on. You can further drill down these KPIs for sales forecasts by brand, country, market, and audience. Similar to sales forecasts, revenue KPIs display the generated revenue (achievement) in relation to planned (target) revenue in a percentage for the current year as well as the previous year.

- The ROMI can be measured with KPIs that display year on year change of average ROMI. You can also drill down on these KPIs to display ROMI by brand, country, market, and audience.

- Planned budget, planned spend, and actual spend KPIs enable you to compare the planned budget against the planned and actual spend for the marketing campaigns for the current year as shown in Figure 5.30. These KPIs provide insights to help analyze marketing success using planned budget, planned spend, and actual spend for the past year. Similar to previous KPIs, you can drill down for planned budget, planned spend, and actual spend by market, country, brand, and spend type.

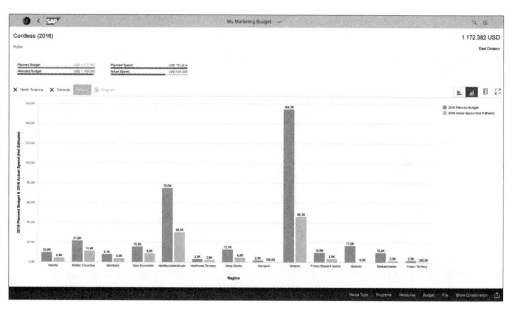

Figure 5.30 Planned versus Actual Marketing Budget

Figure 5.31 and Figure 5.32 show example of analytics to track and measure the effectiveness of various campaigns. In Figure 5.31, you can see the analytics for emails such as **Bounce Rate, Rate of Unopened Messages, Rate of Opened Messages, Click-To-Open Rate**, and so on.

Figure 5.32 shows analytics for campaigns to measure **Calls answered by wrong person, Invalid number, Right Person Reached Campaign Goal Achieved**, and so on.

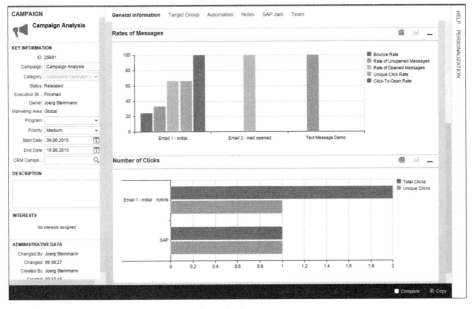

Figure 5.31 Tracking Campaigns: Email Analytics

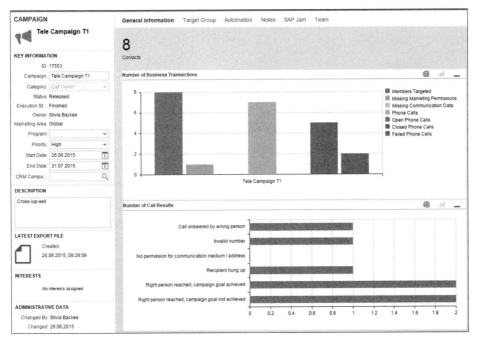

Figure 5.32 Tracking Campaigns: Call Results

- **Performance insight**

  These KPIs provide insights into the performance of leads, active contacts, web visits, and web downloads. You can measure and track how you're performing in these areas and what actions are needed to boost results for lead generation or web visits.

  - The KPIs for leads help you analyze the success of marketing investments in increasing leads as it displays the number of leads generated in relation to the number of leads planned in percentage terms for the current year as well as for the past year, as shown in Figure 5.33. It also shows the trend in increase or decrease in the number of leads in the current year as compared to last year.

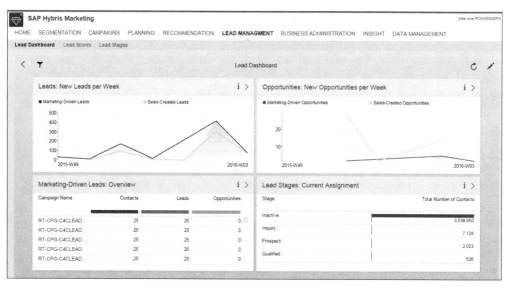

Figure 5.33 Marketing Lead Dashboard

  - Active contact KPIs enable you to review performance figures for a number of interaction contacts and their conversion into marketing prospects and business partners. It monitors contact data to determine the number of active interaction contacts, that is, interaction contacts for which an interaction has occurred (e.g., a phone call or an incoming email) in the last week, by country, channel and interests. Figure 5.34 shows an example of analytics to measure the effectiveness of predictive models you can use to make recommendations to customers regarding online offers and products.

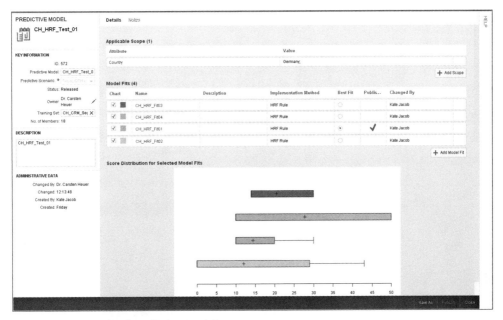

Figure 5.34 Example of Predictive Models

- – The KPIs for web visits display the number of web page visits, unique visitors, page views of a page for this week or this month, and so on, as shown in Figure 5.35. These KPIs allow you to analyze the success of marketing investments to boost traffic to your web pages. You can drill down on these KPIs to see web visits by brand, country, and market. Similar to web visits, web downloads KPIs display the number of PDFs, audio, and audio video web downloads for the past month or past quarter.

- ■ **Sales pipeline**
  These KPIs measure the effectiveness of the sales pipeline, converted pipeline, opportunities, and pipeline acceleration. The key figures supported by these KPIs are YTD achievement and YTD targets, YTD converted to sales, YTD expected revenue, YTD target achievement, YTD number of opportunities, YTD number of opportunities accelerated, and so on. You can drill down these KPIs by brand, country, market, and audience. You can leverage these KPIs to improve the conversion rate and number of opportunities, sales pipeline converted to sales volume in relation to target converted pipeline in percentage, and increased number of accelerated opportunities that are touched by marketing campaigns through the various phases of the sales pipeline. Figure 5.36 shows an example of analytics for conversion rates.

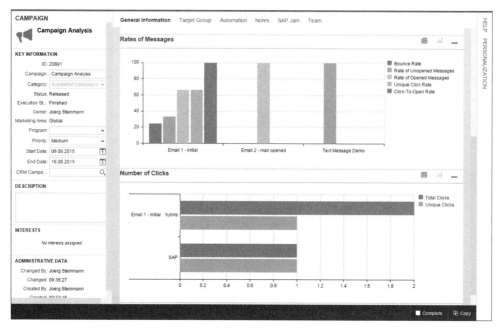

Figure 5.35 Example of Analytics for Web Visits

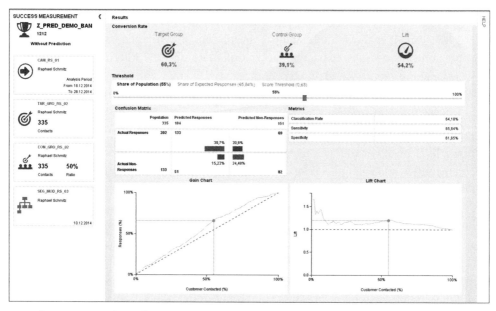

Figure 5.36 Analytics for Conversion Rates

5.2.6   Marketing Lead Management

Lead management integrates business processes between marketing and direct or indirect sales channels to drive higher value opportunities through improved demand creation, execution, and opportunity management. It includes all the measures you can take to convert potential buyers and interested persons into real buyers. Using marketing lead management, you can generate qualified leads, nurture leads to maturity, and seamlessly hand off qualified leads to sales. While handing off leads, marketers can provide sales with insights and intelligence for effective conversion of leads to revenue.

SAP Hybris Marketing Cloud's lead management key capabilities are as follows:

- **Define lead stages**

  The lead management process starts with the determination of those contacts who have demonstrated intent and interest to buy in the next period of time. By defining lead stages and assigning segmentation building blocks, contacts are classified regarding their lead readiness. To track lead readiness for transfer to the sales team, you can define various lead stages such as interested, qualified, product enquiry and so on to structure the marketing base, as shown in Figure 5.37.

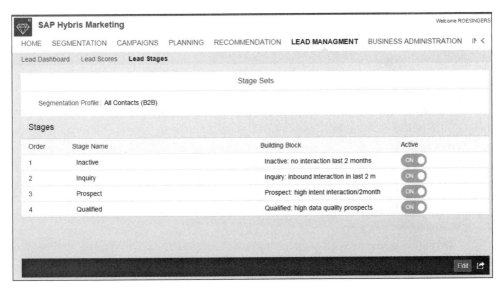

Figure 5.37 Example of Lead Stages

With lead stages, you can classify contacts concerning their lead readiness and build a structure for all available contacts. Figure 5.38 shows an example of a contact profile's **Current Lead Stage** page.

Figure 5.38 Example of Contact profile Showing the Current Lead Stages

The structured contact database provides you with the current stage in the overall lead management process and an overview of how close a contact is from being qualified and finally handed over to sales. The lead stages also provide an insight into the development of the qualification and nurturing process of the underlying contacts over time.

- **Automated transfer of qualified leads**
  You can configure automated transfer of qualified contacts as leads to the sales team.

- **Nurture contacts**
  To qualify leads, you can nurture contacts using multiwave marketing campaigns through progressive qualification steps.

- **Trigger sales activities**
  Using marketing campaign automation, you can trigger various sales activities for leads.

- **Lead scoring**
  You can score leads to measure their maturity and quality as shown in Figure 5.39.

These scores can be used in customer segmentation as segmentation attributes to create building blocks for lead stage calculation, as shown in Figure 5.40.

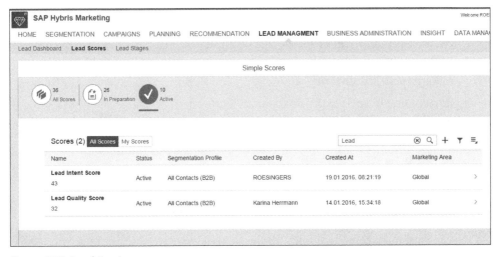

Figure 5.39 Lead Scoring

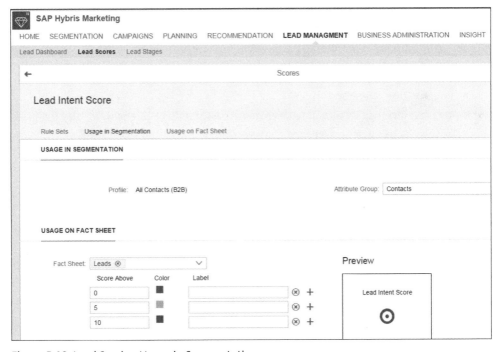

Figure 5.40 Lead Scoring Usage in Segmentation

- **Synchronize leads, opportunities, and activities**
  You can synchronize leads with opportunities and activities from sales.

- **Lead dashboard**
  Standard analytics and the lead dashboard delivered with SAP Hybris Marketing measure the effectiveness of the marketing lead management process. A comprehensive overview of KPIs and benchmarks can help you keep an eye on how lead management is doing.

- **Current and historic lead information**
  This information complements your 360-degree view of contacts.

SAP Hybris Marketing Cloud also contains standard integration with SAP Hybris Sales Cloud for a comprehensive lead management process.

5.2.7 Loyalty Management

The loyalty management application allows businesses to create their own cloud-based loyalty programs. Using loyalty management, you can turn customers into loyal advocates by rewarding them for making a purchase and/or writing positive reviews. You can offer points for sign-ups, purchases, referrals, ratings, and reviews. You can deliver a complete loyalty experience by integrating loyalty programs with core commerce and marketing operations across all channels.

The key capabilities of the loyalty management application are as follows:

- **Loyalty data**
  You can leverage loyalty data to enrich a customer's profile with loyalty insights. Loyalty activity scores ensure that you have additional details about the consumer's buying behavior, as shown in Figure 5.41. You can leverage these insights to better engage with these customers.

- **Loyalty programs**
  Using loyalty management, you can quickly set up loyalty programs, tiers, and rules, as shown in Figure 5.42, and set the limit for the maximum points to be accrued by a member per transaction or activity. For end consumers, points are shown as money equivalents so they can see the exact loyalty discounts they will get when redeeming the loyalty points.

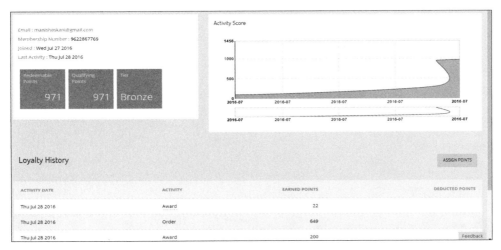

Figure 5.41 Loyalty Insights in the Customer Profile

Figure 5.42 Setting Up Loyalty Programs

- **Targeted offers**

  With integration between loyalty management and SAP Hybris Marketing Cloud, you can send targeted offers from loyalty to marketing and leverage the rich capabilities of segmentation and offers. Offers created in the loyalty application are sent to SAP Hybris Marketing Cloud for enhanced targeting capabilities, as shown in Figure 5.43.

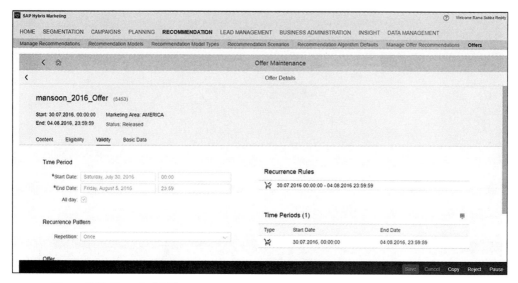

Figure 5.43 Targeted Offers

- **Embedded analytics**

  You can gain insights into loyalty performance using embedded analytics delivered with loyalty management, as shown in Figure 5.44. You can view KPIs for loyalty programs such as total points collectively redeemed by all the members under various loyalty programs, aggregated revenue generated by a loyalty program, total points collectively accrued by members of a loyalty program, total number of activities (order, redeem, etc.) carried out by loyalty members, and total members enrolled under a loyalty program.

- **Location-based marketing**

  You can leverage geofences to send an offer/notification to end users when they enter or exit geofences, or both. You can target customers better by leveraging location contexts through iBeacons and geofence configuration, as shown in Figure 5.45.

Figure 5.44 Loyalty Performance Insights

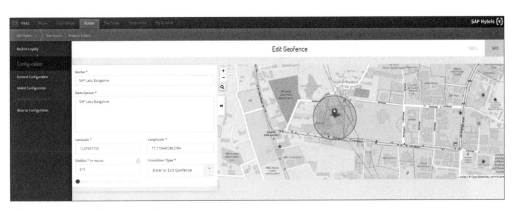

Figure 5.45 Location-Based Marketing

- **Integration**

  With integrated loyalty management, you can deliver a complete loyalty experience by integrating loyalty programs with your core commerce and marketing operations across all the channels.

- **Mobile wallets**

  You can build customized digital loyalty cards and coupons that automatically work across mobile wallets from Apple and Google through the **Wallet Configuration** screen, as shown in Figure 5.46.

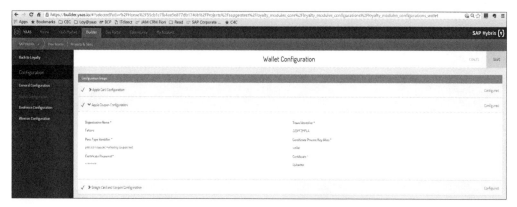

Figure 5.46 Configuring Mobile Wallets

5.3   Integrating with Other SAP Hybris Front-Office Solutions

In line with other SAP Hybris solutions, SAP Hybris Marketing Cloud integrates with key SAP Hybris front-office solutions for sales, service, and commerce. Because SAP Hybris Sales Cloud and SAP Hybris Service Cloud are part of SAP Hybris Cloud for Customer, in this section, we'll review SAP Hybris Marketing Cloud integration with SAP Hybris Cloud for Customer and SAP Hybris Commerce Cloud.

5.3.1   Integration with SAP Hybris Cloud for Customer

You can integrate SAP Hybris Marketing Cloud with SAP Hybris Cloud for Customer to bridge the gap between marketing and sales and build harmonized processes across marketing and sales channels. By sharing the same business partners and business document data, marketing is able to support sales in the process of converting potential buyers and interested persons into real buyers. The integration between SAP Hybris Marketing Cloud and SAP Hybris Cloud for Customer supports marketing lead management, call qualification, and activities for sales, as shown in Figure 5.47.

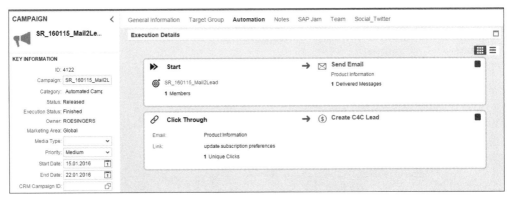

Figure 5.47 Campaign Integration with SAP Hybris Cloud for Customer

From SAP Hybris Cloud for Customer, the system replicates the following data to SAP Hybris Marketing Cloud:

- Business partners
  - Contacts
  - Accounts
  - Individual customers
- Business documents
  - Leads, including product items
  - Opportunities, including product items
  - Phone call, appointment, and visit activities

Similarly, the creation of the following data and documents is triggered in SAP Hybris Cloud for Customer from SAP Hybris Marketing Cloud:

- Business documents
  - Leads
  - Phone call, appointment, and task activities

You can set up the integration of accounts, contacts, and individual customers to SAP Hybris Marketing Cloud with SAP Hybris Cloud for Customer via SAP Cloud Platform Integration, as shown in Figure 5.48.

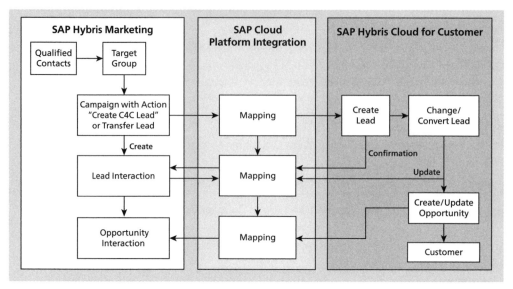

Figure 5.48 Integration between SAP Hybris Marketing and SAP Hybris Cloud for Customer through SAP Cloud Platform Integration

5.3.2   Integration with SAP Hybris Commerce Cloud

Integration between SAP Hybris Marketing Cloud and SAP Hybris Commerce Cloud allows you to use marketing campaigns and product recommendations from SAP Hybris Marketing Cloud to SAP Hybris Commerce Cloud storefronts. You can offer your customers personalized interactions and shopping experiences in online stores. The integration between these two solutions occurs in the following areas:

- **Customer and consumer profile**

  These profiles capture all customer interactions and behaviors to create and enrich continually evolving contextual profiles. Integration with SAP Hybris Commerce allows you to capture events in profiles such as user registration and logon events, order events (creation, shipment, return, etc.), and click events. It offers actionable insights for real-time, 1:1 engagements with every customer across the channels, as shown in Figure 5.49.

- **Segmentation**

  In Chapter 4, you learned that the SAP Hybris Commerce web content management system (WCMS) is used for data presentation and management for storefronts. By using SAP Hybris Marketing Cloud segmentation, you can create campaigns that are used to create customer segment rules in WCMS so that contents can be personalized for specific customer segments.

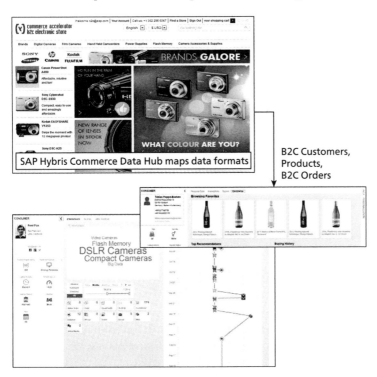

Figure 5.49 Capturing Clickstreams

- **Recommendations**
  You can use SAP Hybris recommendation models from SAP Hybris Marketing in WCMS to create components and boost personalization capabilities in the online stores. Customers receive context-relevant offer recommendations in real time. In addition, data feeds from SAP Hybris Commerce to SAP Hybris Marketing provide data that can be used to create more relevant campaigns and recommendations.

- **Loyalty management**
  Using SAP Hybris Loyalty, you can create loyalty programs for SAP Hybris Commerce storefronts. The integrated loyalty programs can create personalized customer experiences and convert customers to lifetime brand advocates.

- **Back-office admin cockpit**
  Using the admin cockpit in SAP Hybris Commerce, you can configure and enhance integration between SAP Hybris Commerce and SAP Hybris Marketing components.

- **Data replications**
  Standard out-of-the-box data feeds can be leveraged to replicate customers, products, and transactions (activities and orders) directly from SAP Hybris Commerce to SAP Hybris Marketing. The data from the SAP Hybris Commerce database is sent to the SAP Hybris Commerce, data hub and then to SAP Hybris Marketing, where the data can be used to offer more relevant product recommendations in online stores.

5.4   Integrating with SAP S/4HANA and SAP ERP

To leverage the full capabilities of SAP Hybris Marketing, you must bring in data in SAP Hybris Marketing from all possible external sources. Data serve as the fuel for marketing profiles, segmentation, and campaigns. The SAP backend holds the most critical details about your customers and associated transactions. These details are prerequisite in SAP Hybris Marketing to uncover a 360-degree view of customers. To achieve this, you can integrate SAP Hybris Marketing with SAP ERP and exchange master data, sales data, and financial data. These integrations are possible through various options such as OData Services, SAP Cloud Platform Integration/SAP Process Integration (SAP PI), or RESTful Services. The key integration scenarios between SAP Hybris Marketing Cloud and SAP backend systems are as follows:

- Master data and sales transaction data flow from the SAP backend to SAP Hybris Marketing for customers, contacts, sales orders, quotations, contracts, and so on. These details can be used to enrich SAP Hybris customer profiles.

- Financial data flow from the SAP backend system to SAP Hybris Marketing Cloud such as project work breakdown structure (WBS) elements and spends for campaigns, costing data and Profitability Analysis (CO-PA) data for margin decomposition, and relationship and sales analysis.

- Budget planning and campaign data flow from SAP Hybris Marketing Cloud to the SAP backend system to create WBS elements in the SAP backend upon release of campaigns in SAP Hybris Marketing Cloud when spends have been defined. The

WBS elements are updated with budget and planned data, which can be compared with actual expenses when they are settled in the SAP backend. It helps in budget and spend planning and at the same time keeping the chief marketing officer (CMO) dashboards updated with planned verses actual details.

5.5 Integrating with SAP Customer Relationship Management

Integration between SAP Hybris Marketing Cloud and SAP CRM enables you to leverage next-generation marketing segmentation and campaign management functionalities in SAP Hybris Marketing and drive actions in SAP CRM Interaction Center. Marketing professionals can segment SAP CRM data in SAP Hybris Marketing and replicate target groups to SAP CRM. The target groups and segmentation models can be adjusted in real time based on changes to customer data in SAP CRM. The key processes achieved through this integration are as follows:

- Customers, consumers, contacts, sales transactions (e.g., quotations, orders, and opportunities), and interaction center generated business transactions (e.g., activities and interactions) from SAP CRM are sent to SAP Hybris Marketing.

- Target groups created in SAP Hybris Marketing Cloud segmentation can be automatically uploaded to SAP CRM as soon as the target group status in SAP Hybris Marketing is set to **Released**. If business partner information is updated in SAP CRM, dynamic target groups in SAP Hybris Marketing are automatically updated. Using this integration, you can assign target groups from SAP Hybris Marketing in campaigns created in SAP CRM. You can also display the target groups created in SAP Hybris Marketing Cloud as embedded objects in SAP CRM.

- You can execute an action in SAP CRM to create call lists, tasks, activities, and leads from marketing campaigns executed in SAP Hybris Marketing Cloud. You can create a campaign in SAP Hybris Marketing and then assign an action to create a call list, tasks, activities, or leads in SAP CRM. When you release the campaign in SAP Hybris Marketing, the assigned action is activated, and the call list, tasks, activities, and leads are created in the SAP CRM Interaction Center.

- Sales activities, opportunities, and leads can be created in SAP CRM from campaigns in SAP Hybris Marketing through SAP CRM middleware.

5.6   Summary

In this chapter, you've learned that SAP has both on premise (called SAP Hybris Marketing) as well as cloud (called SAP Hybris Marketing Cloud) offerings for the next-generation contextual marketing solution for businesses of any size. These offerings have more or less similar capabilities to cover the entire spectrum of marketing functions such as marketing profiles, segmentation, campaigns, marketing leads, marketing resource management, and marketing analytics and dashboards. The SAP Hybris Loyalty management solution is available in the cloud through the SAP Hybris as a Service marketplace. The SAP Hybris Marketing solution can be integrated with other SAP Hybris front-office solutions such as SAP Hybris Sales Cloud and SAP Hybris Commerce, as well as SAP back-office solutions such as SAP S/4HANA, SAP ERP, and SAP CRM, to achieve end-to-end processes. In the next chapter, we'll cover the last components of the SAP Hybris front-office solutions: SAP Hybris Billing and SAP Hybris Revenue Cloud.

Chapter 6

Revenue

*SAP Hybris Billing, formerly known as SAP Billing and Revenue Innova-
tion Management (SAP BRIM), and SAP Hybris Revenue Cloud are
highly flexible and scalable solutions for automated billing, invoicing,
and revenue management.*

The new and emerging business models in the digital era require new ways of billing
for products and subscription-based services. More and more businesses are transi-
tioning from selling products to selling value-based services and are focused on the
outcome or "experience" the customer has and how they evaluate that as part of the
overall service. The customer relationships are no longer one-directional and a one-
time affair. Now customers are becoming partners in business networks; participating
in marketing, sales, and delivery; and co-defining future innovations. Businesses have
realized that focusing on price, cost, and payment terms only leads to commoditization. Instead, businesses are beginning to focus on overall outcomes in their business
network ecosystem and measuring value creation using real-time data before trans-
lating that into revenue for each partner.

The ability to sense and analyze business outcomes in granular detail across the business network in real time enables you to uncover opportunities for improvement.
The business operating models can be changed or reconfigured quickly and at a lower
cost to take advantage of new opportunities. As the cost to try new business models
goes down, the ability to tolerate failure goes up; therefore, businesses can become
more nimble and agile. Business process transformation is a new way of protecting
current market share and growing new businesses.

In this chapter, we'll discuss SAP's strategy for revenue and billing with SAP Hybris
and how it can be leveraged to support new business models. The key capabilities of
SAP Hybris Billing, such as business model design, subscription order management,
usage metering and transaction pricing, billing receivables and collections, and partner revenue share, will be explained in this chapter along with their business benefits.

You'll also learn about SAP Hybris Revenue Cloud, the newest SAP Hybris cloud offering for configure, price, and quote (CPQ); order orchestration; and subscription billing. In line with other SAP Hybris solutions covered in previous chapters, we'll cover the integration of the SAP Hybris Billing component and SAP Hybris Revenue Cloud with other SAP Hybris front-office solutions such as SAP Hybris Commerce, as well as SAP backend solutions such as SAP S/4HANA, SAP ERP, and SAP Customer Relationship Management (SAP CRM).

6.1   Strategy for Revenue and Billing with SAP Hybris

In response to product commoditization, increased competition, shrinking margins, regulatory pressures, and more demanding customers, you must redesign your business model and launch innovative new services to remain sustainable in the new economy. These trends are apparent in many industries, including telecommunications, media, high tech, transportation and logistics, utilities, and financial services. The global explosion of Internet and mobile networks, the widespread adoption of smart devices, and the emergence of the Internet of Things (IoT) have unleashed a new era of creative services.

However, to launch new services, you must address large numbers of direct customers with huge transactional usage volumes in an increasingly competitive high-cost, low-margin environment. To maintain differentiation and increase the average revenue per customer, you must seek ways to identify your most profitable customers and offer them the services they demand at a compelling price to keep them engaged.

Before we review SAP's strategy for revenue and billing with SAP Hybris, let's review some of the monetization challenges faced by businesses today:

- **Monetizing new business models:**
  - **Moving from products to services and outcomes**
    Businesses are moving away from commoditized product sales to services and subscription- and usage-based business models. Subscription- and usage-based billing are new business models that need new ways to charge customers for the usage of these services.
  - **IoT and connected devices**
    More and more devices are getting connected to intelligent networks, requiring you to gather usage data from these devices in real time. The billing and

pricing needs to take into account the real-time usage data from these connected devices.

- **Digital commerce**
A flexible billing solution with high-volume global payment flexibility is required to handle digital commerce across various channels.

- **Platform business model**
A multisided monetization and revenue sharing model is needed to support Software-as-a-Service (SaaS) and subscription- and usage-based business models.

- **Renovating monetization business processes:**

  - **Agility**
  Businesses need the ability to make fast and flexible offerings to their customers to take advantage of new opportunities. It requires unprecedented financial flexibility and agility to manage such changes.

  - **Revenue management innovation**
  High-volume, automated, and watertight revenue management solutions are needed to seamlessly handle invoicing, collections, dunning, and write-offs.

SAP helps customers meet these challenges head on with SAP Hybris Billing and SAP Hybris Revenue Cloud in the following areas:

- **Agility**
It's essential for companies to embrace change with the ability to simulate new business processes. With SAP Hybris Billing, companies can design new business models and then simulate and validate new pricing and revenue models before committing time and resources to the new products or services.

- **Multisided monetization**
We're in a shared economy, and new business models require multisided monetization. With multisided monetization, companies can expand their business network and develop a platform business model around integrating value chain partners both on the supply side (apps, content, services) and the sell side (channel partners, resellers, distributors) with revenue-sharing models, hence creating additional end-customer value and delivery capabilities. SAP Hybris Billing and SAP Hybris Revenue Cloud allow businesses to create revenue-sharing models for various customers in a single transaction.

- **Massive scalability**
Growing from a small operation to a multibillion-dollar business requires a platform

that provides reliable automation for the complete order-to-cash process for digital customers, subscriptions and usage services, and partner revenue sharing. It needs to operate across geographies and industries to allow rapid market expansion and, most importantly, needs to keep operational costs low, even as the business scales. SAP Hybris Billing and SAP Hybris Revenue Cloud can scale to handle hundreds of thousands of events per second. SAP Hybris Billing is an on-premise solution for high-volume usage and subscription-based billing, whereas SAP Hybris Revenue Cloud is a completely cloud-based solution built on SAP Hybris as a Service on SAP Cloud Platform for CPQ, order orchestration, and subscription billing.

In this chapter, we'll cover both solutions just described, so let's begin by reviewing the key capabilities of SAP Hybris Billing.

6.2   SAP Hybris Billing

SAP Hybris Billing is the next-generation real-time billing solution for subscription- and usage-based services. SAP Hybris Billing will help you launch revenue sharing and customer-centric subscription offers, and ramp up efficiency with a billing and revenue management solution that integrates the entire order-to-cash process. It provides complete coverage of the order-to-cash process for subscriptions and usage-based service monetization that can be integrated with the rest of the SAP Hybris front-office processes. Even though the solution is modular, it allows customers to just deploy smaller pieces of the solution, such as adding flexible metering and pricing to an existing legacy billing system or adding the revenue management functionality from SAP Hybris Billing to complement the backend revenue management capabilities. With SAP Hybris Billing, you can build both simple and sophisticated business models quickly to meet customers' changing needs.

SAP Hybris Billing has been designed for scalability, openness, and modularity with open interfaces. It's proven to scale from small trials to handling multibillion-dollar billing requirements. Modularity and openness offer you flexibility and choice to leverage investments in existing infrastructures. It has been packaged by SAP in a rapid-deployment solution (RDS) with industry best practices for quick deployment and rapid time to value.

Although customers deploy the end-to-end solution offered by SAP Hybris Billing, SAP offers the flexibility to deploy portions of SAP Hybris Billing to address particular pain points and provide a short time-to-value with a nondisruptive approach while leveraging investments in existing systems. Figure 6.1 shows two examples of common modular deployment options for SAP Hybris Billing, with a smaller scope than the full end-to-end solution. Similarly, you can craft other deployment options per your unique business requirements.

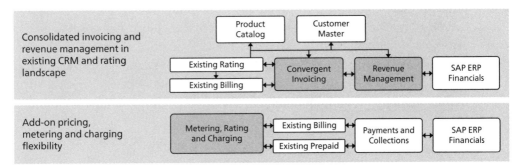

Figure 6.1 Example of Modular Deployment Options for SAP Hybris Billing

The key components of SAP Hybris Billing are as follows:

- Business model design
- Subscription order management
- Usage metering and transaction pricing
- Billing receivables and collections
- Partner revenue share

Let's review the key capabilities and business benefits of these solution components available in SAP Hybris Billing.

6.2.1 Business Model Design

Most service providers set pricing using a combination of instinct and trial and error. However, this unscientific method is ineffective for creating the structured and targeted pricing necessary to compete in the digital economy. For high-volume service providers, adapting quickly to changing business conditions is essential to stay ahead of competition.

One of the key components of SAP Hybris Billing is business model design, which allows you to accelerate time to market. Both marketing and sales professionals can leverage this capability in SAP Hybris Billing to craft new pricing models that reward loyalty, offer partners flexible terms, and ensures accurate settlements. The operations team can consolidate pricing for multiple services and multiple lines of business on a single, high-performance platform that dynamically scales to extreme transaction volumes with high availability.

It further allows business users to design subscription pricing, usage pricing, and bundling through configuration without any need for coding. They can allocate fees and credits to multiple financial accounts: prepaid, postpaid, or hybrid. In addition, they can innovate customer offers with credit, quota, and entitlement pooling across multiple enterprise employees, seats, or devices and interlink partner revenue share terms.

6.2.2   Subscription Order Management

Subscription order management is a core component of SAP Hybris Billing, and it uses SAP CRM as a foundation to drive rich capabilities. This component enables customers to benefit from the product catalog that combines different views of products coming from different systems such as rating, billing, provisioning, and especially other SAP Hybris Billing components that are integrated end to end. It offers built-in subscription management capabilities—such as order capture, order distribution, and change order processes—across the entire order-to-cash processes. Subscription order management supports advanced business-to-business (B2B) capabilities such as B2B master agreements and hierarchies with large enterprise customers, including specific terms for pricing, shared allowance, or credit pooling; order flexibility and restrictions for specific customers; volume discounts; and invoices.

SAP Hybris Billing service order management can be leveraged with call center application in high-volume environments to give service agents a 360-degree view of customer interactions across the entire order-to-cash process, allowing them to provide prompt and expert service to resolve customer queries on the very first call. Back-office managers can manage orders, monitor and control their distribution and fulfillment across the entire order-to-cash process, and have more visibility and control over the subscription management process.

The key capabilities of SAP Hybris Billing subscription order management will be discussed in the following sections.

Product Catalog and Offer Management

Using this functionality, you can create targeted subscription offers quickly and make them instantly available to customers for quoting and ordering across all channels, as shown in Figure 6.2.

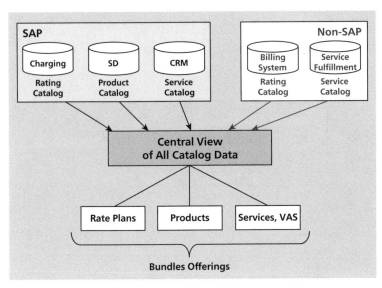

Figure 6.2 Subscription Bundled Offers from Multiple Catalogs

The product catalog can list any types of services (such as rate plans and combined rates) and devices (hardware) with out-of-the-box integration with the SAP Hybris Billing charging capabilities and SAP Hybris Billing invoicing catalogs. The product catalog combines the different views of a product (commercial, rating, and provisioning) using SAP's cross-catalog mapping. The catalog definitions are done in respective systems. The commercial catalog is integrated with other catalogs via mapping instead of data replication to improve efficiency and reduce complexity. Figure 6.3 shows the cross reference of catalog mapping from various catalogs.

The product catalog is split between the charging and subscription order management functionalities of SAP Hybris Billing. The charging function includes the algorithmic definition, such as how the price is calculated based on usage or on a periodic basis, and so on. Subscription order management uses this definition and adds characteristics to the product/service, as shown in Figure 6.4, as well as links with other SAP components if needed.

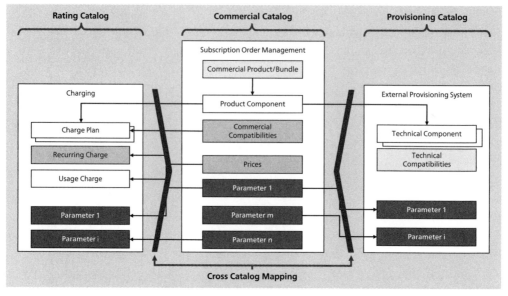

Figure 6.3 Cross-Catalog Mapping for a Centralized View of Catalogs

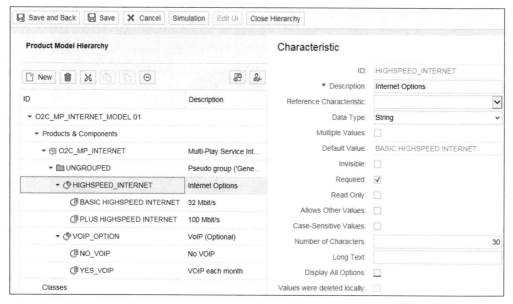

Figure 6.4 Example of Product Model Hierarchy and Adding Characteristics

You can design pricing algorithms for usage and recurring or one-time events using the event-driven pricing engine, graphical configuration of pricing trees by pricing icons, ready-made structures such as tables (regular or range), multipurpose counters, and so on.

Using subscription order management, you can create subscription offerings with bundles to define packages for any type of services and devices, manage tariffs (wireless, wired line, data, and TV) and combined services, define groups and options, create combination rules for product and services bundles, cross-sell and up-sell products and options, and so on.

Order Capture

With subscription order management, you can capture orders and engage and acquire customers across all channels. It provides an order capture solution for customer-specific pricing requirements and supports sales order processing and contract changes also known as move, add, change, and delete services (MACDs), as shown in Figure 6.5.

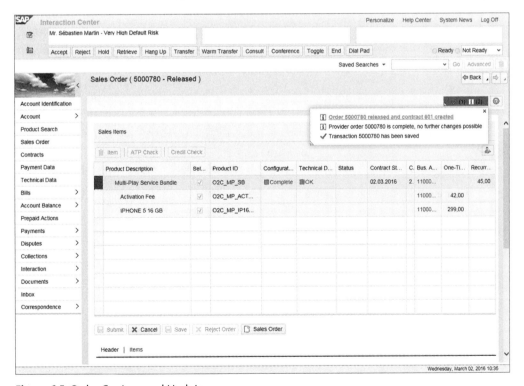

Figure 6.5 Order Capture and Update

You can sell rate plans, combine rate plans, and package and incentivize products with ad hoc pricing for recurrent and one-time fees. During order capture, marketing functions such as up-sell, down-sell, and cross-sell are supported as well. Information from external sources such as provisioning or billing systems can be monitored, and all the ordering processes are integrated with credit management checks from external systems or SAP Financial Supply Chain Management (FSCM) solutions.

With subscription and order management, customer service agents can capture or retrieve customer and account data with payment methods, products can be searched within catalogs, and package components are exploded in fully configurable sales items, as shown in Figure 6.6.

Figure 6.6 Product Packages in a Sales Order

Order capture also supports eligibility, feasibility, and availability checks for products and different payment types for different parts (e.g., one for physical devices and one for services).

Order Distribution

Error-free order distribution to fulfillment systems after order capture is critical to ensure ordered products are accurately delivered and billed. Order distribution controls the execution of actions needed to fulfill the order across billing, charging, and other fulfillment systems. The document distribution is implemented by the Order

Distribution Infrastructure (ODI) framework, which distributes one-off charges to SAP ERP or SAP S/4HANA and distribute provider contract data to SAP ERP or SAP S/4HANA, as shown in Figure 6.7.

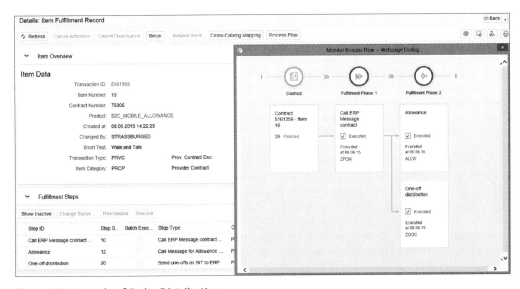

Figure 6.7 Example of Order Distribution

The ODI framework provides functionality to meet order processing and monitoring requirements. It helps you decompose the order, distribute the order to multiple systems, and track the distribution of the order to connected backend systems for provisioning, billing activation, and so on to both SAP and non-SAP systems. It also defines the dependency between distribution steps, monitors contract distribution, and restarts and reschedules distribution in case of errors in a dedicated application (called the distribution monitor) or directly in the contract view of the service agents.

The framework enables the distribution of one-off charges to the SAP Hybris Billing invoicing capabilities (e.g., activation fee), which can then be included together with usage charges on a single invoice or on a separate invoice. Order information can also be sent to SAP Hybris Billing charging and SAP Hybris Billing invoicing for rating/charging and billing/invoices purposes to create or change a provider contract.

Contract Change Processes

The contract change process allows you to make mass changes to existing subscriptions. All contract change processes for existing customers are handled by change orders. When a customer service agent triggers a change process, an order is created based on the contract. Within this order, the changes are applied and later written back to the contract. Change orders can also be scheduled in the future and can include one or a combination of change processes such as product change, contract extension, revocation of cancellation, cancellation of options, revocation of cancellation of options, change of business agreements, change of product configuration, contract cancellation, SIM card change, phone number change, move DSL, move fixed line, and lock and unlock telephone numbers (see Figure 6.8).

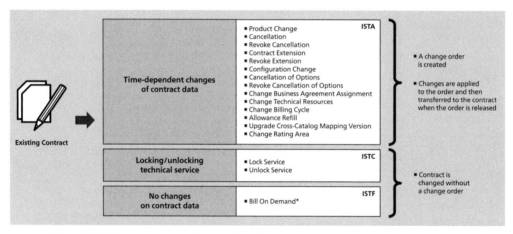

Figure 6.8 Change Contract Process Overview

All contract changes are used to apply the changes to contracts. The contracts always retain their previous ID, and the related change processes are stored in detail as the contract history. The future changes in the contract can be scheduled in the change order for a future date, and when the date is reached, the changes are applied to the contract. Let's review some of the contract change processes as follows:

- **Product change**
  For changing products on a contract, depending on the existing contract, different product recommendations are proposed. After you select and apply the new product (in the master data of the respective product), the change is considered in the contract, as shown in Figure 6.9.

  The product changes can be scheduled for a particular date, and the performed changes can always be seen in the contract history.

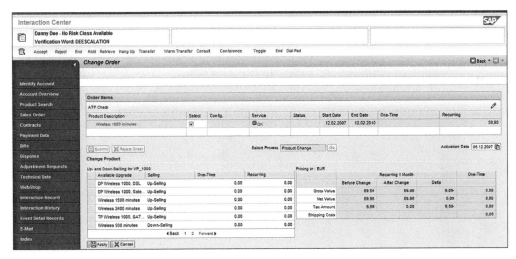

Figure 6.9 Product Change Process in a Contract

- **Contract extension**

  The contract extension process provides different extension periods depending on the product master data, and you can generate process-dependent incentive products such as a new mobile phone or a credit memo. The recurring prices before/after change and the delta amount are calculated to help call center agents share the details with customers, as shown in Figure 6.10.

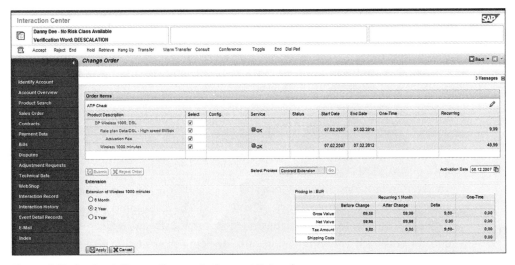

Figure 6.10 Contract Change Process to Support Extension

- **Contract cancellation**
  When a contract cancellation process is initiated by a call center agent, the system automatically calculates the earliest confirmed cancellation date based on the request cancellation date, as shown in Figure 6.11.

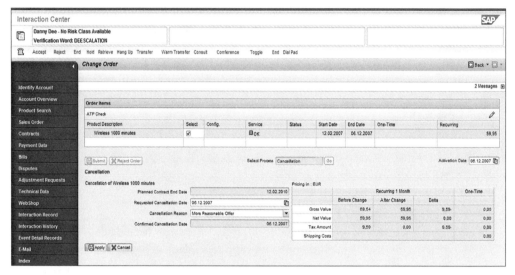

Figure 6.11 Contract Change Process for Cancellation

The cancellation fees can be assessed and applied based on different attributes such as cancellation reasons, dates, and so on. In addition to single contract cancellation, an implicit bundle cancellation functionality is also supported by the contract change process.

- **Change technical resources**
  Figure 6.12 shows how changing a technical resource such as a phone number is supported in the call center application. The system automatically applies a special change fee or activation fee, as the case may be, and triggers distribution of information to the relevant backend system such as billing or rating by ODI.

- **Lock or unlock services**
  The system provides different lock and unlock reasons, such as cell phone lost or subscriber on vacation, as shown in Figure 6.13. These reasons can be set in future dates, and applicable fees are determined automatically and triggered to the backend systems such as billing, rating, and invoicing as needed. It also allows you to set authorization rules for locking/unlocking per business requirements.

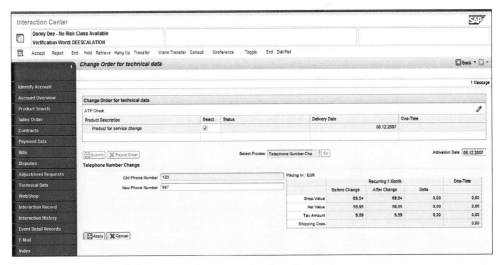

Figure 6.12 Example of Changing a Phone Number in a Contract

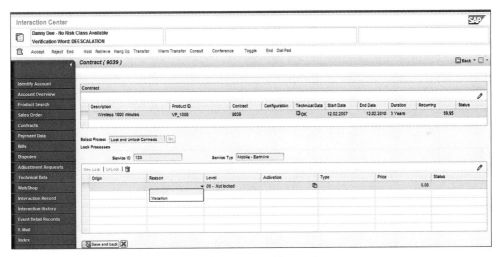

Figure 6.13 Lock and Unlock Service in the Contract Change Process

Business-to-Business Features

With subscription and order management, you can easily manage B2B master agreements and hierarchies with large enterprise customers. You can offer flexible contract terms, flexible order capturing capabilities for master agreements, detailed invoice breakdowns, and credit pooling for large enterprise sales scenarios. B2B features in subscription and order management have the following three capabilities:

- **Manage master agreements and account hierarchies**
  Master agreements, also known as frame agreements, are created to capture special commercial terms for important and large customers. These terms govern
  which items different entities of the enterprise can order, how they are priced, and
  how they are billed and paid. You can set up discounts and tiering levels in the
  pricing agreements that can be driven by a shared allowance of pools of credits/
  entitlements/quotes maintained in real time for large enterprise customers. Figure 6.14 shows an example of a master agreement setup for an account hierarchy.

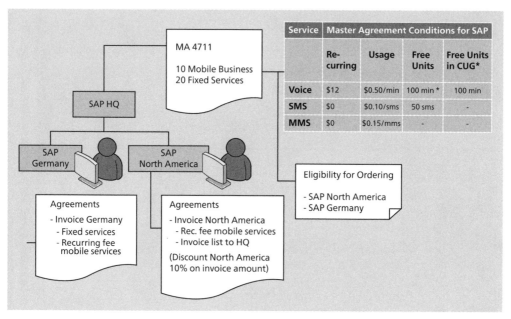

Figure 6.14 Example of Master Agreement and Account Hierarchy

  You can issue consolidated bills to customers for all the services, including billable
  items or complete bills taken in from third-party billing systems and converged
  into a single invoice. Invoice can also be split between different entities who are
  responsible for paying different charges.

- **Flexible partner settlement and revenue sharing**
  The SaaS business model requires managing money flows among developers for
  access to each other's components. You share revenue with developers and also
  charge them for access to SaaS services, passing on the fees for the services of
  other platform providers. Flexible partner settlement and revenue sharing in
  SAP Hybris Billing subscription order management ensures easy developer and

partner on-boarding, allows pricing and revenue sharing flexibility for developers and channels, and enables multilateral netting among developers and platforms, as shown in Figure 6.15.

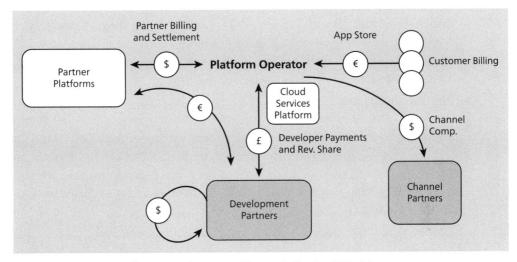

Figure 6.15 Partner Settlement and Revenue Sharing in the SaaS Model

- **Bulk ordering and mass processes**
  Using this functionality, you can plan the mass creation of a preselected number of provider orders and contracts. You can mass create provider orders and also mass change provider contracts if needed. You can also use flexible enhancement options to tailor mass run types per the required processes. Tracking progress and monitoring results enables you to reprocess elements if there are any errors. One of the use cases for bulk ordering and mass processes could be a large customer with a maser agreement in place for phone and mobile services. If the customer hires new employees and orders new mobile service contracts and phones for the new employees, you could use the bulk ordering and mass update capabilities.

Financial Customer Care

Financial customer care provides customer service agents with a 360-degree view of customer interactions across the entire order-to-cash process. Financial customer care is a composite application (based on SAP ERP and SAP CRM) that integrates SAP ERP Financials Contract Accounting (FI-CA) processes into the SAP CRM Interaction Center web client. It supports following processes:

- **Financial customer care**
  Customer service agents can view the financial fact sheet, account balance over-view, dunning history, and payment search.

- **Collection management**
  In collection management, you can trigger outbound calls for customer service agents for the collection process. Customer service agents can also access the col-lection factsheet, payments (credit card, debit memo, credit memo, etc.), install-ment plan, deferral, and promise-to-pay capabilities.

- **Dispute management**
  This SAP CRM-based application is connected with SAP Hybris Billing. SAP Collec-tions and Dispute Management loads and displays invoices from SAP Hybris Bill-ing invoicing or from third-party billing systems in the SAP CRM Interaction Center. Customer service agents can answer customer disputes, create adjustment requests for a complete invoice, and invoice items or a single billable item, as shown in Figure 6.16.

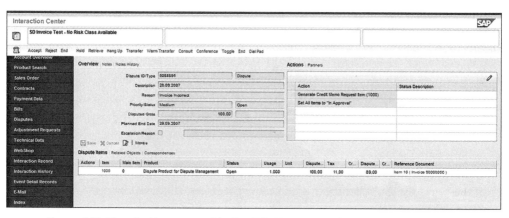

Figure 6.16 Dispute Management in the SAP CRM Interaction Center

6.2.3 Usage Metering and Transaction Pricing

SAP Hybris Billing provides a massively scalable metering, pricing, rating, and charging engine. It's designed to be part of a high-volume, customer-facing quotation process or to manage prepaid or credit limited accounts where service isn't extended to cus-tomers before service is priced and available allowances or balances are reserved. To accomplish this, the solution operates with low latency (typically on the order of 10–50 milliseconds of response time) and with high volume and high availability (no more than 5 minutes of planned downtime per year). The solution supports dynamic scaling for nonstop operation; that is, hardware nodes can be added and removed while service continuity is maintained because the solution doesn't have to be brought down or restarted.

The solution supports prepaid, postpaid, and hybrid models to monitor customer accounts in real time and improve customer sentiment by giving subscribers control over their spending and visibility into their available allowances, quotas, or entitlements.

Pricing for complex B2C scenarios such as family plans and B2B scenarios such as credit pooling and sophisticated tiered models are supported out of the box. With concurrent access to allowances, they can be monitored in real time. For example, tens of thousands of employees of a customer organization can all concurrently share a single pooled allowance with the assurance that all transactions will be correctly accounted for. Sophisticated session-based balance and allowance reservation mechanisms are provided to deal with concurrent access scenarios while ensuring watertight accounting.

You can manage configuration chronologies to handle the late arrival of usage data. Chronologies are provided for pricing and charging configuration objects so that, for example, multiple versions of a price plan are live in the solution at any given time, and the correct one will be applied depending on the customer contract and the date on usage data to handle late charging. This allows you to facilitate the rollout of new pricing changes because new pricing can have an effective date in the future.

SAP Hybris Billing includes a solution for mediation (based on a third-party partner product from DigitalRoute), which enables a standardized approach to data mediation and service policy management. With this flexible workflow functionality, service providers can collect and act on data from a wide range of network technologies and operational systems. The software then filters, transforms, and consolidates data feeds into required formats before routing them to applications such as billing, fraud management, service assurance, and business analytics solutions. The solution comes preintegrated to SAP Hybris Billing, supporting both real-time and batch processing, and provides a single platform for all mediation and policy management activity. This reduces the number of integration points required to manage data across networks.

The hardware-agnostic mediation platform eliminates the requirement for multiple solutions, hence the costs are reduced significantly. The graphical user interface (GUI) with intuitive drag-and-drop features allows for easy in-house configuration.

All mass processes, such as usage management, rating, billing, invoicing, payment reconciliation, and revenue management, run automatically and unattended. Production scheduling for mass processing is precisely controlled with checks and balances; reversals and end-to-end error correction is available to reprocess mass data to automate recovery from hardware/network outages and incorrect data entry. When configuration changes are made to the system, completeness and compatibility checks are run and managed though robust testing and change control processes through quality assurance (QA) and preproduction systems to ensure that errors are caught before affecting the production system.

6.2.4 Billing, Receivables, and Collections

SAP Hybris Billing enables service providers to produce a single customer bill across all the lines of businesses to ensure prompt payments. It allows you to reduce costs associated with printing, mailing, and presenting customer bills and enables you to significantly reduce billing-related customer enquiries and customer service calls. SAP Hybris Billing brings different billing streams from different SAP and non-SAP systems together intelligently on a common platform and then converges them onto a single customer bill, as shown in Figure 6.17.

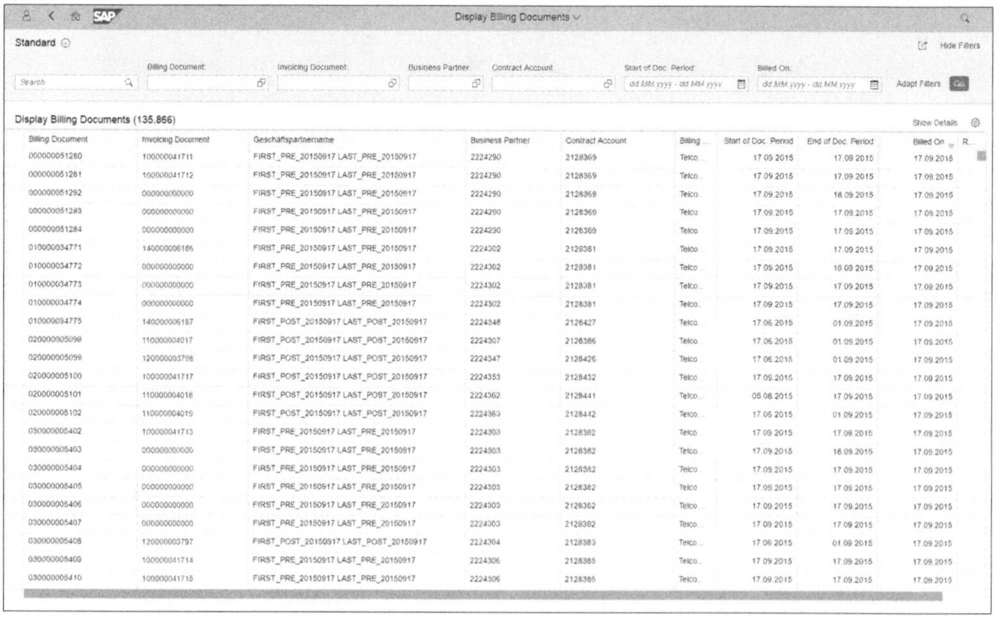

Billing Document	Invoicing Document	Geschäftspartnername	Business Partner	Contract Account	Billing ...	Start of Doc. Period	End of Doc. Period	Billed On	R...
000000051280	100000041711	FIRST_PRE_20150917 LAST_PRE_20150917	2224290	2128369	Telco...	17.09.2015	17.09.2015	17.09.2015	
000000051281	100000041712	FIRST_PRE_20150917 LAST_PRE_20150917	2224290	2128369	Telco...	17.09.2015	17.09.2015	17.09.2015	
000000051282	000000000000	FIRST_PRE_20150917 LAST_PRE_20150917	2224290	2128369	Telco...	17.09.2015	18.09.2015	17.09.2015	
000000051283	000000000000	FIRST_PRE_20150917 LAST_PRE_20150917	2224290	2128369	Telco...	17.09.2015	17.09.2015	17.09.2015	
000000051284	000000000000	FIRST_PRE_20150917 LAST_PRE_20150917	2224290	2128369	Telco...	17.09.2015	17.09.2015	17.09.2015	
010000034771	140000006186	FIRST_PRE_20150917 LAST_PRE_20150917	2224302	2128381	Telco...	17.09.2015	17.09.2015	17.09.2015	
010000034772	000000000000	FIRST_PRE_20150917 LAST_PRE_20150917	2224302	2128381	Telco...	17.09.2015	18.09.2015	17.09.2015	
010000034773	000000000000	FIRST_PRE_20150917 LAST_PRE_20150917	2224302	2128381	Telco...	17.09.2015	17.09.2015	17.09.2015	
010000034774	000000000000	FIRST_PRE_20150917 LAST_PRE_20150917	2224302	2128381	Telco...	17.09.2015	17.09.2015	17.09.2015	
010000034775	140000006187	FIRST_POST_20150917 LAST_POST_20150917	2224348	2128427	Telco...	17.06.2015	01.09.2015	17.09.2015	
020000005098	110000004017	FIRST_POST_20150917 LAST_POST_20150917	2224307	2128386	Telco...	17.06.2015	01.09.2015	17.09.2015	
020000005099	120000003798	FIRST_POST_20150917 LAST_POST_20150917	2224347	2128426	Telco...	17.06.2015	01.09.2015	17.09.2015	
020000005100	100000041717	FIRST_POST_20150917 LAST_POST_20150917	2224353	2128432	Telco...	17.09.2015	17.09.2015	17.09.2015	
020000005101	110000004018	FIRST_POST_20150917 LAST_POST_20150917	2224362	2128441	Telco...	05.08.2015	17.09.2015	17.09.2015	
020000005102	110000004019	FIRST_POST_20150917 LAST_POST_20150917	2224363	2128442	Telco...	17.06.2015	01.09.2015	17.09.2015	
030000005402	100000041713	FIRST_PRE_20150917 LAST_PRE_20150917	2224303	2128382	Telco...	17.09.2015	17.09.2015	17.09.2015	
030000005403	000000000000	FIRST_PRE_20150917 LAST_PRE_20150917	2224303	2128382	Telco...	17.09.2015	18.09.2015	17.09.2015	
030000005404	000000000000	FIRST_PRE_20150917 LAST_PRE_20150917	2224303	2128382	Telco...	17.09.2015	17.09.2015	17.09.2015	
030000005405	000000000000	FIRST_PRE_20150917 LAST_PRE_20150917	2224303	2128382	Telco...	17.09.2015	17.09.2015	17.09.2015	
030000005406	000000000000	FIRST_PRE_20150917 LAST_PRE_20150917	2224303	2128382	Telco...	17.09.2015	17.09.2015	17.09.2015	
030000005407	000000000000	FIRST_PRE_20150917 LAST_PRE_20150917	2224303	2128382	Telco...	17.09.2015	17.09.2015	17.09.2015	
030000005408	120000003797	FIRST_POST_20150917 LAST_POST_20150917	2224304	2128383	Telco...	17.06.2015	01.09.2015	17.09.2015	
030000005409	100000041714	FIRST_PRE_20150917 LAST_PRE_20150917	2224306	2128385	Telco...	17.09.2015	17.09.2015	17.09.2015	
030000005410	100000041715	FIRST_PRE_20150917 LAST_PRE_20150917	2224306	2128385	Telco...	17.09.2015	17.09.2015	17.09.2015	

Figure 6.17 List of Billing Documents

Even though a bill may summarize charges, full transaction-level details are always preserved by maintaining traceability back to the original line items. Figure 6.18 shows an example of an individual billing document.

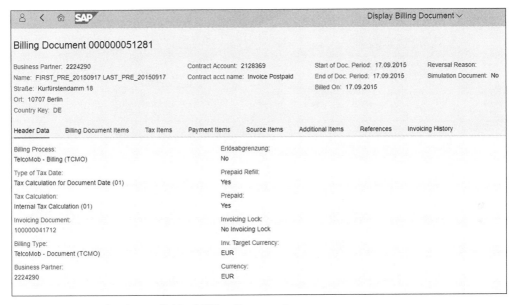

Figure 6.18 Example of an Individual Billing Document

This allows the customer service agents to have access to all details behind charges, discounts, and taxes. The invoice can be enriched with flexible discounts, multiple integrations, different levels of details, and statements about prior payment activities or late payments.

Figure 6.19 shows the list of invoices searched in the system based on search criteria. You can display an individual invoice to see the details, as shown in Figure 6.20.

The final bill can be designed to conform to readability and marketing objectives to ensure that they are easy for customers to read, follow, and use to make prompt payments.

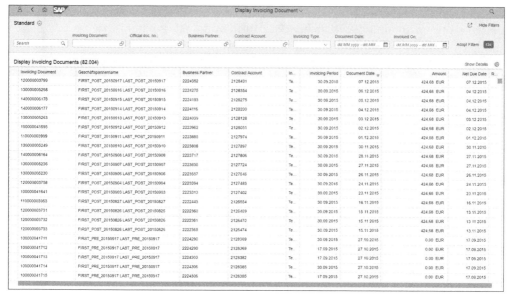

Figure 6.19 List of Invoicing Documents

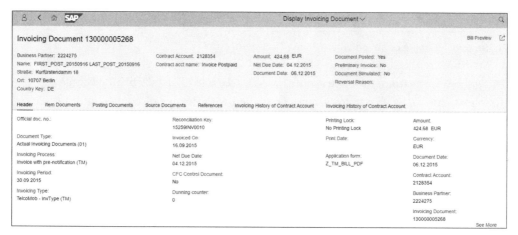

Figure 6.20 Displayed Invoice Document with Details

The revenue management functionality automates routine tasks for every possible payment channel, from credit cards, to checks, to internal or external cash desks, as well as bank transfers that are initiated by the customers or service providers. You can continuously monitor customer payment behavior to get real-time updates on customer risk profiles. Customers can be segmented into different groups based on their credit risk profile, and you can apply different payment collection strategies for each group. You can compare collection and dunning success through out-of-the-box analytics, as shown in Figure 6.21 and Figure 6.22, and then refine these strategies to optimize an efficient cash collection process.

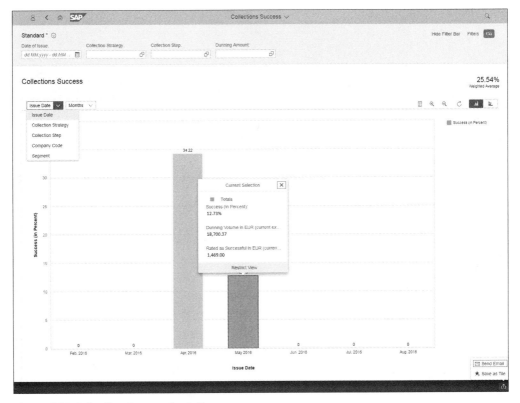

Figure 6.21 Collection Success Analytics

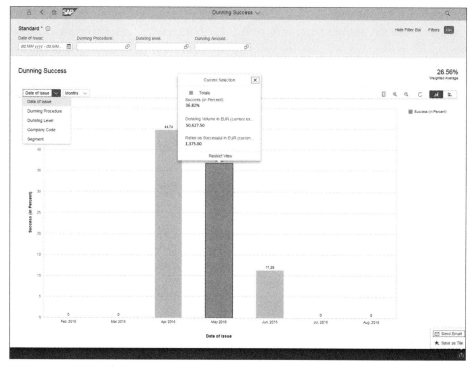

Figure 6.22 Dunning Success Analytics

Integrated financial customer care and dispute management allows customer service agents to access and update data for customer contracts, payment instruments, and accounts as needed. For disputed items, customer service agents can use a guided process and seek approval before deferring individual line items or applying credit notes. These solutions also allow you to recognize revenue for subscription- and usage-based services so that revenues are posted accurately into the SAP General Ledger or non-SAP accounting systems. The account receivables information is continuously updated based on billing, payments, and disputed amounts to provide accurate cash flow projections, as shown in Figure 6.23.

Financial customer care and dispute management supports all financial-related communications with customers. This solution manages both inbound and outbound customer contacts via any communication channel. Because customer service agents have access to all the facts and figures, they are empowered to immediately and accurately answer customer's payment-related queries and resolve customer issues to enable a smooth payment collections and optimal cash flow process. By allowing customers to work out promises to pay or installment plans, service providers can reduce uncollectible account receivables (AR) write-offs.

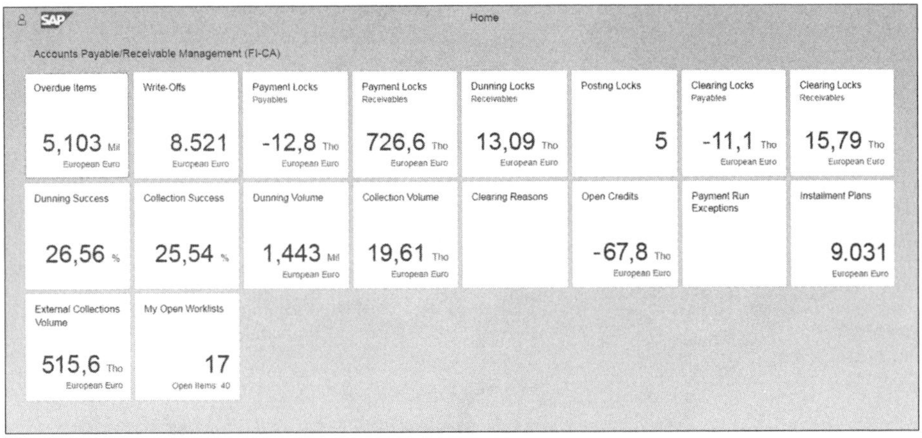

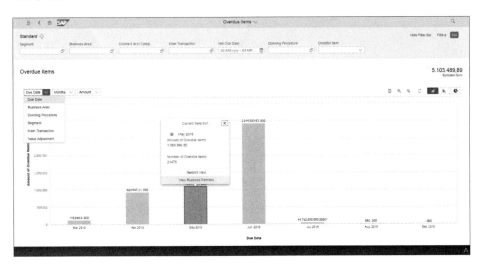

Figure 6.23 Accounts Payables and Receivables Information

Using standard out-of-the-box analytics, you can track overdue payment items (see Figure 6.24) based on various criteria such as due date, business area, dunning procedure, and so on.

Figure 6.24 List of Overdue Payments

You can also track customers with overdue payments for a date range and status of last entry (as shown in Figure 6.25).

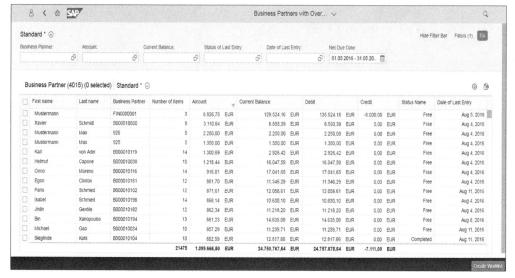

Figure 6.25 List of Customers with Overdue Payments

You can also display customer write-offs such as write-off dates, write-off reasons, dunning procedure, and write-off types for various reasons (as shown in Figure 6.26).

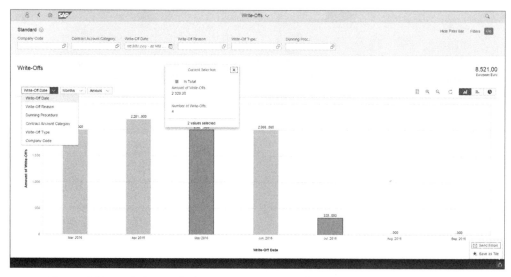

Figure 6.26 Analytics to Display Payment Write-Offs

Finally, you can display payment locks based on payment method, lock reason, total duration in days, and so on (see Figure 6.27).

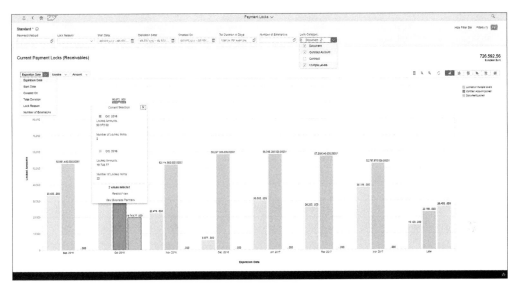

Figure 6.27 Analytics to Show Payment Locks

6.2.5   Partner Revenue Share

Using partner settlement features, you can introduce price plans involving any number of third parties in the value chain. You can manage royalties, commissions, and sponsorship structures in a single pricing configuration tool and model complex revenue sharing between multiple partners. The customer usage transactions can trigger the required related transactions so that all involved partners are properly compensated with no limit on the number of partners that can be involved in a single transaction. By designing unique revenue-sharing deals between partners, you can launch new services and lines of business to meet current and future customer needs. With convergent invoicing, you can partner with third parties and ramp up new services with select partners. When you configure the software to share revenues with specific third-party providers, such charges are distributed to them only if the end customer has paid the corresponding charges.

Discounts can be configured to trigger automatically in the invoice if the total charges exceed certain threshold values or if a subtotal across certain services or products exceeds a defined limit. During the actual invoicing process, functions in account receivables and payables in contract accounts are triggered to calculate interest, trigger dunning, update accounts receivables, and include all the relevant information on the final invoice.

The partner revenue-sharing models can be designed alongside revenue-generation models. Partner payments can be made dependent on receipt of customer payments to minimize the credit exposure and share the risk with partners. With transparent statements and prompt payments, you can grow your loyal partner base with the partner revenue sharing functionality in SAP Hybris Billing.

6.3   SAP Hybris Revenue Cloud

SAP's cloud solution for revenue known as SAP Hybris Revenue Cloud is a growth engine for a new way of doing business, that is, enabling companies to monetize and run their businesses in the digital economy. It's a comprehensive cloud-based solution for CPQ, order management, and subscription billing. Built completely on SAP Hybris as a Service, SAP Hybris Revenue Cloud is based on a microservices architecture. With this solution, you can deploy highly effective and innovative sales and monetization processes in an agile, flexible, and scalable environment. It's built on the flexible SAP Cloud Platform and is available in the public cloud through SAP Hybris as a Service.

SAP Hybris Revenue Cloud uses the SAP Fiori 2.0 UI for engaging user experience, while it also integrates with backend solutions such as SAP S/4HANA, SAP CRM, and SAP ERP to complement your investments. Being in the public cloud, the SAP Hybris Revenue Cloud solution is on accelerated innovation path and follows faster release cycles and extensions.

In today's increasingly disrupted business landscape, SAP Hybris Revenue Cloud helps companies become more agile. They can open new revenue streams by tapping into new markets and by delivering fast pricing and product releases. The solution also allows lower total cost of ownership (TCO) and provides business insight to deliver the exact experience end customers are looking for.

The three components of SAP Hybris Revenue Cloud—CPQ, order orchestration, and subscription billing—are shown in Figure 6.28.

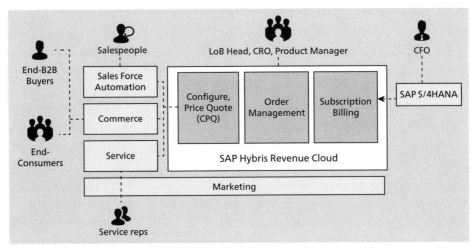

Figure 6.28 SAP Hybris Revenue Cloud

In the following sections, we'll review the key capabilities of these three components of SAP Hybris Revenue Cloud.

6.3.1 Configure, Price, and Quote

Product configuration and pricing has been one of the most limiting factors for businesses to alter their product offerings and engage in more flexible business models to acquire new customers. Emerging business models and competitive pressure are forcing companies to rethink their product and services offerings and revenue models. Many new product categories, usage-based pricing, and product/price bundles have made product configuration and associated pricing extremely complex.

To help these businesses meet the new challenges with product configuration and pricing, SAP Hybris Revenue Cloud offers the most flexible, powerful, and innovative CPQ solution available. With the cloud-based solution delivered as part of SAP Hybris Revenue Cloud, you can scale, simplify, and accelerate your customer-facing sales channels and processes. It helps you improve sales effectiveness, monitor customer behavior, measure sales performance, and track the overall health of your business in real time. SAP Hybris Revenue Cloud enables you to effectively implement an end-to-end digital quote-to-cash process.

6.3.2   Order Orchestration or Order Management

The ability to configure, price, and quote isn't sufficient if you don't have an integrated order management or order orchestration process. In fact, any discrepancy between order fulfillment and product configuration might not only result in loss of revenue but also unwanted customer complaints and unhappy customers. Hence, it's critical that your CPQ process has a seamless handoff with your order management process. Your customers should not be able to configure, price, and quote a product bundle, if your order management process can't successfully fulfill that product configuration.

The order orchestration or order management component of SAP Hybris Revenue Cloud enables seamless integration between CPQ and the order orchestration process. You never have inconsistent product models and pricing between CPQ products and finally ordered products. You can create new revenue streams and sell more and faster through your direct sales and commerce channels. Unnecessary customer complaints related to incorrect product configuration, pricing, and order fulfillment are also avoided. The user interface in SAP Hybris Revenue Cloud makes is easier to search and view sales transactions, including quotes, as shown in Figure 6.29.

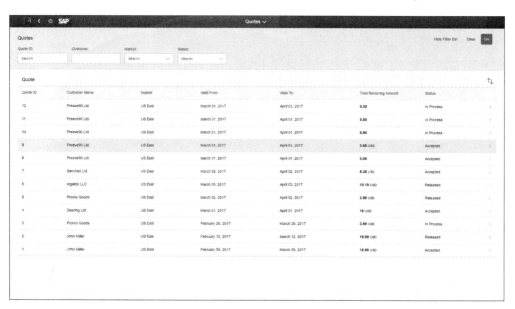

Figure 6.29 Quotes Overview Screen

From here, you can navigate to look at a single quote, as shown in Figure 6.30.

Figure 6.30 View of a Single Quote

You can also view additional details about a quote, as shown in Figure 6.31.

Figure 6.31 Quote Details

6.3.3 Subscription Billing

Traditionally, the subscription- or usage-based business model has been restricted to just a few industries such as utility, telecom, media, and so on. However, in the digital economy, consumers believe in only paying for what they use, not for what they own. Most of the traditional business models are being challenged and are in the process of being replaced by usage- and subscription-based business models. Businesses are struggling with trying to use their rigid legacy billing applications to support these new flexible and innovative business models. Subscription-based billing is no longer just a back-office necessity but a key enabler for new business models.

The subscription billing solution part of SAP Hybris Revenue Cloud is a strategic revenue management system that functions as a core enabler rather than a barrier to change. The SAP Hybris Revenue Cloud user interface makes it much easier for business users to navigate through the subscription details, as can be seen in Figure 6.32.

Figure 6.32 Subscription Overview Screen

You can also access subscription product details, as shown in Figure 6.33.

It enables the management of digital and connected products and services, subscription- and usage-based pricing and one-time fees, and any configuration thereof. Figure 6.34 shows example of subscription product defined in SAP Hybris Revenue Cloud.

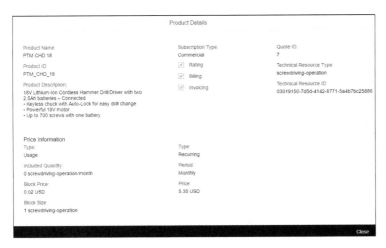

Figure 6.33 Subscription Product Details

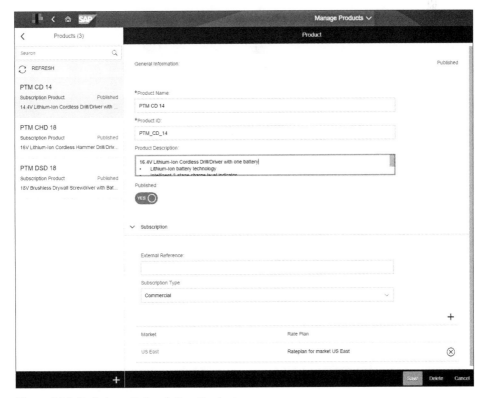

Figure 6.34 Defining a Subscription Product

Subscription billing is integrated with CPQ and order orchestration as part of SAP Hybris Revenue Cloud to provide the foundational application infrastructure to sell digital products and monetize new and emerging business models. Most importantly, by subscribing to SAP Hybris Revenue Cloud and integrating with your back-end system, you can get up and running in just a few weeks. You don't need to reinvent the wheel and build your own subscription-based billing solution.

6.4   Integrating with Other SAP Hybris Front-Office Solutions

Among all the SAP Hybris front-office solutions, SAP Hybris Billing and SAP Hybris Revenue Cloud integrate with SAP Hybris Commerce Cloud to provide a rich commerce experience with subscription- and usage-based billing capabilities. Leveraging this integration, businesses can extend to their customers complete control over their orders and contracts and sell subscription-based products and services through an omnichannel commerce platform. Businesses not only deliver consistent experiences to customers from CPQ and subscription, to delivery, billing, and payment, but they also innovate and transform their business models. Figure 6.35 shows the solution scope for SAP Hybris Commerce and SAP Hybris Billing or SAP Hybris Revenue Cloud integration.

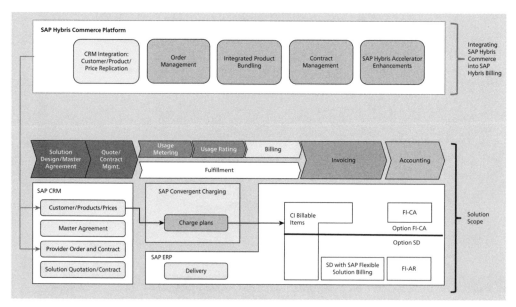

Figure 6.35 SAP Hybris Billing and SAP Hybris Commerce Integration

The key capabilities achieved through end-to-end digital commerce and billing solutions integration are as follows:

- **Master data replication**

  For SAP Hybris Billing and SAP Hybris Commerce integration, the leading system of record for master data is the SAP CRM backend. The integration fully reuses the mast data replication provided by the SAP CRM integration. Customers, contacts, products and service materials (subscription and consumption based), and catalog prices are replicated from SAP CRM. Product bundles aren't replicated, but rather the bundle structure information is derived synchronously during runtime from SAP CRM. Business agreements aren't contained in the SAP Hybris Billing and SAP Hybris Commerce integration, but they can be provided through custom-specific implementation.

- **Order management**

  Order management is made up of the following functionalities:

  - **Logon and products**

    SAP Hybris Billing and SAP Hybris Commerce integration only supports early logon. Customers must log on to the web shop before they can add products to the shopping cart. This is also prerequisite for identifying the customer to enable customer-specific pricing in the SAP backend. Customers can browse the product catalog in the online store and add products to the shopping cart. As soon as a product is added to the cart, a stateful order is created in the SAP backend. Customers can change the product quantity or add and remove the products in the shopping cart, and these changes are updated in the backend stateful order. As soon as the customer places the order in the online store, the stateful order in the backend is persisted and committed to the database.

  - **Product bundles**

    In the catalog search, only the product bundle is available, not the components of the bundle, but customers can personalize the bundle from the catalog, search results, or product details. During personalization, the full bundle structure with all dependent components is available. As soon as the customer starts personalizing a bundle, a simulated order combined with the bundle structure information is created in the SAP backend. Customers can choose between alternative components, selecting additional options, and adding the personalized bundles to the cart. As soon as the customer adds the personalized bundles to the shopping cart, a stateful order is created. If there are already products in the cart, the stateful order is updated in the SAP backend. After the customer places the order in the online store, the order is persisted, and the actual order is created in the SAP backend.

- **Pricing**
Product list prices (which are mostly based on the embedded Apache Solr index) are shown in the catalog products in SAP Hybris Commerce storefront from. However, the special pricing, including customer-specific pricing, is provided as part of the bundle personalization or checkout process from the SAP CRM Internet Pricing Configurator (IPC) in the backend through a synchronous call.

- **Checkout and order placement**
During the checkout process, the customer can select an alternative shipping address. The shipping addresses available in SAP Hybris Commerce includes the address of the sold-to party and the address of all the ship-to parties belonging to the sold-to party in the SAP backend system. In addition, during checkout, only the preselected and supported payment method invoice is displayed. As soon as the customer places the order in the online store, the order is committed in the backend, and the order confirmation email is sent to the customer. Figure 6.36 shows the process flow for customer interaction with order management.

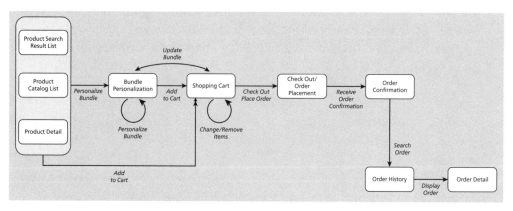

Figure 6.36 Order Management Interaction

- **Cart restoration**
SAP Hybris Billing and SAP Hybris Commerce Cloud integration allows cart restoration and enables customers to log out from the web shop without placing an order and come back at a later point. The backend session closes when the customer logs out or after the session times out in SAP Hybris Commerce, without an order being saved in the backend. The cart is restored with personalized

product bundles when the customer logs back in to the online store, the order is created synchronously in the backend, and the results are displayed in the cart. When the customer places the order, the order in the backend is persisted, and the cart information is deleted from SAP Hybris Commerce.

- **Shopping experience: order search**
  The order search and order history functions allow customers to search for orders created for their company (within a predefined period of time set in the SAP Hybris Commerce back office administration cockpit) and view the order details. The results list covers all the orders independent of the channel through which orders were placed (backend, call center, online store, mobile app, etc.).

- **Contract management**
  Subscriptions cause long-term contractual agreements that are subject to change. Customers can search for contracts created for their company and view contract items. If needed, customers can navigate into contract details and initiate a change process or a contract extension process by maintaining change process parameters. As soon as customers start a change process, an order is created in the SAP backend. They can directly confirm the change process without adding the change order to their cart, and as soon as they confirm the change order, the order is persisted in the SAP backend, and a change confirmation email is sent to the customer. Figure 6.37 shows the process for the customer interaction process during contract management.

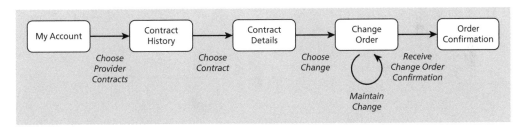

Figure 6.37 Customer Interaction during the Contract Management Process

6.5   Integrating with SAP S/4HANA and SAP ERP

As mentioned earlier, with SAP Hybris Billing, you can leverage existing SAP investments in SAP ERP Sales and Distribution (SD) and SAP ERP Financials Accounts Receivable (FI-AR) to implement subscription- and usage-based services to an existing product based on project-centric quoting and billing solutions for B2B customers.

You can add SAP Hybris Billing components (due to the flexible deployment option) to an existing SD and FI-AR landscape nondisruptively. This allows you to sell and bill solution packages to B2B customers with a one-time fee and/or project-based billing, along with new subscriptions, metered, and pay-per-use services. You can create these solution packages, build a single quote and a single contract for the entire solution package, and then manage changes over time against that contract.

In SAP Hybris Billing, with its modular deployment flexibility, the key components use open interfaces and enterprise web services to communicate with third-party non-SAP systems. The data models and data flows are exposed so that they can be redirected and reused to achieve particular customer use cases. Each subcomponent is architected to use master data from a third-party non-SAP system. Even with modular deployment, the solution deployment, administration, and monitoring activities across the systems can operate as one end-to-end solution.

Figure 6.38 shows different operation systems running different components of the solution package (e.g., SD) and billing of the hard goods products, the existing third-party billing system for some other line of business, and SAP Hybris Billing for metering, rating, and charging for subscription- and usage-based charges. All of these different streams can be brought together in a combined invoice for the customer. By extending SD, you converge multiple billing streams from SAP and non-SAP systems into a single invoice, and this invoice is processed through FI-AR for accounts receivable just like any other invoice but with full traceability back to potential high-volume line-item details captured in SAP Hybris Billing usage-based services. This way, enterprise B2B customers get the convenience of a single quote, a single contract, and a single bill, hence enhancing customer satisfaction and lowering days sales outstanding (DSO).

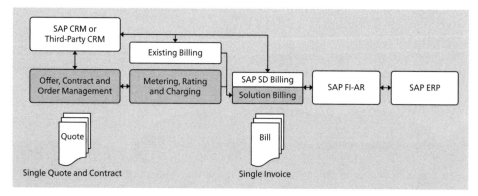

Figure 6.38 Deploying SAP Hybris Billing Components with an Existing SAP Landscape

To enable SAP Hybris Billing (or SAP Hybris Revenue Cloud) integration with the SAP backend, you can either integrate SAP Hybris Commerce with SAP CRM and SAP ERP or with SAP S/4HANA's digital core in the backend, or you can integrate SAP Hybris Commerce with SAP S/4HANA or SAP ERP. All these integrations are possible through SAP Hybris Commerece, data hub. We'll review the integration with SAP CRM in the next section. Figure 6.39 shows the integration with SAP ERP or SAP S/4HANA for the billing solution.

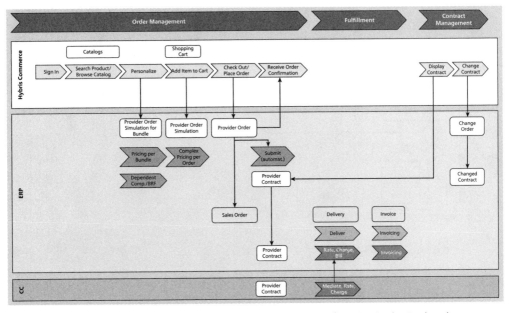

Figure 6.39 SAP Hybris Billing Integration with SAP ERP or SAP S/4HANA in the Backend

In this scenario, SD and FI–AR capabilities are leveraged from the SAP ERP or SAP S/4HANA backend. From an SAP Hybris Commerce web shop, customers can view invoices, open balances, and look at detailed billing overviews from the SAP backend system. The product catalogs, pricing and customer information, and product stocks are available in the SAP Hybris Commerce web shop from the SAP backend. Customers can view catalogs for products and services and display price information, such as the one-time price, one-time activation fee, installment price, recurring fee, and special price, along with stock information. Customers can view invoices for the last billing period, see detailed usage information such as on demand service consumption, pay for selected invoices, and view payment history. All these details are pulled from SAP ERP or SAP S/4HANA.

6.6   Integrating with SAP Customer Relationship Management

As stated earlier, SAP Hybris Billing leverages master data and transactions from SAP CRM to enable seamless product bundling, product pricing, order management, and contract management in SAP Hybris Commerce web shops.

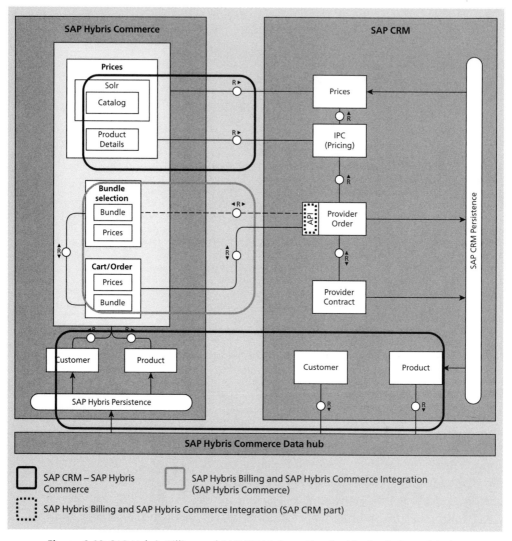

Figure 6.40 SAP Hybris Billing and SAP CRM Integration for Master Data and Order Management

Figure 6.40 shows the integration among SAP Hybris Billing, SAP Hybris Commerce, and SAP CRM for pricing, bundle selection, and order management. For contract management from the web shop, the integration among SAP Hybris Commerce, SAP Hybris Billing, and SAP CRM is shown in Figure 6.41.

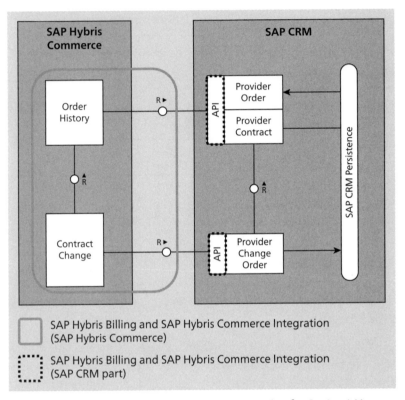

Figure 6.41 SAP Hybris Billing and SAP CRM Integration for Contract Management

Figure 6.42 shows all the components of integration among SAP Hybris Billing, SAP Hybris Commerce, SAP ERP, and SAP CRM.

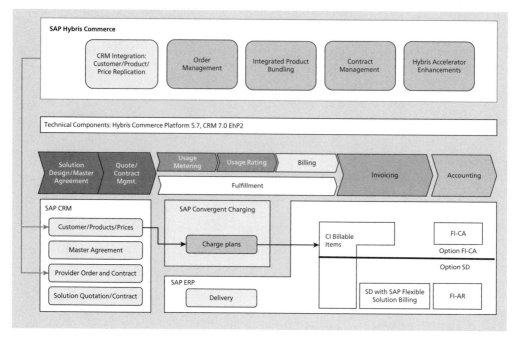

Figure 6.42 SAP Hybris Commerce, SAP Hybris Billing, SAP ERP, and SAP CRM Integration

6.7   Summary

In this chapter, you've learned that SAP Hybris Billing, previously known as BRIM (Billing, Revenue, and Innovation Management), and SAP Hybris Revenue Cloud are SAP's initiative to help customers monetize their usage- and subscription-based services. We've reviewed the key capabilities of the SAP Hybris Billing on-premise solution as well as the SAP Hybris Revenue Cloud solution and their business benefits. Because SAP Hybris Billing leverages backend SAP solutions such SAP S/4HANA, SAP ERP, and SAP CRM, we've reviewed integration of SAP Hybris Billing with SAP Hybris Commerce and SAP backend systems. SAP Hybris Billing is the last component of the SAP Hybris front-office solutions (SAP Hybris Sales Cloud, SAP Hybris Service Cloud, SAP Hybris Marketing, SAP Hybris Commerce, and SAP Hybris Revenue Cloud). In the next chapter, you'll learn about SAP Hybris as a Service.

Chapter 7

Microservices and SAP Hybris as a Service

SAP Hybris as a Service is a nonproprietary, open standard solution, based on microservices architecture to help customers digitally transform their businesses. In this microservices ecosystem, businesses can rapidly augment and build new, highly flexible cloud solutions.

Businesses can no longer remain agile and adaptable to new market realities with old monolithic architecture applications. They must transform their application landscape to make it flexible and scalable, and they also must, more importantly, open their systems (via application programming interfaces [APIs]) to try new business models and business processes. Many companies are generating revenue by exposing their APIs as business building blocks for third-party applications.

Microservices are a new way of building software systems that have gained tremendous popularity in recent years due to the emergence of cloud and mobile computing. More and more developers prefer microservices to building enterprise applications. The microservices architecture offers enormous flexibility and scalability, and it enables you to support a wide range of devices and platforms, such as mobile, web, Internet of Things (IoT), wearable devices, and cloud. Essentially, microservices architecture allows you to build applications into a suite of independently deployable, small, and modular services in which in each service runs as a unique and independent process, communicating with another process through predefined communication to deliver unique business functions.

To offer flexibility to customers and partners in deploying SAP Hybris solutions, SAP is leveraging microservices architecture to offer SAP Hybris as a Service on SAP Cloud Platform. SAP Hybris as a Service is changing the landscape for SAP customers and SAP partners for deploying, using, and extending SAP Hybris solutions. In this chapter, we'll discuss the important concepts behind the microservices architecture, compare the monolithic and microservices architectures, and explain some of the key consider-ations for investigating microservices for building enterprise applications. We'll provide examples from leading companies that are using business applications built on microservices architecture and how they are transforming themselves in this API economy. To clearly define the architectural components of microservices and some of the key components of SAP Hybris as a Service, we've used few techni-cal terms in this chapter that are only relevant to developers. We've tried your best to keep the concepts at a high level for the broader audience. However, we've pro-vided references to SAP Hybris as a Service online documentation for developers to gain additional insights for building and deploying SAP Hybris as a Service applica-tions.

> **Note**
>
> SAP Hybris as a Service is commonly abbreviated as YaaS. Throughout this chapter and book, we're using the official name, but don't be surprised if you see YaaS crop up when reading further about the product.

With some background on microservices, we'll review how SAP has leveraged the microservices architecture to offer SAP Hybris as a Service. We'll introduce SAP Hybris as a Service concepts and how you can use the solutions available through the SAP Hybris as a Service marketplace to extend the capabilities of your SAP Hybris solutions. To help with building and deploying applications in SAP Hybris as a Service, we'll review some of the key steps toward building your own SAP Hybris as a Service.

7.1   Microservices Architecture

The microservices architecture is a specialization of the service-oriented architecture (SOA) and is used to build independently deployable software applications. Each ser-vice in microservices is independent and delivers a self-contained functionality that other services can leverage, as shown in Figure 7.1.

These services communicate over a light protocol to deliver a larger and more com-prehensive business functionality. These services are technology-agnostic, giving developers' flexibility to use any development framework and programming lan-guage they choose.

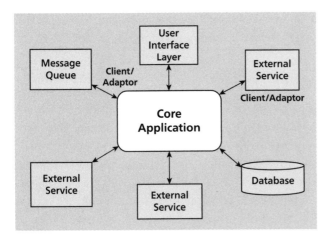

Figure 7.1 Microservices Architecture

Although there is no industry consensus on the definition of microservices architecture, the following standard guidelines define their characteristics:

- In microservices architecture, the protocol used for the services to communicate should be lightweight, and the services should be small and granular.

- The services should be independently deployable, which makes it easier to add and change functions in a system at any time without affecting other constituting services in the application.

- The services are organized around capabilities such as shopping cart, user interface (UI) frontend, sales order, product catalog, product recommendations, loyalty, logistics, billing, and so on.

- Services can be implemented in different programming languages, hardware environments, and software environments, as preferred by the developers and organizations building these services.

- The application development process using the microservices architecture generally adheres to industry-accepted principles such as well-defined interfaces to enable independently deployable services, business requirements-driven development approach, ideal cloud application architectures, lightweight container deployment, decentralized continuous delivery, and service monitoring.

There are some distinct advantages to using the microservices architecture over the traditional monolithic architecture, which we'll look at in the following sections. We'll also explain why you need to investigate microservices for your application design and deployment, and then we'll conclude with a few examples of microservices.

7.1.1 Monolithic Architecture versus Microservices

Monolithic architecture, as the name suggests, is a single piece of software. For example, imagine you're building an e-commerce application. The application is deployed as a single monolithic application to handle multiple functions such as product catalog, shopping cart, ordering, inventory verification, credit check, shipping, and so on. It consists of a single file that runs on a web container with a single directory hierarchy. If needed, you can run multiple instances of this application through a load balancer to scale the application and offer improved availability. These types of applications are deployed through a traditional web application architecture, as shown in Figure 7.2. They are simple to develop, test, and deploy. Most importantly, you can scale these types of applications by running multiple copies of the application behind a load balancer.

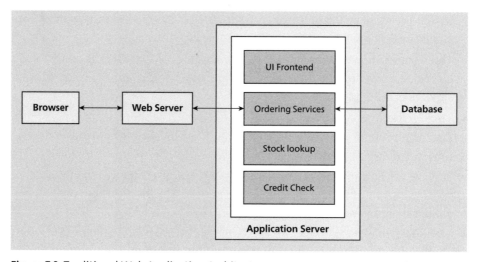

Figure 7.2 Traditional Web Application Architecture

However, after the application becomes large, and the team size supporting this application grows, it becomes increasingly difficult to maintain and support the application. The large monolithic code base can be difficult for the developers to understand and modify, particularly if they aren't the ones who originally wrote the application. The larger code base overloads and slows down the integrated development environment (IDE), making developers less productive. In short, the larger the application, the longer it takes to load in the web container and the longer the application start time is. In a large monolithic application, even a minor change to code requires redeploying the entire application, which is a huge obstacle in deploying frequent changes.

Scaling a monolithic application can be difficult because the application scales in only one direction. It can scale with an increase in transaction volume because you can run the application on multiple instances; however, this architecture can't scale with increasing data volume. Each copy of application data must access the entire data, which makes caching less effective and increases memory consumption and input/output (I/O) traffic. Another dimension concerns the application-specific requirements for system resources. Some applications might be CPU intensive and others might be memory intensive. With a monolithic architecture, you can't scale each component independently.

A monolithic architecture requires a long-term commitment to a technology stack you chose at the time of building the initial application. It's difficult to adopt a newer technology. If your application uses a platform framework that becomes obsolete later, you'll likely have to rewrite the entire application to adopt a newer platform, which could be risk-prone and time-consuming.

The microservices architecture, on the other hand, is an alternative approach to building applications over monolithic architecture. In the microservices architecture, you structure the application as a set of loosely coupled and collaborative services. Each of these services implements a narrowly defined function. For example, an application may consist of services such as customer registration, order management services, credit management services, and so on. These services communicate either using a synchronous protocol such as HTTP/REST or an asynchronous protocol and can be deployed independent of one other. Each service has its own database to keep these services decoupled from other services. Figure 7.3 shows an example of a set of deployed services that are decoupled from each other.

These types of application deployments have some unique benefits. First, because each microservice is relatively small, it's easier for the developer to understand, the IDE isn't overloaded, and the application starts faster, making developers more productive. Second, the new versions of each service can be deployed frequently and independent of other services. It's easier to scale development because each team member can develop, deploy, and scale their services independently of other team members working on different services. Whereas one faulty component of a monolithic application can bring down the entire application, in the microservice deployment, a memory leak in one service or component doesn't affect the other services. Other services will continue to handle requests. Each service can scale independently of the other services in this architecture. Finally, with this approach, there is no long-term commitment to a technology stack. While developing a new service, you can easily pick a new technology stack. While making changes to an existing service, you can easily rewrite using a new technology stack.

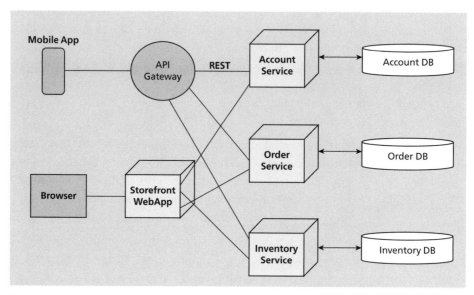

Figure 7.3 Example of an Application Consisting of Set of Microservices

However, the advantages of decoupled services come with a few trade-offs. First, most of the development tools and IDEs are designed to build monolithic applications and lack explicit support for developing distributed applications, hence developers need to deal with additional complexity while building distributed applications. Second, testing is more difficult for such applications. It's difficult to deploy and manage a system comprised of many different service types. Finally, resource requirement and memory consumption is higher for these types of applications.

7.1.2   Why Use Microservices?

The microservices architecture can be leveraged by businesses as well as by software vendors or developers for different reasons. Let's consider their motivations separately to better understand the utility of microservices for each group.

Business Reasons

Some of the reasons that a business might want to look into using microservices are as follows:

- **Gain speed to market**

  With a microservices architecture, customers can quickly deploy new solutions and fast-track their speed to bring their new products or services to market.

- **Support iterative/agile business approach**

  Due to their modular deployment, microservices enable businesses to support agile and iterative development processes. Microservice can be deployed quickly and you can test how they are resonating in the market.

- **Scale flexibly**

  You've already seen that a microservices architecture offers multidimensional scalability. Hence, businesses have the flexibility to start small and then scale to an enterprise-wide application by adding modular services.

- **Infrastructure and project savings**

  The independent and simple deployment of services using a microservices architecture helps businesses keep their IT infrastructure fairly simplified, resulting in substantial project cost savings in deploying and running microservices applications compared to monolithic architecture-based enterprise applications.

- **Transform IT landscape into manageable building blocks**

  Companies can mix multiple languages and development frameworks, and deploy business applications in manageable building blocks. By transforming their IT landscape using microservices, organizations can manage more applications with fewer resources.

- **Increase productivity**

  As stated earlier, applications developed using microservices are easier to build, deploy, and modify compared to their monolithic counterparts, which increasing software developer's productivity.

- **Cooperate efficiently with third-party software and service providers**

  More and more solutions from software vendors are based on a microservices architecture. To take advantage of this API economy and new solutions becoming available in the marketplace, customers are moving toward microservices as their integration and application development pattern.

It's evident that customers have sufficient motivation to investigate the microservices pattern of application building and deployment. However, it's important to note that you must not overlook some of the inherent challenges of deploying this pattern. Microservices provide business benefits to remain agile and scalable but that comes with a cost. Microservices reinforce a modular structure by providing strong module boundaries, which is extremely important for large software team. However, the fact remains that distributed systems are harder to program because remote calls are slow and are prone to risk of failure. Though services are easier to deploy because they are independent, maintaining strong consistency is extremely difficult for a distributed system, which means everyone has to manage eventual consistency. Microservices provide technology diversity (choice of using language or platform), so you need a mature operations team to manage the many services that are deployed and redeployed regularly.

Developers and Partners Reasons

Companies are moving toward utilizing microservices for their enterprise applications, which creates an opportunity for a microservice market for companies such as SAP; however, it offers partners greater opportunities to build and market their own solutions and services using a microservices architecture. Some of the key factors for partners to investigate into this API economy are as follows:

- **Helps customers innovate**
  By developing solutions using microservices, partners can help their customers in their journey to innovate their business processes and deliver fast, scalable, and iterative solutions.

- **Enable customers' transformation**
  Customers have embarked on their digital transformation journey and need help. Partners can build microservices expertise and enable customers' digital transformation.

- **Innovate new ways of building and delivering software and services**
  By leveraging microservices architecture, partners can build new software and solutions to reach out to new markets and customers in new and innovative ways.

- **Productize and Monetize IP**
  The new products and services built using microservices can be productized and offered to customers for consumption on a subscription basis, hence opening new streams of revenue.

- **Shifting industry focus**
  The role of mega software vendors and their partners are changing. The focus is shifting from selling and shipping software to a network of value that connects

customers with smaller software vendors, business data, and partners. Microservices can help partners realign and reposition per new market realities.

7.1.3   Adoption of Microservices

To underline the importance and wide acceptance of microservices architecture in the design of enterprise applications, it's important to note that some of the largest global businesses have been successfully using microservices architecture for their flagship applications. Netflix, eBay, Amazon, Twitter, PayPal, and many other large-scale websites and applications have evolved from a monolithic architecture to a microservices architecture.

Netflix receives more than 1 billion calls every day from more than 800 different types of devices from all over the world to its streaming-video API. Each API call then prompts around 5 additional calls to the backend services. These services have evolved from a monolithic to a microservices architecture. Amazon has also similarly migrated from older applications to microservices. It receives a massive number of calls from a variety of applications, which are handled efficiently by different services. For eBay, the core application consists of several autonomous applications with each one executing business logic for different business functions as separate services. Likewise, many applications companies have successfully adopted a microservices architecture to build their core business applications.

In the next section, we'll discuss SAP's approach to microservices, that is, SAP Hybris as a Service, and how you can leverage it to build, deploy, and consume your own SAP Hybris microservices.

7.2   SAP Hybris as a Service

SAP Hybris as a Service offers an innovation workbench for building and assembling data-driven front-office microservices and Software-as-a-Service (SaaS) applications to enable new commercial model and digital products and services, and a microservices marketplace for commercialization and consumption of prepackaged front-office microservices. SAP Hybris as a Service is based on open standards (e.g., Cloud Foundry) and requires no vendor lock-in. Microservices built on SAP Hybris as a Service can run on any platform-as-a-service (PaaS). SAP Hybris as a Service is free for developers, and there are no limitations on the number of services deployed by you or the number of objects per user. You only pay if you consume any services deployed in the SAP Hybris as a Service marketplace by another provider. Utilization of services on SAP Hybris as a Service is paid on a pay per-use basis, and usage is billed in arrears monthly, which provides full cost control and usage transparency. In subsequent sections, we'll review key features of SAP Hybris as a Service.

7.2.1 Introduction to SAP Hybris as a Service

SAP Hybris as a Service can help you discover and consume software while leveraging existing investments by adding new features as needed. SAP Hybris as a Service lets you build new API-driven custom and commercial apps faster. It increases productivity with developer tools, software development kits (SDKs) and UI frameworks. Applications are made ready for the enterprise with a simple publishing model. Using SAP Hybris as a Service, you can easily add new features, enable social commerce experiences, increase revenue with the assisted sales and service model, reduce churn with loyalty programs, and excite customers with personalized experiences and rewards. It helps you simplify business relationships, reduce commercial complexity, simplify paying for service, and monitor usage. You can lead digital transformation in organizations by rapidly creating proof of concepts at a minimal cost and discover valuable and relevant services through the SAP Hybris as a Service marketplace.

The key features of an API economy based on SAP Hybris as a Service are as follows:

- **Open standards**
  SAP Hybris as a Service is built on Cloud Foundry, which is the industry-leading PaaS for applications and microservices, and it uses RESTful APIs and JavaScript Object Notation (JSON).

- **Flexible and no lock-in**
  The services you build can be deployed on any PaaS and not just on the SAP-preferred Cloud Foundry services on SAP Cloud Platform.

- **Built especially for microservices and ecosystem**
  SAP Hybris as a Service is based on the microservices architectural style. The included productivity tools, guidance, SDKs, UIs, and team management are all tailored to the microservices approach.

- **Pay-per-use business functionality**
  Charges are based on simple metrics and usage, and you pay for only what you use. Payments are monthly in arrears and pay as you go. There are no up-front costs, and services include free tiers to enable cost-effective evaluation and proof of concepts.

- **Marketplace of secure and trusted functionality**
  SAP Hybris as a Service offers secure, trusted, scalable applications, APIs, and services. You can choose services that matter most to your business. Instead of using one large application, you can use a part of an ever-increasing ecosystem of new functionalities.

- **Connect to SAP Hybris**
  To launch additional storefronts and go faster into new markets in a matter of days, you can connect to SAP Hybris Commerce as a Service.

- **Increase customer lifetime value**
  To drive customer loyalty, you can subscribe to the loyalty management services available in SAP Hybris as a Service and integrate with your SAP Hybris Commerce suite or SAP Hybris as a Service Commerce services.

- **Enable customers to buy from tweet**
  The Stripe Relay In-App & Social Sales package enables you to sell products and receive orders that are managed on SAP Hybris as a Service via social channels and shopping apps supported by Stripe Relay. You can easily offer your products in more sales channels to increase your commercial reach as well as let customers place orders directly from their favorite apps.

SAP Hybris as a Service is a commercial, legal, billing and development network for microservices, which consists of the following: SAP Hybris as a Service Market, SAP Hybris as a Service Builder, SAP Hybris as a Service Dev Portal, and SAP Hybris as a Service Community.

SAP Hybris as a Service is a cloud-based application development framework that allows rapid, agile, and cost-effective development and deployment of applications and services from concept to reality based on microservices. With SAP Hybris as a Service, you primarily get an innovation workbench and microservices marketplace as explained here:

- **Innovation workbench or builder**
  This workbench allows you to build and assemble data-driven front-office microservices and SaaS applications to enable new commercial models and digital products and services. It offers a rapid development model based on open web standards with built-in scalability, resilience, security, and data privacy. It also provides built-in consumption billing and metering. It's independent of the runtime environment, hence microservices can be deployed on SAP Cloud Platform or, for example, the Amazon Web Services (AWS) cloud platform. These features allow

you to test and experiment with new commercial models and digital products and services. You can reinvent customer experiences based on customer and product interactions, and, most importantly, you can develop new channels to monetize daily product interaction.

- **Microservices marketplace**
  This marketplace is for the commercialization and consumption of prepackaged front-office microservices from SAP Hybris and its partner ecosystem. It provides prepackaged business services through on-demand microservices with trusted components built and run by SAP. You can get complete SaaS applications based on microservices that are safe, secure, resilient, and auto scale individually. These services are continuously evolving and automatically updating with newly added capabilities and functionalities by their providers. Using microservices available in the marketplace, you can dramatically reduce the time required to build and deploy custom applications. With an API-first approach, services can be brought online immediately and easily replaced or extended as needed. You pay only for services you use and when you use them through subscription/usage billing supported by SAP Hybris as a Service Market.

- **SAP Hybris as a Service Dev Portal**
  SAP Hybris as a Service Dev Portal is a centralized source of information and a dynamic community for software developers. It includes information on getting started, solutions, API documentation, tools and resources, news, and UI design guidelines. The documentation, tool kits, and guidelines contained in SAP Hybris as a Service Dev Portal help developers quickly create services, APIs, or even storefronts. SAP Hybris as a Service Dev Portal can be accessed through *https://devportal.yaas.io*.

- **SAP Hybris as a Service Community**
  This is a community of experts to collaborate and exchange information on SAP Hybris as a Service (Figure 7.4). It showcases SAP Hybris as a Service packages for product recommendations, trending products, product comparison, call back services, inventory service, etc. SAP Hybris as a Service Community also shows planned and past SAP Hybris as a Service events. In the **hybris Experts** section under **Community**, you can also browse through posts and post your own questions related to SAP Hybris as a Service. All of these valuable tools under **Community** help you quickly build, deploy, and consume services from the SAP Hybris as a Service marketplace.

Figure 7.4 SAP Hybris as a Service Community

Next, let's review the architecture, communication mechanisms, and key components of SAP Hybris as a Service microservices.

SAP Hybris as a Service Architecture

The core design principles of SAP Hybris as a Service are based on the microservices architecture style as mentioned earlier. It enables you to build a flexible API on the SAP Hybris scalable platform and then publish it. Software is often bundled into components that use various technologies. The microservices architecture allows you to partition software into smaller, independent, and manageable components. With this approach, you can build any application as an orchestration of microservices.

The microservices architecture style is based on standard, widely accepted technology and design principles for seamless interaction among services. It provides flexibility to use any technology to implement each specific microservice. Every provider of microservices has the freedom to choose the technology, programming language, and development tools to fulfill their business requirements and find the best fit for their application domain. The autonomy of microservices is achieved through three layers, namely RESTful APIs, business logic, and integration logic. The RESTful API implementation exposes business functionality as a web source. Business logic encapsulates the actual implementation of your business requirements, and integration logic is used when services need to interact with another services or with databases.

The SAP Hybris as a Service architectural approach defines two technical types of services as follows:

- **Independent services**
  These kinds of services are self-contained and independent services; they don't have any dependency on any other services. These types of services maintain their own backing services, such as a native database. The backing services aren't shared between multiple services.

- **Dependent services**
  These types of services leverage other services to provide high-level services. To function correctly, these kinds of services depend on the functions of other services, for example, a mashup of more than one service.

The SAP Hybris as a Service ecosystem of services provides an array of building blocks to create a wide range of applications to suite your unique needs.

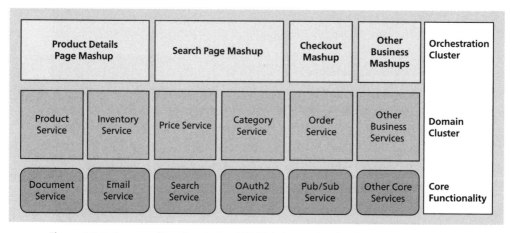

Figure 7.5 Category of Services in the SAP Hybris as a Service Ecosystem

At a high level, these services are categorized under three clusters as shown in Figure 7.5:

- **Core functionality cluster**
  The bottom component is the core functionality cluster that provides a wide range of core functionality such as an email service, search service, document repository service, user authentication service, and so on. The services in this cluster provide

general-purpose functionalities, and they are independent of any business domain. The core services in their cluster are provided to implement basic functionalities, such as repository, search capabilities, and messages. All of these services are ready for the cloud, and you can reuse them to speed up your implementation instead of creating your own services.

- **Domain cluster**
  The middle layer provides services focusing on specific domain, business, or commerce functionalities such as product, customer, catalog, order, and so on. A pure business service focuses on the actual implementation of some specific business functionality, such as calculation of a customer-specific price, calculation of shipping charges, and so on.

- **Orchestration cluster**
  The top level provides high-level services to build domain-specific applications by leveraging and orchestrating services from the bottom two levels (the other two clusters). These types of services aggregate information from multiple other services, such as a service that relays data to the customer browser or a service that orchestrates a business process across multiple services such as the check-out process that uses a cart, prices, and tax service.

Services Communication

Because microservices in SAP Hybris as a Service interact with each other to deliver overall business functionality, it's critical that their communication is robust and fail-proof. Essentially, these services use two mechanisms to communicate, that is, synchronous or HTTP/REST requests and asynchronous or message-based communication:

- **Synchronous or HTTP/REST requests**
  SAP Hybris as a Service services primarily uses HTTP as the communication channel, and each service exposes its web resources through well-defined RESTful APIs. These APIs are described in a natural and intuitive way. In addition to web resources that implement its API, each service also exposes its own API definition through HTTP, and the API console enables API consumers to browse through the API documentation and interact with the service APIs directly. The exposed APIs of services aren't directly accessible by service consumers; instead, they have a component API proxy in front of it. Each service request reaches the API proxy, which analyzes and verifies certain parameters and headers before forwarding the request to the service implementation. The API proxy serves the purpose of

enforcing security, central logging and tracing, and HTTP header rewriting, and it ensures platform resiliency by implementing the rate-limiting and circuit breaker mechanisms.

- **Asynchronous or message-based communication**
  In addition to synchronous HTTP communication, services in SAP Hybris as a Service also communicate asynchronously using the central publish/subscribe (pub/sub) message infrastructure pattern. Services can publish information about the specific topics being managed in the central messaging infrastructure, and other services can subscribe to those topics. When a message is published to a specific topic, it's automatically available to subscribers. The messaging provides a high-level and cross-boundary exchange of asynchronous events, which is critical for building flexible, loosely coupled, and highly scalable solutions.

Components of SAP Hybris as a Service

Figure 7.6 shows all the components of SAP Hybris as a Service.

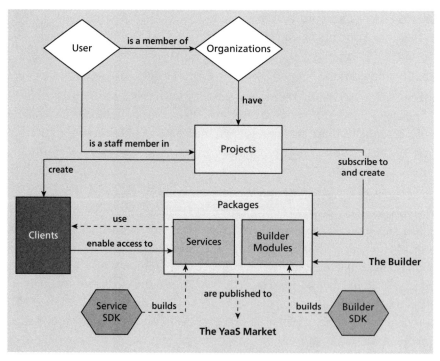

Figure 7.6 Putting All the SAP Hybris as a Service Building Blocks Together

Let's briefly review all these components:

- **User**
  To participate in the SAP Hybris as a Service ecosystem, you must register as a user at *https://www.yaas.io*, as shown in Figure 7.7. Registration is free, and users can be linked to multiple organizations so that one developer can work on projects with multiple organizations.

Figure 7.7 Registering for SAP Hybris as a Service

- **Organization**
  This is the company with which the user is associated.

- **Projects**
  Just like any other project, you need to create a project in SAP Hybris as a Service before you can build any services there. It can be an individual or collaborative created and managed project such as a storefront.

- **Packages**
  A package is a bundle of services. It can include builder modules as well. In SAP Hybris as a Service marketplace, you sell or subscribe to packages, which are the main commodity.

- **Services**
  These are small isolated applications called microservices in SAP Hybris as a Service. They deliver a single piece of functionality and are exposed over a RESTful API.

- **Builder modules**
  These are UIs provided in the builder to manage back-office functionality. Builder

modules are registered with Builders. Using Builder modules, you can manage all the services you offer and consume in the SAP Hybris as a Service marketplace.

- **Builder**

  As the name suggests, it's the main tool that you use to build, publish, and manage packages in the SAP Hybris as a Service marketplace. You need to register at *https://builder.yaas.io* to use Builder services as shown in Figure 7.8.

Figure 7.8 SAP Hybris as a Service

- **SAP Hybris as a Service Market**

  In the marketplace, you share your packages that others can subscribe to, or you can subscribe to packages others have created, as shown in Figure 7.9. This is similar to iTunes and Google Play app stores.

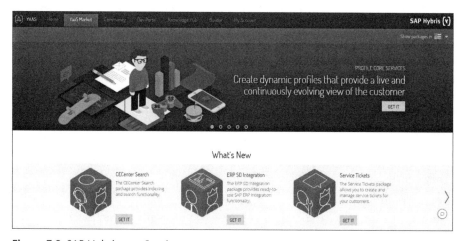

Figure 7.9 SAP Hybris as a Service

- **Service SDK**

  This is one of the SAP Hybris as a Service tools to enhance services based on your business requirements.

- **Builder SDK**

  If you don't like the UI provided by the Builder module, you can build your own interface to manage your services in Builder using this SDK. It's a command-line interface to run Builder in developer mode.

- **SAP Hybris as a Service Storefront**

  This ready-to-use template sets up a fully functional and transactional storefront within minutes, or you can use this template as a starting point to customize your features and functionality. The template is implemented fully with SAP Hybris Commerce as a Services and third-party services. Some of the key features of SAP Hybris as a Service storefront are single-page application written in AngularJS, responsive design with mobile support, extensible architecture, single-tenant and multitenant deployment modes, and multisite and localization capabilities.

7.2.2   SAP Hybris Commerce as a Service

It's estimated that by 2018, more than 50% of commerce sites will integrate technologies from more than 15 vendors to deliver a digital commerce experience to their customers. Today, commerce is all about being where the customer is, from pulling the customers to web storefronts and helping them navigate through the products they might need to presenting personalized and compelling purchase opportunities on demand. Hence, online commerce is no longer about just having a web shop, an optimized mobile website, or a native mobile application. You need to be able to embed commerce in any web- and mobile-connected devices customers use to present them with the right product offering at the right time. Providing a product display and transaction capability isn't sufficient; you need an integrated solution to provide data and algorithms that can predict what the customer wants.

Though individual microservices can be subscribed and consumed from SAP Hybris as a Service, you can also build a fully functional e-commerce site using SAP Hybris Commerce as a Service on SAP Hybris as a Service. It's an API-first approach to build commerce applications across channels and devices using loosely coupled architecture. You need the ability to quickly bring new products and services to market. SAP Hybris Commerce as a Service enables you to build beautiful and fully functional commerce storefronts in days. You can have fully responsive sites that can be accessed from any devices. The SAP Hybris Commerce services are built using the microservices architectural style with RESTful APIs and common standards such as JSON and OAuth2, which makes it easier to embed such services into any application.

SAP Hybris Commerce as a Service is a collection of APIs and UI modules built on SAP Hybris as a Service. To use these services, you need to register for SAP Hybris as a Service and subscribe to these services from the SAP Hybris as a Service marketplace. After subscribing, you need the Builder, a tool for managing and publishing microservices by an API proxy. You can access the SAP Hybris as a Service Dev Portal provided as part of your access to SAP Hybris as a Service for extensive documentation, toolkits, and guidelines for building and integrating microservices. SAP Hybris as a Service Market acts as an ecosystem of microservices to be discovered and easily subscribed to. SAP Hybris as a Service pricing is straightforward. You pay for commerce package microservices based on usage, including a base fee usage. As soon as certain aspects of a service exceed predefined limits, you only pay for what you're using, for example, the number of transactions or volume, and so on. Some of the key microservices available in SAP Hybris as a Service for SAP Hybris Commerce as a Service are cart, customer accounts, coupon management, and order management.

To help customers meet these challenges, SAP has created SAP Hybris Commerce as a Service, which adds speed, agility, and flexibility to SAP Hybris Commerce. SAP Hybris Commerce as a Service enables businesses to present purchasing opportunities to their potential customers, whenever and wherever they are most likely to buy. SAP Hybris Commerce as a Service allows merchants to experiment with different sales channels across platforms by embedding commerce in their applications through flexible API structures and commerce components available in the SAP Hybris as a Service marketplace. These commerce components available in SAP Hybris as a Service have been taken from SAP Hybris Commerce, hence the name SAP Hybris Commerce as a Service. However, it's still part of the SAP Hybris as a Service ecosystem. Figure 7.10 shows the components of the SAP Hybris solutions that can be integrated with the SAP Hybris as a Service solution.

SAP Hybris Commerce as a Service is a full set of out-of-the-box digital commerce microservices available for you to build an ideal e-commerce solution. These digital commerce microservices are deployed in the cloud through SAP Hybris as a Service. SAP Hybris as a Service is used for building and assembling data-driven front-office microservices and SaaS applications to enable new commercial models and digital products and services. It allows you to choose the exact commercial services and modules suited to your business requirements. You can replace any microservice with your own software or freely customize it based on your needs.

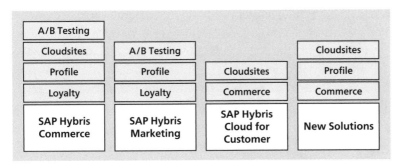

Figure 7.10 Integrating SAP Hybris Solutions with SAP Hybris as a Service

You can even integrate with third-party microservices. Each microservice can scale independently, and the entire application can scale based on traffic and demand. Some of the business benefits of using SAP Hybris Commerce as a Service are as follows:

- **Pop-up shops**
  You can easily set up transactional commerce functionality within days—not months—by choosing commerce microservices from SAP Hybris as a Service. You can test new markets and experiment with new channels by quickly turning on new functionality.

- **Embedded commerce**
  With open architecture and plug and play features enabled by the SAP Hybris as a Service partner ecosystem, you can embed commerce capability in your existing applications by adding Buy Now buttons. This allows you to integrate new commerce capabilities easily with existing solutions in your landscape.

- **Custom build commerce**
  You can choose the best-of-breed commerce components and customize them to meet your specific data and process requirements. The chosen solutions have no vendor lock-in, and you can sign up for short subscription cycles and scale as your business grows.

- **Extend SAP Hybris Enterprise Commerce**
  SAP Hybris Commerce as a Service expands the capabilities of SAP Hybris Commerce Cloud and enables a level of deployment speed (in days not months), flexibility (pick and choose functionality), and agility via microservices extensions, emerging channel penetration, and continuously evolving features.

To make SAP Hybris solutions integrate with SAP Hybris as a Service services, you can leverage SAP Hybris as a Service Connect. SAP Hybris as a Service Connect provides an easy way for you to integrate the SAP Hybris Commerce solution with SAP Hybris as a Service to enhance the native SAP Hybris Commerce platform capabilities with cloud-based microservices built on SAP Hybris as a Service. SAP Hybris as a Service Connect is a module that allows you to connect data between SAP Hybris Commerce and the SAP Hybris as a Service instance asynchronously through SAP Hybris Commerce, Data Hub. It provides an implementation for moving data in both the directions between SAP Hybris Commerce and SAP Hybris as a Service.

7.2.3   Augmenting and Enhancing SAP Hybris Solutions Using SAP Hybris as a Service

The SAP Hybris as a Service marketplace is growing with new solutions available as services from SAP and SAP Partners. These services can be consumed to augment and enhance SAP Hybris Solutions. In this section, we'll provide examples of a few of the services currently available in the SAP Hybris as a Service marketplace and how they extend the core capabilities of SAP Hybris solutions:

- **Shop the Look service**
  One such solutions is Shop the Look, which allows retailers to integrate SAP Hybris Commerce solutions with the Shop the Look service to offer their end customers the ability to upload an arbitrary image. The service will automatically identify various items in the picture and find the best matching products on the retailer's website. This solution augments the capabilities of the SAP Hybris Commerce site and increases the customer's engagement with the retailer's web shop.

- **Social Media Service package**
  Social media has become one of the most powerful communication channels of your time. Businesses can't afford not to interact with their customers through social media. They must connect and engage with their customers through social media to improve customer service experiences and strengthen loyalty with online customers. The Social Media Service package available in the SAP Hybris as a Service marketplace provides you with a ready-to-use service so that you can easily engage with customers via social media. It provides integration with your community's major social media providers such as Facebook and Twitter. You can integrate this service with your storefront customer service application.

- **Address Verification Service**
  You can integrate this service with an SAP Hybris Commerce storefront to validate

shipping and billing addresses during the checkout process. Verifying an address is required for tax verification, and it reduces the risk of missed deliveries and fraud.

Along with these few examples, there are many other useful services available now and more are being added by SAP and SAP Partners. Instead of building your own enhancement or extension to an SAP Hybris solution, review the available services in the marketplace first. If you have a unique idea to augment your current SAP Hybris solution, you can build your own services and publish them in the marketplace to monetize them. In the next section, we'll discuss how to get started with developing your own SAP Hybris as a Service solution.

7.2.4   Develop Your First SAP Hybris as a Service Solution

Now that you have the background on SAP Hybris as a Service, let's review what you need to build your first solution. This is just an overview of the resources and steps you need to build, deploy, and manage your own packages on SAP Hybris as a Service. For detailed steps and work instructions, visit the SAP Hybris as a Service Dev Portal (*https://devportal.yaas.io*), as shown in Figure 7.11.

Figure 7.11 SAP Hybris as a Service Dev Portal

First, you need to create a free user account on SAP Hybris as a Service (*https://www.yaas.io*). Developing applications on SAP Hybris as a Service requires a basic understanding of modern, object-oriented programming languages, such as Java,

Java Development Kit (JDK), or Open JDK; Eclipse IDE; or a similar development environment. For developers, the best way to get familiar with building SAP Hybris as a Service services is to review SAP Hybris as a Service Bites on SAP Hybris as a Service Dev Portal. SAP Hybris as a Service Bites are small, focused, incremental coding exercises. Each bite provides basic guidelines to make the journey to SAP Hybris as a Service as smooth as possible. These resources are as follows:

- **SAP Hybris as a Service Bites First Steps**
  This resource provides information on how to make secure connections to SAP Hybris as a Service services. Making a RESTful call to SAP Hybris as a Service services requires a valid token. You need to acquire an access token and include it in the header of any RESTful calls you make to services you need to consume for your applications or processes.

- **SAP Hybris as a Service Bites Essentials**
  This resource helps you with developing your own SAP Hybris as a Service services. It includes step-by-step instructions to deploy, call, and debug your first web service, take a web service to the cloud, use Build Packages and Builder Modules, call other web services, and so on.

- **SAP Hybris as a Service Bites Sequel**
  This resource helps you explore coding beyond Java, for instance, microservices written in Scala, Akka, and Node.js.

SAP Hybris as a Service Dev Portal provides comprehensive documentation and work instructions for developers to go quickly from zero to fully skilled in building, deploying, and consuming services from SAP Hybris as a Service Market.

With this background, let's review the high-level steps for building and deploying your own services in the SAP Hybris as a Service marketplace:

1. **Set up the environment.**
   Before you create your own service, you need to set up your environment. The SAP Hybris as a Service SDK uses Maven to resolve all additional software dependencies that are necessary to create, build, rest, and debug your new service. You need to install Maven before you can develop your services using SAP Hybris as a Service SDK.

2. **Create your service.**
   After setting up your environment, you can create your service. The best way to start is to create a wish list of services you have in mind to create. You develop a REST web service that is deployable in the web.

3. **Create a Builder module.**
   Next, you create a Builder Module and integrate your service so that you can manage your services using the Builder Module. Builder Module lets you easily manage your wish list services data from a UI.

4. **Set up the storefront.**
   In this step, you set up the storefront for your service. The SAP Hybris as a Service storefront is a ready-to-use template that can be set up as a fully transactional storefront, or you can use the template as a starting point to customize your own features and functionalities. Its architecture makes the SAP Hybris as a Service storefront easy to extend with the creation and implementation of new or existing services. To set up the storefront, you must clone the SAP Hybris as a Service storefront, run it locally on your machine, examine the storefront files, and familiarize yourself with the cloned storefront directory structure.

5. **Integrate your service in the storefront.**
   Finally, you can implement your wish list functionality by establishing a connection between your service and your storefront.

For detailed documentation on these steps, please visit SAP Hybris as a Service Dev Portal at *https://devportal.yaas.io*.

7.3 Summary

In this chapter, you've learned that the microservices architecture is becoming the standard for building and deploying distributed enterprise applications that can be consumed across devices and across channels. With SAP Hybris as a Service, SAP has taken a leadership position in offering an open cloud platform and marketplace for customers and partners to build, deploy, and consume SAP Hybris as a Service solutions. For many organizations, SAP Hybris as a Service is a stepping stone into the new API economy, by generating revenue from exposed microservice APIs. SAP Hybris as a Service includes everything you need to build and deploy fully functional and transactional commerce storefronts in days by orchestrating services available in the SAP Hybris as a Service ecosystem. The SAP Hybris as a Service marketplace is growing with new offerings and solutions, and customers can evaluate and integrate these services with their existing commerce solutions without needing to build their own. Partners can leverage SAP Hybris as a Service to build, deploy, and monetize complementary SAP Hybris as a Service solutions. In the next chapter, we'll cover what you need to successfully on-board SAP Hybris and how you can make your SAP Hybris journey as smooth and successful as possible.

Chapter 8
First Steps to SAP Hybris

The first steps to taking the SAP Hybris journey are all about defining business ambitions and crafting your to-be state for the customer experience processes. Beginning with an end state in mind will help you pick appropriate SAP Hybris solutions and target architecture to serve your business objectives best.

Based on the information shared in previous chapters about the key capabilities and business benefits of the SAP Hybris cloud portfolio, you can transform your operations to engage with your customers and prospects in new meaningful ways. You can attract and retain customers to grow your revenue and market share profitably in the new digital era.

In this chapter, you we're focusing on your first steps into SAP Hybris and the tasks and activities you need to accomplish before embarking on the SAP Hybris journey. How do you evaluate your current front-office processes and application landscape and compare it with where you want to be? With end business goal in mind, you choose the SAP Hybris solution components and roadmap for your deployment plan.

Because you can deploy SAP Hybris solutions in a public cloud, private cloud, or on premise, each with their own unique advantages and challenges, we'll compare these deployment options so that you can make an informed decision about the best deployment option to pursue. Next, we'll review various target architectures for deploying SAP Hybris solutions integrated with SAP S/4HANA, SAP Customer Relationship Management (SAP CRM), and SAP ERP applications. After you've finalized the solution to be implemented with the most suitable deployment option and target architecture, the next logical activity in your SAP Hybris journey is to adopt and implement best practices so that your SAP Hybris implementation goes as smooth and risk free as possible. We'll review some of the resources available from SAP such as SAP Hybris training courses and SAP Hybris Best Practices rapid-deployment solutions (RDSs) to help you with your SAP Hybris implementation.

8.1   Evaluating your Operations

Before you evaluate your operations relating to commerce and customers, you must define your business ambitions for growing your revenue and market share. The following questions can help you define the underlying business objectives:

- Do you engage with your customers in the right way, and do you meet their expectations?

- Do you have real-time visibility into your customers and your business?

- How and what data do you need to get additional and actionable insights into your customers?

- How can the new and extended data help you serve your customers even better?

- What does the digitization of data and interactions mean to you?

- Is your current commerce application integrated with your sales, service, and marketing applications?

- Can you uniquely identify and engage your customers across channels and devices?

- Is your current customer relationship management (CRM) and commerce application giving you what your business is asking for?

Answering these questions will help you uncover where you are and where you want to be in your journey to attract and retain new customers and prospects. While brainstorming new ideas, let your imagination race unchecked; you need to define your business ambitions—the ideal state you want to achieve. Without restricting yourself with current systems and infrastructural challenges, you should define your new face to your customers, new ways of meaningfully engaging with customers and prospects, new business models to deliver your products and services to your customers, and so on. You can't start your journey without clearly defining your end state.

Although business ambitions for growing customers can vary from business to business and industry to industry, let's briefly review some of the potential goals that could help you define your own business objectives:

- **Omnichannel commerce powered by contextual marketing**
  This is one of the key goals for many organizations. You want to engage with your customers through the channel of their choice. Your customers should be able to connect with you consistently, and you can offer them a seamless experience irrespective of the channel or device they choose to use. Whether they are calling your

customer service agent, chatting with you through your storefront, or sending you a service request from an online help portal, you should be able to recognize them and offer them appropriate answers to satisfy their queries. You want to offer omnichannel commerce capabilities such that customers can buy online and pick up in store, view a product catalog online and call your customer contact center to place an order, or place an order online on your web storefront and then modify the shipping address from a mobile app.

You may want to leverage contextual marketing to accurately identify registered and nonregistered customers and engage with them contextually through in-moment marketing. Contextual marketing helps improve the click-to-commerce ratio. You may want your marketing campaigns to be targeted with precision, based on dynamic customer profiles and target groups. When customers are browsing the product catalog in your storefront, you want your customer service agents to assist customers with queries through chat and even help customers by taking over the shopping cart and placing orders on behalf of the customers. You want to constantly and dynamically enrich customer profiles with information coming from various sources to accurately model their behavior.

To achieve this, you would plan to deploy SAP Hybris Commerce Cloud and SAP Hybris Marketing Cloud, not only integrated together but also with SAP or non-SAP backend systems. This solution will help you deliver true omnichannel capabilities backed with contextual and in-moment marketing to attract, engage with, and retain customers to grow your revenue and increase your market share.

- **Leverage marketing intelligence to improve sales productivity**
  For businesses heavily focused on field sales, this could be an ideal end state. You want to improve the productivity of sales professionals by helping them with more qualified leads and giving them marketing intelligence they so dearly desire to close their opportunities faster. Sales reps want flexibility to use applications from any device they choose, and they want access to information from their backend system, such as product availability, product pricing, delivery status, customer complaints status, and so on, at their fingertips so they can proactively engage with their customer contacts. Sales managers need real-time analytics to accurately measure the state of their business and devise strategies to fast-forward their sales opportunities.

  SAP Hybris Sales Cloud integrated with SAP Hybris Marketing Cloud lets you achieve this business ambition. SAP Hybris Sales Cloud can get sales team up and running on the new solution in as early as three to four weeks.

- **Transform service operations to a profit center**

  In most organizations, service operations are categorized as a cost center not a profit center. Service team members have more credible relationships with their customers, and any product or service recommendations they make are more likely to be taken seriously by their customers compared with their sales counterpart. They want to be making productized service offerings to prospects and customers as part of the sales opportunities. Service technicians need to have the ability to create leads for their sales counterparts as part of their service calls. You can leverage your analytics on service tickets and service orders to execute marketing campaigns for new products and services. By giving storefront access to customer service agents, you can assist your customers while they are browsing through your catalog and help them make purchasing decisions.

  SAP Hybris Service Cloud integrated with SAP Hybris Commerce Cloud and SAP Hybris Marketing Cloud can be leveraged to bring customer service, field service, sales, commerce, and marketing together to achieve these goals.

- **Offer new subscription-based products and services**

  If your business is planning to offer new products and services using a subscription-based model, then your current billing system may not be able to handle the new billing process and transaction volume. Application restrictions have prevented businesses from exploring new business models and business opportunities. They have no way to simulate new pricing and revenue models due to inherent infrastructural challenges. However, with SAP Hybris Revenue Cloud, you have the power to explore and charter new business models. You can participate in the new digital economy with new digital products and services using SAP Hybris solutions for billing innovation.

  These types of business ambitions are easier to achieve with integrated SAP Hybris Commerce Cloud, SAP Hybris Revenue Cloud, and backend SAP CRM and SAP ERP or SAP S/4HANA.

Using the preceding use cases as a reference, you can define your own end state for SAP Hybris solutions. Figure 8.1 shows the building blocks of SAP Hybris solutions to enable a digital customer experience and engagement landscape. Depending on your use case and business ambitions, you can pick the corresponding SAP Hybris components and create an application landscape for your end state.

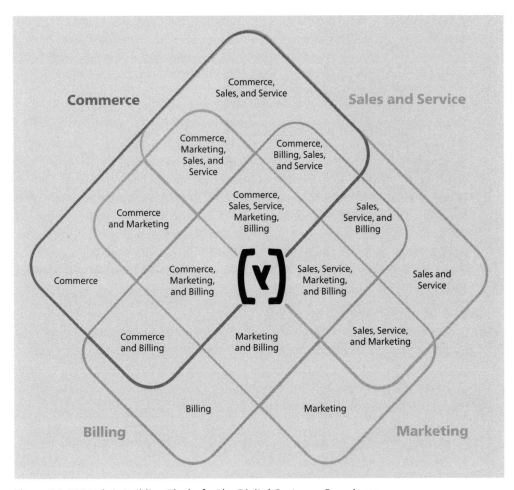

Figure 8.1 SAP Hybris Building Blocks for the Digital Customer Experience

Next, you need to prioritize your SAP Hybris solution deployment based on your business area urgency and available resources. It may not be feasible to deploy SAP Hybris Commerce Cloud and SAP Hybris Marketing Cloud at the same time, although it's not impossible. You may need to sequence and map your deployments for various SAP Hybris components. Mapping the deployment of your SAP Hybris solution is key to making the most positive impact to your business operations without causing any disruption. You can get help from SAP or SAP Hybris partners to map your SAP Hybris solution deployment.

After you have a road map for your SAP Hybris deployment, you need to compare and decide what deployment option works best for you. In the next section, we'll review and compare on-premise and cloud deployment options for these SAP Hybris components.

8.2   Comparing Deployment Options

As you've learned in previous chapters, SAP offers various deployment options for SAP Hybris solutions—on premise, private cloud, and public cloud—and they all come with their own advantages and trade-offs. Before committing to one deployment option over another, you must take a closer look at these options particularly in the backdrop of your current infrastructural limitations and available resources. For some SAP Hybris solutions, there is no on-premise deployment option, and you can only deploy cloud versions. Although we've covered the SAP Hybris portfolio of solutions in the previous chapters, let's review these deployment options again:

- **Sales and service**
  SAP Hybris Sales Cloud and SAP Hybris Service Cloud are only available through subscription in the public cloud, and there is no on-premise deployment option. As far as deploying SAP Hybris Sales Cloud and SAP Hybris Service Cloud are concerned, you can be up and running in as early as four weeks by subscribing to public cloud-based SAP Hybris Cloud for Customer.

- **Commerce**
  SAP Hybris Commerce is available on premise, and SAP Hybris Commerce Cloud is available for private cloud deployment. You can also use SAP Hybris Commerce as a Service from the SAP Hybris as a Service on SAP Cloud Platform marketplace as covered in the previous chapter.

- **Marketing**
  SAP Hybris Marketing can be deployed on premise as well as in a private cloud, whereas SAP Hybris Marketing Cloud is the public cloud solution offering.

  For the SAP Hybris Marketing on-premise solution you have three possible deployment scenarios as shown in Figure 8.2:

  - SAP Hybris Marketing is deployed as a standalone system on the SAP HANA database.

- SAP Hybris Marketing is deployed side-by-side with SAP ERP/SAP CRM or SAP S/4HANA. In this side-by-side deployment, you have two separate databases. In this case, SAP data such as accounts, contacts, and interactions are replicated between SAP Hybris Marketing and SAP ERP/SAP CRM or SAP S/4HANA.

- SAP Hybris Marketing is co-deployed with SAP ERP/SAP CRM on SAP HANA or SAP S/4HANA. In this case, both systems share a common database, and you don't need to replicate the accounts, contacts, and transactions data from one database to another as in the previous deployment option.

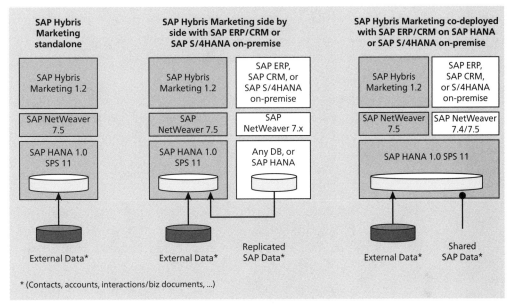

Figure 8.2 SAP Hybris Marketing On-Premise Deployment Options

- **Revenue**

  The SAP Hybris Billing solution can be deployed on-premise as well as in the private cloud. SAP Hybris Revenue Cloud is available for cloud deployment, is built on SAP Hybris as a Service, and includes configure, price, and quote (CPQ), order management, and subscription billing.

With this background on availability of SAP Hybris solutions for cloud and on-premise deployments, let's compare and evaluate their advantages and restrictions:

- **Public cloud versus private edition**

  When deploying SAP Hybris Sales Cloud or SAP Hybris Service Cloud (SAP Hybris Cloud for Customer), most companies typically choose a single system, multitenant public cloud environment (which is the default option offered by SAP). In the multitenant public cloud, multiple customers use the application on the same system with multiple tenants, and each customer uses a separate tenant. In the public multitenant cloud application, the upgrade schedule is controlled by SAP, and customers are aligned with the published upgrade schedule. SAP offers a standard maintenance window for each region such as the Americas, Europe, and Asia Pacific. The private edition for SAP Hybris Cloud for Customer provides a multitenant system for single customer usage with customizable maintenance windows. The private edition is intend for larger companies with policies against the use of public cloud systems for customer information.

- **Cloud versus on premise**

  In recent years, businesses have come to prefer cloud deployment to on-premise deployment. Figure 8.3 shows a comparison of the public cloud versus the on-premise or private cloud deployment option. Cloud-based solutions have the least investment requirements. You can be up and running with some SAP Hybris solutions in just a few weeks. You don't need to set up your own servers, networks, databases, and so on. SAP provides you access to your tenant in the public cloud with an initial user ID and password, and you can start configuring the system per your business requirements. In this option, you pay a small subscription fee based on the number of users.

  However, for on-premise deployment, investment requirements are much higher to account for up-front software license cost, and costs for the system, hardware, database, networks, and so on. With the public cloud offering, you have go-live much sooner than with on premise or private cloud. Because you're forced to participate in SAP's upgrade schedule in public cloud, you're closer to the innovation and always working on the latest release of an application. However, for on-premise or private cloud deployment, you control your own upgrade schedule. Lastly, with public cloud, you have limited flexibility to extend the application. However, in the on-premise version, you have more flexibility to extend the application because you're using a dedicated system that isn't shared with any other customer.

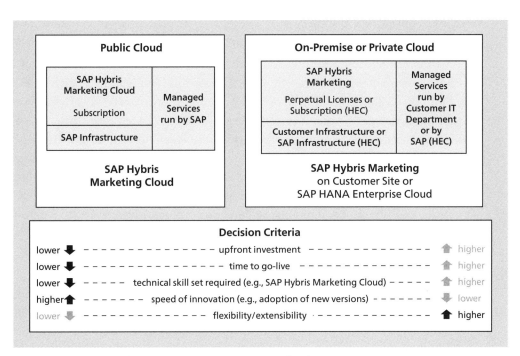

Figure 8.3 Public Cloud versus On-Premise or Private Cloud

Based on these comparisons between public cloud, on premise, and private cloud, you should be able to choose which deployment option works best for you. In the next section, we'll review what target architecture to choose for your SAP Hybris solutions deployment.

8.3   Choosing a Target Architecture

We've already reviewed the key capabilities of SAP Hybris front-office solutions and their deployment options. Next you need to determine the target architecture for implementing your solution. The motivation to choose a specific target architecture for your SAP Hybris solution deployment largely depends on the business ambition you're pursuing as briefly discussed in the beginning of this chapter. Business ambitions vary from organization to organization and industry to industry. For one organization, omnichannel is more critical than field sales, whereas, for another organization, contextual marketing is more compelling than high volume and subscription- and usage-based billing. Depending on your business aspirations, you pick the appropriate front-office SAP Hybris solution.

Another important variable in target architecture is what you're running in the back-end for order fulfilment, inventory management, accounting, and so on, and how your SAP or non-SAP backend system integrates with the SAP Hybris front-office solutions. You can create a target architecture most suited to your business drivers. Many business ambitions can be fulfilled by a combination of SAP Hybris front-office and backend solutions; however, for sake of example, we'll only discuss the following four business scenarios and the corresponding target architectures you can use to implement SAP Hybris solutions and achieve your business objectives.

Omnichannel Commerce and Contextual Marketing

In this business ambition, your primary goal is to achieve omnichannel commerce capabilities backed with contextual marketing. You know that to achieve this, you need to deploy SAP Hybris Commerce and SAP Hybris Marketing solutions along with your backend enterprise application. To get the most value for your investment, you can choose an architecture to transform your digital landscape, implement SAP S/4HANA as the backend system, and integrate SAP Hybris Commerce and SAP Hybris Marketing, as shown in Figure 8.4.

SAP Hybris also offers standard integration with SAP ERP, SAP CRM, and open APIs to integrate with non-SAP systems as well. The customers, products, and pricing information are replicated to SAP Hybris Commerce from the backend system. Using customer profile information from SAP Hybris Marketing, you can augment customer information in SAP Hybris Commerce to engage contextually with your customers. By using segmentation models, target groups, campaigns, and offer models in SAP Hybris Marketing, you can make personalized recommendations, offers, and storefronts in the SAP Hybris Commerce storefront. Customers can place orders in SAP Hybris Commerce, and the orders will replicate to the backend system for fulfilment. Using clickstream with SAP Hybris Commerce, you can capture customers' online behavior and augment customer profile information for better insights and contextual intelligence about customers' actions and intentions.

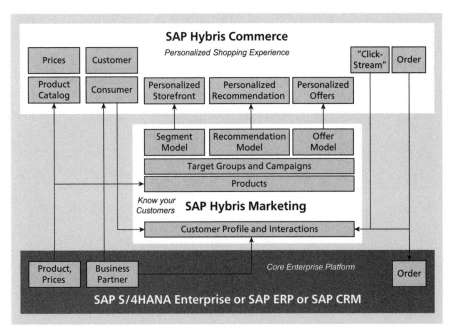

Figure 8.4 Architecture Driven by Omnichannel Commerce and Contextual Marketing

In this scenario, the marketing component can be implemented as the SAP Hybris Marketing on-premise solution or in the public cloud with SAP Hybris Marketing Cloud. Similarly, SAP Hybris Commerce can be deployed using the SAP Hybris Commerce solution in the cloud through SAP Hybris as a Service. In this architecture, you haven't included SAP Hybris Sales Cloud, SAP Hybris Service Cloud, or SAP Hybris Revenue Cloud because your business drivers are aligned toward the omnichannel commerce and contextual marketing solution.

Services Sales and High-Volume Subscription Billing

In this scenario, you're driven by your need to sell digital services through omnichannel commerce, which requires high-volume subscription- and usage-based billing and revenue management. Figure 8.5 shows the architecture to support this business ambition. To enable this business process and support key business drivers, you need to implement SAP Hybris Commerce and SAP Hybris Billing (or SAP Hybris Revenue Cloud) together and integrate these with the SAP S/4HANA and SAP CRM backend system. As mentioned earlier, you can leverage this architecture even with SAP ERP in the backend if you haven't transitioned to SAP S/4HANA. As covered in Chapter 6, you need SAP CRM integrated with SAP Hybris Billing to support product bundles, prices, contract, usage prices, and charging and subscription order management.

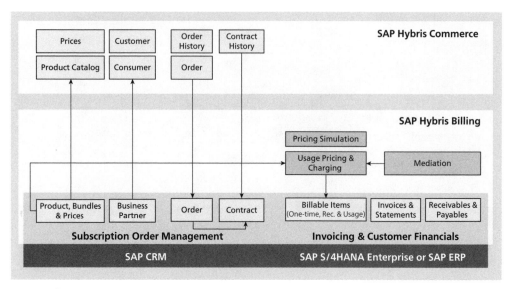

Figure 8.5 Architecture Driven by Digital Services Sales with High-Volume Subscription Billing

SAP Hybris Commerce integrated with SAP Hybris Billing provides pricing simulation, usage pricing and charging, mediation, order management, and contract management. However, invoicing and customer financials, including invoices and statements, receivables, and payments, are still managed in the SAP S/4HANA or SAP ERP backend system. This architecture demonstrates on-premise deployment for both SAP Hybris Commerce as well as SAP Hybris Billing; however, you can still use this architecture in the cloud by deploying both SAP Hybris Commerce and SAP Hybris Billing solutions in the cloud.

This type of architecture is used predominantly for digital services and usage-based products that require high-volume billing. Customers normally subscribe to digital services such as software-as-a-service (SaaS), network or system usage, wireless phone services, and so on, and they are charged a one-time or recurring fee based on the usage of services. If high-volume billing for digital usage-based services isn't the prime motivation, then this architecture may not be the target architecture for such scenarios.

Sales and Service Teams Productivity

If your business ambition is driven primarily by increasing revenue through high-touch sales and service, then you need to focus on solutions around increasing productivity of sales and service teams. When you talk about sales and service, you must include SAP Hybris Cloud for Customer in the landscape as it offers major capabilities for SAP Hybris Sales Cloud and SAP Hybris Service Cloud solutions. As you saw in Chapter 3, the Assisted Sales Module (ASM) provides real-time sales/service support. Customer service agents can use ASM to handhold customers during online shopping and provide support as needed by being in the same storefront that the customer is using.

Figure 8.6 shows the architecture to support this business ambition. In this case, we've included SAP Hybris Commerce, SAP Hybris Cloud for Customer, and SAP Hybris Marketing in the architecture with the SAP backend if it's preexisting in the current system landscape. As you know, SAP Hybris Cloud for Customer is only available in the cloud, but you can deploy SAP Hybris Commerce as well as SAP Hybris Marketing in Cloud instead of on premise without altering this architecture. SAP Hybris Marketing provides contextual marketing and feeds into SAP Hybris Commerce for personalized offerings and product recommendations to customers. SAP Hybris Marketing can also leverage orders and clickstream data coming from SAP Hybris Commerce to enrich customer profiles. SAP Hybris Cloud for Customer uses customer and product information from the backend system (SAP S/4HANA, SAP ERP, or SAP CRM). The service tickets and quotes can be created in SAP Hybris Cloud for Customer by customer service agents. Using the SAP Hybris Commerce ASM, customer service agents can take control of a customer's shopping cart and place an order on behalf of the customer.

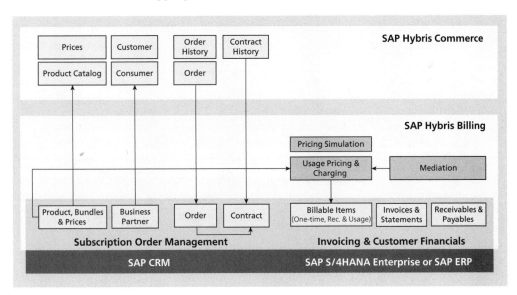

Figure 8.6 Architecture to Support Improved Sales and Service Productivity

This target architecture to deploy SAP Hybris solutions is definitely more comprehensive and brings more value across commerce, sales, service, and marketing. It allows you to increase sales revenue and sales pipeline through high-touch sales and service by leveraging capabilities in SAP Hybris Sales Cloud and SAP Hybris Service Cloud in conjunction with SAP Hybris Commerce and SAP Hybris Marketing. Except for SAP Hybris Billing, this target architecture leverages all the SAP Hybris front-office solutions. In the next and last business scenario covered in this section, we'll evaluate how you can leverage customer insights and marketing intelligence to grow your sales pipeline and enhance the chance of winning opportunities, along with other benefits around improving sales and service team's productivity.

Identify New Sales Opportunities through Digital Marketing Intelligence

This business scenario builds on the previous target architecture by augmenting digital marketing intelligence from data collected in SAP Hybris Marketing from various internal and external sources and leveraging predictive analytics and marketing intelligence to uncover new sales opportunities. From an SAP Hybris front-office solutions perspective, this still uses SAP Hybris Commerce, SAP Hybris Cloud for Customer, and SAP Hybris Marketing with the backend system. The only difference from the previous scenario is that in this architecture, the sales capabilities in SAP Hybris Sales Cloud are leveraged with insights and information from SAP Hybris Marketing. Here you leverage digital marketing intelligence from SAP Hybris Marketing to enrich your sales pipeline, create or qualify leads, and create and enrich sales opportunities in SAP Hybris Cloud for Customer (see Figure 8.7).

Note

In these business scenarios, we've covered four target architectures you can use to drive business objectives around enabling omnichannel commerce powered with contextual marketing, manage high-volume digital services subscription-based usage billing, increase revenue through improved productivity of sales and service teams, and increase the sales pipeline though digital marketing intelligence. Using these target architectures, you can craft an SAP Hybris deployment road map and target architecture for any business or industry.

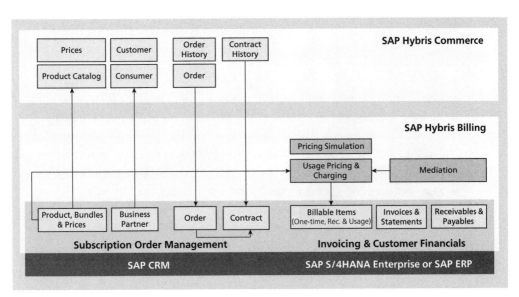

Figure 8.7 Architecture to Identify New Opportunities through Digital Marketing Intelligence

8.4   Applying Implementation Best Practices

SAP has made it much easier for customers to implement SAP Hybris Cloud solutions by applying SAP Best Practices. These best practices are easy, step-by-step instructions to implement SAP Hybris Commerce, SAP Hybris Marketing, SAP Hybris Revenue Cloud, SAP Hybris Sales, and SAP Hybris Service solutions. For customers who aren't comfortable implementing themselves, SAP offers fixed-scope, fixed-fee RDSs to implement SAP Hybris Cloud solutions.

> **Note: DIY**
>
> When you decide to implement the SAP Hybris solution for your business, it's important that your business process owners are leading the design sessions, system configuration, testing, and end-user training. No one knows your business better than your business process owners, and it's critical that they are fully engaged at every step in the SAP Hybris implementation. Business process owners are often only involved during the requirements gathering phase, and then later, they come back to test the system only to find to their surprise that the system isn't par with their expectations.

For successful adoption of SAP Hybris solutions by your business users, it's important that your own team members configure the system. Of course, you need help from SAP and SAP Partners to configure the system and make enhancement or change extensions to suite your unique business requirements, but the goal for your team should be to learn and do it themselves. By doing so, you know what and how you've designed and configured your SAP Hybris system. You'll be in a better position to support your business users and derive business value from your investments in the SAP Hybris solutions. To succeed at this, your team must be fully trained in SAP Hybris.

Knowing SAP Hybris best practices and standard capabilities will also help you better evaluate your current processes and make a case for potential process change. Change management initiatives meet least resistance if business process owners are involved throughout the project activities, and they're ready to accept the system when it's delivered because they've designed the system and they own the system, unlike in the past when systems were forced on business users.

In the following sections, we'll look at best practices, RDS solutions, and other suggested recommendations for successfully implementing SAP Hybris solutions.

8.4.1   Implementation Best Practices

At the time of writing this book, the following best practices were available from SAP to deploy SAP Hybris solutions. For the most recent information on SAP Hybris best practices, however, contact SAP and its partners.

- **SAP Hybris Commerce best practice**
  Currently, the only best practice available for SAP Hybris Commerce is for SAP Hybris Commerce and SAP S/4HANA integration. This prebuilt scenario can help you accelerate the integration between SAP Hybris Commerce and SAP S/4HANAs' digital core to set up an end-to-end order management process for business-to-business (B2B) and business-to-consumer (B2C) commerce. These integration scenarios can serve as a starting point for your implementation projects. You can download this best practice from the following link (you need an SAP S-user ID to log in and download the content): *https://rapid.sap.com/bp/HYB_COM_S4H*.

- **SAP Hybris Marketing best practice**
  The best practice for SAP Hybris Marketing Cloud includes preconfigured scenarios for consumer and customer profiling, segmentation, campaign execution, commerce marketing, marketing resource management, marketing lead management,

and loyalty management. SAP Best Practices provide preconfigured integration contents, preconfigured data load, and easy-to-use guides for the required manual steps. The link for SAP Hybris Marketing best practice is as follows: *https://rapid.sap.com/bp/#/BP_CLD_MKT*.

- **SAP Hybris Billing best practice**
  The SAP Hybris Billing and commerce integration best practices document serve as a starting point for business information, configuration information, and technical information about SAP Hybris Billing integration. You need login access to *https://wiki.hybris.com* (only available for SAP customers and partners) to view and download this best practice. The link to this best practice is as follows: *https://wiki.hybris.com/x/ps67Eg*.

- **SAP Hybris Cloud for Customer (Sales and Service) best practices**
  For SAP Hybris Cloud for Customer, currently you have three best practice documents:
  - SAP Hybris Cloud for Customer – SAP Hybris Commerce Integration: *https://help.hybris.com/6.0.0/hcd/914cd3278df94d13ba328a1a45adfda2.html*
  - SAP Hybris Cloud for Customer – SAP Hybris Marketing Integration: *https://help.sap.com/saphelp_sapcloudforcustomer/en/SAP_Hybris/index.html*
  - SAP Hybris Cloud for Customer – SAP Hybris Marketing Cloud Integration: *https://rapid.sap.com/bp/BP_S4H_MC_C4C*

  These three documents provide best practices configuration instructions to integrate SAP Hybris Cloud for Customer with SAP Hybris Commerce and SAP Hybris Marketing Cloud. You may need SAP login access to view these best practice documents.

8.4.2 Rapid Deployment Solutions

As mentioned earlier, SAP offers productized implementation services to customers in the form of RDSs. These are fixed-scope, fixed-deliverable, and fixed-fee engagements. Customers can engage SAP professional services for these RDS services to get started with their SAP Hybris implementation. RDSs are great ways to engage SAP professional services and leverage their expertise to kick off SAP Hybris deployments. The scope of RDSs may not be sufficient to cover the entire SAP Hybris implementation for customers, but they serve as great starting points. Customers may need to engage SAP Partners to implement SAP Hybris Solutions fully per each customer's unique business processes and requirements.

Table 8.1 summarizes the RDSs, as well as the SAP Best Practices from the previous section, for SAP Hybris solutions. You should contact SAP Professional Services to learn about SAP Hybris RDS offerings.

Area	Rapid Deployment Solutions and Best Practices
Commerce	▪ SAP Hybris Commerce – SAP S/4HANA Integration: *https://rapid.sap.com/bp/HYB_COM_S4H* ▪ SAP Hybris Commerce Integration RDS: *https://rapid.sap.com/bp/RDS_HYB_INT*
Marketing	▪ SAP Best Practices for SAP Hybris Marketing Cloud: *https://rapid.sap.com/bp/#/BP_CLD_MKT* ▪ SAP Hybris Marketing RDS: *https://rapid.sap.com/bp/RDS_CEI_HANA* ▪ SAP Hybris Marketing Rapid Data Load: *https://rapid.sap.com/bp/RDS_DAT_LOAD*
Billing	▪ SAP Best Practices for SAP Hybris Billing: *https://rapid.sap.com/bp/RDS_O2C* ▪ SAP Hybris Billing – Commerce Integration: *https://wiki.hybris.com/x/ps67Eg*
Sales and Service	▪ SAP Best Practices for SAP Hybris Cloud for Customer – SAP S/4HANA Integration: *https://rapid.sap.com/bp/RDS_CFC_S4_INT* ▪ SAP Best Practices for SAP Hybris Cloud for Customer – SAP ERP Integration: *https://rapid.sap.com/bp/RDS_CFC_ERP* ▪ SAP Hybris Cloud for Customer Integration with SAP ERP RDS: *https://rapid.sap.com/bp/RDS_CFC_ERP_INT* ▪ SAP Hybris Cloud for Customer – SAP Hybris Commerce Integration: *https://help.hybris.com/6.0.0/hcd/914cd3278df94d13ba328a1a45adfda2.html* ▪ SAP Hybris Cloud for Customer – SAP Hybris Marketing Integration: *https://help.sap.com/saphelp_sapcloudforcustomer/en/SAP_Hybris/index.html* ▪ SAP Hybris Cloud for Customer – SAP Hybris Marketing Cloud Integration: *https://rapid.sap.com/bp/BP_S4H_MC_C4C*

Table 8.1 SAP Best Practices and Rapid Deployment Solutions

8.4.3   SAP Education

A critical success factor to ensuring successful implementation of SAP Hybris solutions, is training team members on the SAP Hybris solutions that you plan to implement. SAP training should never be considered as an expense. It's as important as investing in software licenses and consulting services. There is no substitute for keeping the knowledge and expertise in-house during and after implementation. The first and foremost task is to identify team members who should be involved in SAP Hybris implementation and who will be responsible for supporting business users after go-live. After you've identified the team members, then you need to design the appropriate training and knowledge transfer plan. It's critical that team members are trained on SAP Hybris solutions before commencing the implementation project.

The best place to start learning about SAP Hybris solution is to review the free SAP Hybris online courses available at Open SAP (*https://open.sap.com/course/hyb1*). You need to register before viewing these courses. In these overview courses, SAP Hybris solutions are explained through a series of videos and PDF slides. You can download these videos and slides to go through them at your own pace.

SAP Education has a portfolio of SAP Hybris training courses available both online and through in-class training for SAP Hybris Commerce, SAP Hybris Marketing, SAP Hybris Billing, SAP Hybris Commerce, and SAP Hybris Cloud for Customer. Table 8.2 shows SAP Hybris Commerce training for functional, technical, developer, and end users. Depending on your team members and project team requirements, you can choose various trainings such as functional, developer, or technical. The first course in the SAP Hybris Commerce portfolio is HY100, which is an online course of essentials to get the fundamentals of the SAP Hybris solutions portfolio. We strongly recommend that both business and project team members take this training before starting any other SAP Hybris Commerce training course.

SAP Hybris Education Track	Level	Training Details
SAP Hybris Commerce	Essentials	HY100, HY100E – Essentials Online
	Functional	HY200, HY200E – Functional Analyst Training
	Technical	HY300, HY300E – System Administrator
	Developer	HY400 – Developer Part-1
	Developer	HY410 – Developer Part-2

Table 8.2 SAP Hybris Commerce Training Portfolio

SAP Hybris Education Track	Level	Training Details
	Developer	HY412E – Commerce Front End Developer
	Developer	HY430 – Data Hub Training
	Technical	HY440 – SAP Hybris Commerce OMS (Order Management)
	End User	HY500, HY500E – Commerce End User
	Technical, Functional	HY460E – Commerce Cockpit NG Fundamentals
	Technical	HY465 – Commerce Cockpit NG
	Technical, Functional	HY600 – Hybris (Commerce) – SAP Solution Integration

Table 8.2 SAP Hybris Commerce Training Portfolio (Cont.)

For SAP Hybris Marketing (including SAP Hybris Marketing Cloud) and SAP Hybris Billing, the portfolio of training courses is listed in Table 8.3. Note that some of these courses may not be available in your country; check with your SAP training contact or visit *https://training.sap.com* for availability and pricing information.

SAP Hybris Education Track	Level	Training Details
SAP Hybris Marketing	Essentials	HY700E – Essentials Online
	Functional	HY730E – Functional Analyst Training
	Technical, Functional	HY710/750 – Customization & Integration
	Technical, Functional	S4MC50 – Implementing SAP S/4HANA Marketing Cloud
SAP Hybris Billing	Essentials	AC230 – Overview
	Functional	AC233 – Hybris Billing, Sales and Order Management in SAP CRM
	Functional	AC235 – Convergent Charging

Table 8.3 SAP Hybris Marketing and SAP Hybris Billing Training Portfolio

SAP Hybris Education Track	Level	Training Details
	Functional	AC240 – Contract Account Receivable and Payable
	Functional	AC245 – Convergent Invoicing
	Functional	E2EYB – End-to-End Enablement of Hybris Billing
SAP Hybris Revenue Cloud	Planned	TBD

Table 8.3 SAP Hybris Marketing and SAP Hybris Billing Training Portfolio (Cont.)

Table 8.4 lists the SAP courses available for SAP Hybris Cloud for Customer (including the SAP Hybris Sales and SAP Hybris Service Cloud solutions) and SAP Hybris as a Service. Some of these courses are still under development (at the time of writing this book) and should be available soon through SAP Education. To see the details of these courses, please visit the SAP Education website.

SAP Hybris Education Track	Level	Training Details
SAP Hybris Sales Cloud and SAP Hybris Service Cloud	Essentials	C4C10 – SAP Cloud for Customer Project Implementation
	Functional	C4C12 – SAP Hybris Cloud for Sales
	Functional	C4C14 - SAP Hybris Cloud for Service
	Functional	C4C30 – SAP Cloud Application Studio
	Technical, Functional	C4C50 – SAP Cloud for Customer – Integration with on-premise SAP Solutions
SAP Hybris as a Service	Essentials	YaaS Essentials Online
	Essentials	YaaS Profile Essentials
	Essentials	YaaS Technical Essentials
	Essentials	YaaS Developer

Table 8.4 SAP Hybris Sales, SAP Hybris Service, and SAP Hybris as a Service Training Portfolio

8.5   Summary

In this chapter, you learned about some important activities required to take a first step toward SAP Hybris. After evaluating your current solutions and business ambitions, you can pick the most compelling SAP Hybris solutions and craft your own target architecture for deployment. SAP Hybris offers flexibility for choosing cloud or on-premise deployment options. You can utilize SAP Hybris training courses to ramp up your team members on SAP Hybris solutions and leverage SAP Hybris best practices and RDSs for your SAP Hybris deployment. With this book, we hope that we've been able to enlighten you with SAP Hybris knowledge to help you successfully embark on a digital transformation journey for your front-office customer engagement processes.

The Authors

Sanjjeev K. Singh is a managing partner at ASAR America, Inc., and a former SAP America client partner. For the past 17 years, he has helped customers implement SAP Hybris Cloud for Customer, SAP Hybris Commerce, SAP CRM, and SAP ERP Sales and Distribution. He has been involved in many large-scale SAP implementation projects. He is extremely passionate about helping customers develop their road map and implement customer engagement solutions using the SAP Hybris product portfolio. In his current role, he leads the SAP Hybris practice at ASAR America, Inc., an SAP Hybris services partner.

Sven Feurer is a senior member of the Solution Management and Strategy team for SAP Hybris. He has more than 10 years of experience in SAP Business Suite, SAP CRM, SAP Hybris Sales Cloud, SAP Hybris Service Cloud, and SAP Cloud Platform. In his current role, he's responsible for the overall architecture, technology, and integration strategy of the SAP Hybris solutions. For years, Sven has been driving strategic programs and rollout activities in the context of customer engagement and commerce, as well as supporting long-term customer relationships and strategic business development. To learn more about SAP Hybris products, industry solutions, best practices, implementation, and optimization, visit *www.hybris.com.*

 **Marcus Ruebsam** is the senior vice president of solution management for SAP Hybris. He is responsible for global solution strategy, product definition, and go-to-market activities for the Customer Engagement and Commerce solution portfolio. The global solution management organization includes solution experts for marketing, sales, service, revenue, and commerce.

Marcus has an extensive track record of leading sales and marketing organizations for business-to-business and business-to-customer activities, including sales, brand management, marketing communications, product marketing, and business development. Prior to his current role, he held a number of other strategic positions within SAP, including vice president and general manager for line-of-business marketing solutions, director of small and medium enterprise marketing (SME), and director of integrated marketing communications.

Index

- ▶ Learn how SAP S/4HANA enables digital transformation
- ▶ Explore innovative financials and logistics functionality
- ▶ Understand the technical foundation underlying SAP S/4HANA advances

Baumgartl, Chaadaev, Choi, Dudgeon, Lahiri, Meijerink, Worsley-Tonks

SAP S/4HANA

An Introduction

Looking to make the jump to SAP S/4HANA? Learn what SAP S/4HANA offers, from the Universal Journal in SAP S/4HANA Finance to supply chain management in SAP S/4HANA Materials Management and Operations. Understand your deployment options—on-premise, cloud, and hybrid—and explore SAP Activate's implementation approach. Get an overview of how SAP HANA architecture supports digital transformation, and see what tools can help extend your SAP S/4HANA functionality!

449 pages, pub. 11/2016
E-Book: $59.99 | **Print:** $69.95 | **Bundle:** $79.99

www.sap-press.com/4153

- ▶ Explore SAP HANA in all its forms: as database, as application platform, as driver for SAP S/4HANA

- ▶ Learn about data modeling, data provisioning, and administration

- ▶ Get the basics you need to speed into the world of SAP HANA

Silvia, Frye, Berg

SAP HANA

An Introduction

What does SAP HANA mean for you? This book is your introduction to all the essentials, from implementation options to the basics of data modeling and administration. With cutting-edge coverage of SAP HANA smart data access, SAP HANA Vora, and more, this bestseller has everything you need to take your first steps with SAP HANA.

549 pages, 4th edition, pub. 10/2016
E-Book: $59.99 | **Print:** $69.95 | **Bundle:** $79.99

www.sap-press.com/4160

- ▶ The complete resource for implementing SAP CRM for marketing, sales, and service

- ▶ Set up product determination, campaign management, service functions, and more

- ▶ Apply expert tips for maximizing your SAP CRM solution

Chandrakant Agarwal

SAP CRM

Business Processes and Configuration

Master the business processes and configuration for SAP Customer Relationship Management! This guide offers the details you need about key SAP CRM functionality and customization. Understand the key SAP CRM business processes and then configure the system for marketing, sales, and service. From master data to middleware to the web UI, get the answers you need to tailor SAP CRM for your own requirements.

737 pages, pub. 11/2014

E-Book: $69.99 | **Print:** $79.95 | **Bundle:** $89.99

www.sap-press.com/3648

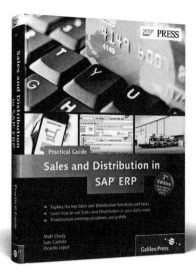

- ▶ Explores the key sales and distribution functions and tasks
- ▶ Teaches how to use SD in daily processes, including sales, pricing, delivery, transportation, and billing
- ▶ Guides you in troubleshooting common problems and pitfalls

Chudy, Castedo, Lopez

Sales and Distribution in SAP ERP— Practical Guide

It's time to focus on your tasks in SD. In this book, you'll find the most common duties you'll need to perform in the SD component explained in a simple manner, with helpful screenshots and lists of transaction codes you'll use. Start the journey with master data setup, and then move on to explore sales, shipping, and billing tasks. Push your skills to new heights by mastering reporting and financial supply chain activities.

520 pages, 2nd edition, pub. 11/2014
E-Book: $59.99 | **Print:** $69.95 | **Bundle:** $79.99

www.sap-press.com/3672

- Learn to easily navigate the SAP system
- Work with SAP components step by step
- Includes many examples and detailed SAP screenshots

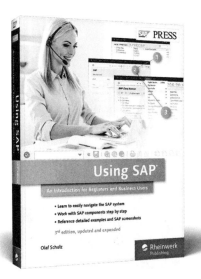

Olaf Schulz

Using SAP

An Introduction for Beginners and Business Users

Do you need to learn SAP for your day-to-day work? Get the detailed steps and screenshots that walk you through the processes you need to do your job. Get comfortable with logging on to and navigating the system, maintaining your data, creating reports, printing, and so much more. Whether you're entering data, automating tasks, or building your foundational knowledge of the SAP system, this book has your back.

387 pages, 3rd edition, pub. 12/2016
E-Book: $24.99 | **Print:** $29.95 | **Bundle:** $39.99

www.sap-press.com/4155

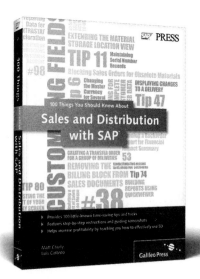

- ▶ Provides 100 little-known time-saving tips and tricks
- ▶ Features step-by-step instructions and guiding screenshots
- ▶ Helps increase profitability by teaching you how to effectively use SD

Matt Chudy, Luis Castedo

Sales and Distribution with SAP

100 Things You Should Know About...

If you've worked with Sales and Distribution in SAP ERP, you know it can sometimes be overwhelming, but it doesn't have to be. This book unlocks the secrets of SD. It provides users and super users with 100 tips and work-arounds to increase productivity, save time, and improve overall ease-of-use of SAP SD. The tips have been carefully selected to provide a collection of the best, most useful, and rarest information.

363 pages, pub. 03/2014
E-Book: $44.99 | **Print:** $49.95 | **Bundle:** $59.99

www.sap-press.com/2946